WYLLIE, ACTON & GOLDBLATT'S

TIME TRAVEL
HANDBOOK

A SELECTION OF TRIPS AND TOURS
FROM THE ERUPTION OF VESUVIUS
TO THE WOODSTOCK FESTIVAL

P

First published in Great Britain in 2015 by
Profile Books:
3 Holford Yard, Bevin Way
London WC1X 9HD
www.profilebooks.com

1 3 5 7 9 10 8 6 4 2

Typeset in Caslon, Sancreek and Copperplate Gothic
to a design by Henry Iles.

Thanks to Sally Holloway, Sonia Land, Karim Noorani, Nikky Twyman,
Henry Iles, Dominic Beddow and Mark Ellingham.

A CIP catalogue record for this book is available from the
British Library.
336pp

ISBN 978-1781254042
e-ISBN 978 178283 1327

Printed and bound in Great Britain by Clays, Bungay, Suffolk
on Forest Stewardship Council (mixed sources) certified paper.

THE
TIME TRAVEL
HANDBOOK

RESEARCHED AND WRITTEN BY

JAMES WYLLIE, JOHNNY ACTON
& DAVID GOLDBLATT

PHOTO CREDITS

Francis I by Jean Clouet (p.8), Louvre Museum; *Henry VIII at the English Camp* (p.10–11), Royal Collection Trust/Her Majesty Queen Elizabeth II; *Henry VIII after Hans Holbein* (p.15), Walker Art Gallery. *V For Victory* (p.45), Picture Post/Getty Image; *Dancing in the streets* (p.50), Photo12/UIG/Getty Images; *Piccadilly Circus* (p.52) and *Churchill, Attlee and Bevin* (p.55), Keystone/Getty Images. *Michael Lang and Artie Kornfeld* (p.60), Bill Eppridge/Life/Getty Images; *Breakfast* (p.65), John Dominis/Life/Getty Images; *Undress Code* (p.69), Silver Screen/Movipix/Getty Images; *Swami Satchidananda* (p.72), Mark Goff/WikiCommons; *Country Joe* (p.75), Jason Laure/Woodfin/Getty Images; *Lost girl* (p.78), Three Lions/Hulton Archive/Getty Images. *Charles I* (p.85), Fine Art Images/Superstock/Getty Images. *Tardivet and Miomandre* (p.116), Bibliothèque Nationale de France. *Berlin Wall 'Death Strip'* (p.133), Thierry Noir/WikiCommons; *Brandenburg Gate* (p.139), Sue Ream/WikiCommons; *Rostropovich* (p.145), L. Emmett Lewis Jr. © Stars and Stripes. *Charlie Parker* (p.189), Gilles Petard/Getty Images; *Lindy Hoppers at The Savoy* (p.192), Charles Peterson/Hulton Archive/Getty Images; *Outside Minton's Playhouse* (p.197), William Gottlieb/Redferns/Getty Images. *Fab Five* (p.203), Astrid Kirchherr/K&K/Redferns/Getty Images; *The Beatles at The Top Ten Club* (p.210), Ellen Piel/K&K/Redferns/Getty Images; *The Beatles at The Star Club* (p.215), Ulf Kruger/K&K/Redferns/Getty Images. *Mobutu introduces Foreman and Ali* (p.218), George Walker/Liaison/Getty Images; *Foreman in training* (p.224), Neil Leifer/Sports Illustrated/Getty Images; *Ali prepares* (p.227), Stringer/AFP/Getty Images; *Ali throws the Big One* (p.231), The Ring Magazine/Getty Images. *Kublai Khan* (p.243), Dea/Getty Images. *Tahitian women* (p.263), Time Life Pictures/Mansell/Life/Getty Images; *The Endeavour* (p.270), SSPL/Getty Images. *Up Pompeii!* (p.282), Art Media/Print Collector/Getty Images. John Ball (p.289), British Library Board. *Union artillery unit* (p.308), *Zouave uniform* (p.313), *Colonel Dixon Miles* (p.316), *Union attack* (p.319), *Federal Cavalry at Sudley Springs* (p.320), *Senators Zachariah Chandler and Benjamin Wade* (p. 321), all Library of Congress.

All MAPS by Magnetic North.

CONTENTS

EPIC JOURNEYS & VOYAGES

EXTREME EVENTS *

* These events are not covered under the Company's insurance policy.

WYLLIE, ACTON
& GOLDBLATT'S

TIME TRAVEL
TOURS

'History repeats itself. First time as tragedy, second time as vacation.'

SOME SAY THE PAST IS A FOREIGN COUNTRY. We say get your passport. At WYLLIE, ACTON & GOLDBLATT (WAG) TIME TRAVEL TOURS, we take you back, set you down and bring you home from some of the finest moments in human history. With our unique Chronoswoosh™ time exchange plasma shuttle technology, we not only offer the most accurate return to the past, but minimal interference with the time-space continuum. No more getting abandoned in the wrong century, no more returning to find you are your great aunt.

At WAG we believe that history second time round need not be farce, but a celebration, a party and a vacation. If that sounds like your idea of a good time past, then our CELEBRATIONS & EXHIBITIONS suite of trips is for you. Try the late feudal pomp of the FIELD OF THE CLOTH OF GOLD, where the nobilities of France and England gathered in great alfresco camps, drink, feast, joust and doff their caps to King Henry VIII and King Francis I. The GREAT EXHIBITION OF 1851 certainly deserves another look and we give you the opportunity to explore Victorian London and the cornucopian contents of the Crystal Palace. For the more hedonistic, VE DAY IN LONDON 1945 and the 1969 WOODSTOCK FESTIVAL in Upstate New York offer contrasting experiences of collective ecstasy.

For more experienced time travellers we recommend moving on to an event that has really made a difference. Our carefully curated selection of MOMENTS THAT MADE HISTORY show the wheels of change in motion while delivering the most extraordinary sensory experiences. Feel the ancient régime crumble and the modern world emerge as CHARLES I IS EXECUTED at the end of the English Civil War or MARCH WITH THE WOMEN OF PARIS in the heat of the French Revolution. For those with more contemporary tastes we offer the poles of the short twentieth century: the ASSASSINATION OF ARCHDUKE FERDINAND IN SARAJEVO that triggered the First World War in 1914; and the FALL OF THE BERLIN WALL in 1989 that brought the long European struggle to a close.

For a more reflective journey to the past, WAG also offers a great treasure trove of CULTURAL & SPORTING SPECTACULARS. Our selection of classic moments takes you to events that seemed un-repeatable and offers them up in all their replayed glory. From the spectacle of the ANCIENT OLYMPICS to the opening night of SHAKESPEARE'S GLOBE, from the BIRTH OF BEBOP in war time New York City to the invention of the BEATLES IN HAMBURG, or Muhammad Ali fighting George Foreman in THE RUMBLE IN THE JUNGLE, there is something to suit all tastes.

For the more adventurous and stoical of our travellers, we have recently developed the long form EPIC JOURNEYS & VOYAGES: six months with MARCO POLO IN XANADU in thirteenth-century China; or the chance to crew on the THREE-YEAR VOYAGE OF CAPTAIN COOK to Australia. For those with the strongest nerves and most balanced dispositions we are pleased to include our EXTREME EVENTS: the ever popular ERUPTION OF VESUVIUS and cataclysmic destruction of Pompeii, the late medieval madness of the PEASANTS' REVOLT that set London alight, and our newest offer, a front seat view of our first American Civil War trip, the hubris and the chaos of the FIRST BATTLE OF BULL RUN.

Whatever trip you choose, the TIME TRAVELLERS' HANDBOOK is your Owl of Minerva. In putting together this guide we've been where you are going, we've flown home at dusk and, at last, with the wisdom of hindsight actually available to us, charted a course through the past on your behalf. We really will take you to the right place at the right time, every time. Alongside the key moments, we let you know WHERE TO STAY, WHAT TO EAT and HOW TO PAY, and of course HOW TO GET HOME. Our Uncle Karl thought that 'Man made history but not in circumstances of his own choosing'. We can't let you make history – it's already a done deal – but we can let you choose the circumstances. Welcome to the past; we'll take you there.

THE SMALL PRINT: TERMS AND CONDITIONS OF TRAVEL

APPEARANCE AND DRESS CODE

It is important to blend in with the crowd as far as possible and for this reason WAG will provide you with suitable attire for all of your journeys. You may, however, already possess appropriate clothing or want to try making your own. If so, please read the guidance notes carefully. In cases where having a skin tone and physiognomy markedly differ from that of the locals would attract undue attention, WAG's experienced prosthetic and make-up department will swing into action.

HEALTH ISSUES

All travellers will be subject to stringent HEALTH CHECKS ahead of their journey. An innocuous seeming virus could have devastating consequences for a historical community which has not developed immunity to it. For similar but reverse reasons, travellers to high-risk destinations will be subject to health checks on their returns, and quarantine will be enforced if necessary. Some trips are more strenuous than others, the long voyages and extreme events in particular. We reserve the right to refuse time travel to clients whose medical condition renders them vulnerable. We advise all travellers to take out appropriate backdated medical insurance.

LANGUAGES AND COMMUNICATION

Travellers should assume that in all but the most contemporary journeys their mother tongue will be of limited use. English speakers who go unprepared to Elizabethan London will find it hard to understand others or to make themselves understood. Consequently WAG provides a basic grounding in the LOCAL LANGUAGE of your journey and an introductory course to body language, ritual, customs and deportment. The quoted price of each trip includes a two-day residential preparation and orientation programme. Please note: these courses are compulsory and a minimal standard of competence is required of all travellers.

THE TIME–SPACE CONTINUUM

All of our trips have been carefully selected so that you can blend into the past without drawing special attention to yourself. (It is for this reason, of course, that we cannot offer Moon Landings or intimate liaisons with the likes of Caesar or Napoleon). Even so, you must exercise great care not to do anything that might interfere with the events you have chosen to visit. The time–space continuum is sufficiently robust to cope with your presence and your minor interactions with the events of the past, but grand gestures are simply not on. WAG reserves the right to transport any customer who appears poised to infringe this regulation instantly back to the present, with no compensation payable.

Minor interactions with other members of the crowd are permitted, as are everyday activities such as EATING AND DRINKING. Any changes such interactions make to the course of history will be negligible and tolerable (e.g. you may return to find that you like speed metal rather than jazz, or that your partner is called Lionel rather than Pam). Such alterations must be regarded as an occupational hazard. It goes without saying that bringing back SOUVE-NIRS is not permitted, as this would play havoc with the market for antiques. Strictly no mobile phones and no cameras. Don't even think about selfies.

WAG will accept no responsibility for the consequences of failing to adhere to these terms and conditions.

PART ONE

CELEBRATIONS & EXHIBITIONS

The Field of the Cloth of Gold

8–24 JUNE 1520 ❋ NEAR CALAIS, ENGLAND

FOR JUST OVER TWO WEEKS IN JUNE 1520, Henry VIII and Francis I, the kings of England and France, and most of their feudal nobility, gathered for a great outdoor meeting in northern France. They came together ostensibly to make peace and celebrate the betrothal of Francis's son and Henry's daughter but it was an occasion soaked in sixteenth-century realpolitik. THE FIELD OF THE CLOTH OF GOLD (as it was dubbed by eighteenth-century historians) provided an extraordinary opportunity for two great Renaissance princes to display themselves to each other and their followers as warrior kings, chivalric gentlemen and luminous stars in Europe's political firmament.

Settled into vast and ostentatious tent cities, equipped with splendid temporary palaces, the two sovereigns first met and then joined together to stage a great knightly tournament of jousting and foot combat, punctuated by intense merrymaking, feasting and dancing.

> **PLEASE NOTE** that this trip is based on attendance in the English camp. For those that prefer a more Francophone experience, we hope to be able to offer *le champ de la toile d'or* experience in the near future.

BRIEFING: GRAND SUMMITS

Grand summit meetings between the French and English kings had a considerable track record. In 1254 Henry III of England met Louis IX of France in Chartres and rode together to Paris for a great banquet. Things went so well they did it all again in 1259 and signed a peace treaty. Things were taken up a notch in scale and splendour by the 1396 meeting of Richard II and Charles VI. Held in the midst of the Hundred Years War it secured a temporary peace by marrying Richard to seven-year-old Princess Isabelle of France.

Like nearly every European monarch since the fall of the Roman Empire, Henry VIII of England and Francis I of France spent a great deal of time and money on warfare; that, after all, was the very purpose of the sovereign, to defend and expand the realm (and in his own body and demeanour express the warrior manliness of the feudal nobility). However, in the early sixteenth century there were countervailing trends. Intellectually, the new humanism of writers like Erasmus argued that monarchs' power was best expressed by keeping the peace, and the warrior creed shifted towards the restraints of the chivalric code. Politically, two of Europe's most important statesmen had reasons for wanting to halt the internecine warfare. Pope Leo X sought unity because he feared the rising power of the Ottoman Empire in the east. England's Cardinal Wolsey, who was pushing England from the periphery to the centre of European politics, sought stability.

The 1518 Treaty of London was the outcome of a short period of competitive peacemaking with Wolsey and the Pope inviting all European states to agree an enduring peace. The French signed up and to seal the deal the Dauphin Francis was betrothed to Henry's daughter, Princess Mary. The small print included an agreement that the monarchs would meet and hold a tournament. The combination was essential, for the jousts and tourneys would allow both sovereigns to demonstrate warrior credentials but simultaneously show they could forsake war for chivalric reasons.

There then followed eighteen months of competitive gift-giving between the kings and petty-fogging, super-politicised debate over the details and protocols of the event, led by Gaspard de Coligny, Marshal of France, and Charles Somerset, Earl of Worcester and Lord Chamberlain. However, by April 1520 the deal was done and the senior officers of both Royal Households bent to the enormous logistical task of staging the event, transporting over 6,000 people, their horses and baggage from England and an equal number of the French court from around the country.

THE TRIP

Your POINT OF ARRIVAL on the morning of 8 June 1520 will be the very rutted road that runs between the small towns of ARDRES and GUINES (in what is now northern France). When you arrive on the path about a mile short of Guines you will actually be in England, or rather the PALE OF CALAIS, an area of land extending about ten miles from the English port ceded by the French in 1347. You will need to return here on 24 June for your departure.

The main body of the English court, nearly 6,000 strong, will have arrived a day beforehand but the road is still likely to be busy. As you head east towards the English camp in GUINES you might see the French nobles Lord Chancellor Antoine Duprat and Admiral Bonnivet riding brusquely past you. They are paying a final courtesy call on Henry. A half dozen English nobles will, on their part, ride out to Ardres to see King Francis. There will also be a steady flow of carts and mules carrying the enormous quantity of supplies required to build and feed the English camp. Expect a selection of vagabonds, beggars and thieves to be lurking around the fringes of the camp sensing that plentiful scraps and charity will be made available over the coming days.

THE ENGLISH CAMP

When GUINES first comes into view it will not be the town's stone castle, church spire or cluster of housing that catches your eye, but the vast tent city of over 300 pavilions in front of it. Almost the entirety of the Tudor nobility and their retinues are here under canvas. Round, square and rectangular tents draped in sparkling coloured cloth are clustered to create instant noble houses, some with as many as a dozen tents linked by covered corridors and galleries. Glastonbury Festival it isn't – though the flags, banners and pennants flying from every mast and central tent pole are vaguely reminiscent, and around the edges is less salubrious accommodation where servants, scullery maids, armourers and stable hands are based. Right at the heart of the site, directly before Guines castle, is the King's Palace: a magnificent set of canvas-roofed, double-storeyed, brick buildings.

ACCOMMODATION

As you make way down to the English camp you will be able to see that the pavilions are all trimmed with fixed and painted wooden boards, the grandest with skirting and flooring too. Tudor roses and Beaufort portcullis arms are much in evidence. Do look up, though; on top of the masts that hold up the tents there is a menagerie of beautifully carved heraldic beasts, including dragons, griffins and greyhounds, lions, stags and antelopes.

Your host for the next fortnight or so is SIR ADRIAN FORTESCUE and you will be looking for his pavilion, marked with the Fortescue coat of arms: a blue shield with a white diagonal stripe and wavy edges, paralleled by two gold diagonal lines, or, in the Latin heraldic vernacular, *azure a bend engrailed argent cotised or*.

Sir Adrian, a knight of the bath with land holdings in Hertfordshire is recently widowed and will be in deep mourning for much of the next five years. Thus distracted, he will, as long as he is not directly approached, barely notice your presence in the pavilion. Please stick rigidly to using the SMALL CIRCULAR TENT at the far end of the Fortescue pavilion. Note the Fortescue livery, here for your use, will get you into the banqueting halls, but do not expect a seat. The slop buckets are strictly your responsibility.

THE KING'S PALACE

HENRY'S PALACE at Guines, a hundred yards square, consists of four blocks round an atrium courtyard. The buildings have stone foundations, brick walls to eight feet high, then wattle and daub with clerestory windows, and an Italianate wooden cornice decorated with cross and leaf work. Above this, large timbers form a frame over which vast decorated canvas sheets are hung. The building has been completed in under three months by thousands of skilled artisans using timber and prepared wall sections from England, glass from Flanders and cloth from all over Western Europe.

As you walk up to the ornate mock guardhouse at the front of the palace, note the splendid FOUNTAIN with its depiction of Bacchus carved from wood. On feast and banquet days this will be running with two streams of wine – one red, one white – pumped under pressure. Earthenware vessels will be available to help yourself; you won't be alone. The gatehouse itself is adorned with a statue of SAINT MICHAEL, a deliberate compliment to France's patron saint of chivalry.

Once inside the palace in the main quadrangle, you will see two sets of very ornate pavilions on either side; to your left are CARDINAL WOLSEY'S QUARTERS; to the right are those of the

King's sister MARY, Duchess of Suffolk. Behind these pavilions are two long brick-walled building: on the left-hand side HENRY'S APARTMENTS and on the right those of QUEEN CATHERINE. The two are connected by an UNDERGROUND PASSAGE, while Henry's apartments have their very own box-tree-planted corridor leading back into Guines Castle. These tents will be closely guarded and difficult to enter, but should you get a glimpse inside look out for Catherine's set of nine floral tapestries stitched in gold and silk. In Wolsey's main waiting chamber you can observe sumptuous TAPESTRY work, rumoured to include a set depicting the TRIUMPH OF PETRARCH. Even from outside you will smell the sweet aroma of freshly cut rushes and flowers that fill the Royal Apartments.

Immediately opposite the entrance, and the building you are most likely to gain access to, is the LARGE HALL. A two-storey building, the ground floor will be a hive of activity at almost any time, housing the offices of the Lord Chamberlain, Lord Steward and Treasure Comptroller – the three most senior positions in the Royal Household. It also provides space for the royal service departments, including the warehouse and jewel house, the pantry, spicery, buttery, ewery (responsible for water and the vessels one drinks from and washes with), poultry, pitcher and larder. The upper floor is reached by an internal staircase over which hovers a sculpture of an armoured footsoldier. Inside the BANQUETING HALL look up at the canvas roof, whose intricate decoration includes the popular if enigmatic homilies of ALEXANDER BARCLAY. He is currently a theological favourite at court, and the Benedictine monk's satirical poem, *The Ship of Fools*, published in 1513, is a good ice-breaker in conversation in 1520.

A short gallery leads out of the back of the Large Hall and into the PALACE CHAPEL. This large open space is decorated with gold and silver and overlooked by the two royal oratories, on the first floor; known as HOLYDAY CLOSETS, they are the box seats for the royal houses. The altar will be set with golden candlesticks and a fabulous pearl-encrusted crucifix over four foot high. Note that the English have brought their own church organ with them. Mass is held daily.

EATING AND DRINKING

Catering at the Field of the Cloth of Gold is a very stratified affir. While you may be able to gain entrance to some of the major BANQUETS to be held over the fortnight, you will for the most part be eating in the FORTESCUE PAVILION. For proper nobles and their households most meals will be self-catered. Expect a lot of pottage, broth and tough black bread. Keep your ears open as there will be a certain number of meals communally provided for gentleman and perhaps their staff. Camp followers, beggars, lepers and locals trying their luck will be ever present around the camp's kitchens.

Water is strictly for washing in. The main drink available in the English camp is ALE, thrice-brewed in ever declining quality. The third brew called SMALL BEER is the least alcoholic of the ales and consumed by servants and children. WINE, as noted previously, will be freely available on feast days but harder to come by at other times.

You will observe at the banquets that courses consist of a multitude of DISHES, both savoury and sweet. There will be a great deal of poultry, game birds, baked and steamed fish, pies and potted animals and above all roast meats. Exotic birds, such as swans, may well be served and even reconstituted after cooking with head, neck and feather to create an edible sculpture. The English court's account will later record that 6,475 birds of various kinds were purchased and nearly 100,000 eggs, not to mention 3,406 sheep and lambs, 842 veal calves and 373 oxen.

THE FRENCH CAMP

It would be a considerable breach of protocol for lowly members of Sir Adrian Fortescue's household to enter the FRENCH CAMP and we advise you strongly not to. However, from a safe distance it is perfectly fine to take in the view. The French court will have made camp in the small town of ARDRES, five miles east and slightly south of the English camp and reached by the same road on which you arrived. You will see that the King's orders to build a vast ditch around the encampment and to repair the town's walls have been accomplished and the two together mark out a camp site filled with nearly 400 pavilions and a considerable swathe of the French peerage and nobility.

FRANCIS I BY JEAN CLOUET – AT AROUND THE TIME OF THE KINGS' MEET.
THE MEDALLION IS SAINT MICHEL. THE DRESS IS CLASSIC RENAISSANCE.

The KING'S APARTMENT should just be visible on the west side of the town, where a whole series of town houses have been combined with large pavilions to create his temporary palace. Of particular note is the huge BANQUETING HOUSE at the foot of the town connected by a long gallery to the palace. The English knight Edmund Hall will describe it as 'house of solas and sporte, of large and mightie compass'. Built like a multistorey amphitheatre, with three levels of stone wall, the interior is lined with balconies and, as Hall will report, decorated with 'frettes and knottes made of Ive buishes and other thynges that longest would be grene for pleasure'. The canvas roof is set with golden stars.

The transformation of Ardres has been overseen by the Marshal of France, GASPARD DE COLIGNY, and Grand Master of the Royal Artillery, JACQUES DIT GALIOT DE GENOUILLAC, whose logistical triumphs in the past include shipping the French cannon across the Alps and winning a great victory at Milan in 1513. Most of the work on the camp has been done in Tours, over 300 miles away, where the local textile industries have provided enough skilled labour to service the enormous order from the French court. For over three months thousands of cloth, silk and leather workers have been stitching and assembling the camp's pavilions, working in shift around the clock in the palace of the Archbishop of Tours. Among the most eye-catching of these is the main tent of the Royal Household, draped in golden cloth with three wide stripes of blue velvet, themselves encrusted with golden fleurs-de-lis. Atop this, balanced on a golden ball you should be able to make out a six-foot-high gold and blue wooden statue of Saint Michael holding a lance and shield, a slain serpent at his feet. Many of the other tents in the encampment feature a large golden apple carved from walnut instead. Queen Claude's pavilion, close by can be picked out for its lighter, brighter golden cloth. The Queen Mother's tents feature violet and crimson material.

DAY BY DAY

THURSDAY 8 JUNE: THE KING'S MEET

You should arrive mid-morning on Thursday, when preparations in the camp will be at fever pitch as horses are brushed and tack polished amid an air of nervous, growing anticipation. At around 5pm you will hear three cannons, signalling the departure of Henry's entourage to THE KINGS' MEET. Soon after this the distant sound of three cannons being fired in Ardres announces that Francis and his party are on their way.

Henry's entourage will be led out by one hundred archers drawn from the Royal Guard and Wolsey's personal guard. They will be followed on horse by a large retinue of household gentlemen and knights. SIR ADRIAN FORTESCUE, if he manages to make it, will be in with this pack. Then you will see the senior nobility, and in their midst the King. HENRY will be preceded by the MAR-QUESS OF DORSET holding upright the sword of state; to his left

HENRY VIII ARRIVES AT THE ENGLISH CAMP. NOTE THE ROYAL PALACE AND
WINE FOUNTAIN ON THE RIGHT, TOURNAMENT FIELD (TOP RIGHT) AND THE
DRAGON WHICH WILL APPEAR AT MASS ON THE FINAL DAY.

CARDINAL WOLSEY in brilliant crimson red silk; to his right SIR
HENRY GUILDFORD, Master of Horse, leading a spare mount for
the King. The King's back is covered by a dozen young henchmen
and hunting mates and then another tranche of senior nobles es-
corting bishops and foreign ambassadors. Finally come musicians
and stewards: twelve mace-bearers, twelve trumpeters, then twelve
heralds, all in Tudor livery. Expect plenty of MUSIC en route.

Francis's entourage will be similar if smaller. We strongly advise that you observe them at the meeting point – the Vale of Arden – rather than at the French camp or on the road. You will see two hundred mounted archers of the Royal Guard dressed in golden coats heading the cavalcade, followed by two hundred gentlemen of the royal household, and a hundred Swiss Guards on foot. Twelve trumpeters then precede the major nobles of France: the DUC DE BOURBON, ADMIRAL BONNIVET and KING FRANCIS himself. The man next to him holding the French sword of state in a sheath of blue velvet covered with golden fleurs-de-lis is GALEAZZO DA SAN SEVERINO, Master of Horse. Behind them will come the DUKES OF LORRAINE, ALENÇON AND VENDÔME, all the Cardinals of France, and the Knights of the Order of Saint Michel.

As the English caravan leaves its camp it will suddenly be joined by an enormous phalanx of INFANTRY, including the entirety of the ROYAL GUARD all decked out in Tudor livery adorned with golden roses. They will take up positions at the front and back of the entourage as well as forming up on the King's flanks in a parade now 4,000 strong. You may well note a certain amount of toing and froing as scouts are sent off to check the progress of the French, while French scouts scurry back to report to their masters. On at least one occasion the whole troupe will come to a halt as the King and his counsellors discuss whether it is safe to proceed. However, by around seven o'clock you should be entering into the VALE OF ANDREN, where the two entourages will take up positions opposite each other on raised earthen mounds.

The music will now fall silent as the two sides come to a silent halt. Look for King Francis to make the first move, shuffling his horse forward a couple of steps, followed by his three main attendants. Henry with Sir Henry Guildford, the Earl of Worcester, Sir Richard Wingate (ambassador to the French court) and of course CARDINAL WOLSEY. Note, Wingate is wearing a splendid brocade cloak given to him by Francis. It is, as you will see, no match for the KING'S OWN OUTFITS. Henry will be dressed in a silver doublet and cloak slashed with gold and hung with jewels. Around his neck you will see the Order of the Garter and a huge Saint George pendant, all topped by a black hat and plume. Francis is dressed in the currently fashionable latticework jerkin called a chammer combining gold, silver and gems set off by white leather riding boots and, like Henry, a black bejewelled velvet cap.

A sudden blast of the sackbuts will see both Kings' companions halt as the monarchs ride on to the appointed meeting place – a spear stuck in the ground. Both entourages will cheer lustily as the Kings doff their hats and then, still on horseback, embrace. They will suddenly be joined by running footmen who will accompany them arm-in-arm as they disappear into a small tent. While the kings are within you will notice that the English entourage does not break ranks and remains on the mound. The French, however, will become curious and drift over to the English side for slightly awkward conversations. After about an hour the Kings will reappear and there will be a great deal of hugging and embracing of each other's companions before a worried-looking Wolsey calls a halt to proceedings and both sides return to camp before sunset.

FRIDAY 9 JUNE: THE TREE OF HONOUR

The TOURNAMENT proper will begin with the hanging of shields on the TREE OF HONOUR. Located on the edge of the tournament field, the tree is made from entwined branches of hybrid raspberry and hawthorn, symbolising the new links between France and England. The whole thing is fixed to a stone column and surrounded by wooden railings. At about half past nine, the two kings, sixty noblemen and sixty guards, drawn from both camps, will be meeting at the tree to HANG SHIELDS.

Pride of place, acknowledging that the field is on English soil, will be going to Francis, whose shield is the first to be hung; Henry's will follow to his right. The shields of fourteen nobles who issue the tournament challenge to all-comers will be added below. Finally, three shields will be added to the lower branches to signify the three components of the tournament to come: a

GREY AND BLACK SHIELD for jousting, GOLD AND TAWNY for the tourney and SILVER for foot combat. Over the next couple of hours, the CHALLENGERS IN THE TOURNAMENT will come to the Tree, touch the three shields and place their own shields on the railings. Eventually there will be over 200 challengers and their coats of arms.

SUNDAY 11 JUNE: BRING ON THE BANQUETS

At some point in mid-afternoon the sound of CANNON will signal Henry's departure for the French camp and Francis setting out for the English camp. They will meet briefly at the field before being received by each other's QUEENS. If you are able to slip into the BANQUET you will find that the monarchs have their own dining zone (not to be entered), while the rest of the hall has been divided into two by a hanging wall of tapestries.

On one side, over a hundred LADIES OF THE ENGLISH COURT will dine, attended by twenty gentlemen who hover but do not eat. On the other side the leading French nobles DUC DE BOURBON and ADMIRAL BONNIVET dine with their entourage. After dinner there will be DANCING to music from tabors, pipes and viols, with a guest spot for Francis's own band of FIFES AND TROMBONES who will be laying down a dance 'in the Italian style'. The key feature of this dance is that, unlike most court masques, the dancers call upon members of the audience to join them.

MONDAY 12 JUNE: JOUSTING BEGINS

On Monday morning much of the English camp will be making its way to the FIELD OF THE CLOTH OF GOLD (as it is not yet known). Located just inside the Pais de Calais, midway between Guines and Ardres, the field is 900 feet long and 300 foot wide, enclosed by an eight-foot ditch which in turn has created a high earthen bulwark. Within, the field is marked by wooden railing and posts. Both ends of the field are entered through temporary

HENRY DISPLAYS THE CROWN JEWELS, IN A PAINTING AFTER
HANS HOLBEIN. BEFORE THIS DEPICTION, STANDING WITH LEGS
APART WAS CONSIDERED IMPOLITE.

TRIUMPHAL ARCHES and at the Guines end this is flanked by two sturdy ARMING CHAMBERS for the two monarchs. The Tree of Honour can be seen at the Ardres end just beyond the arch. On the left of the field is the just completed QUEEN'S PAVILION, from which the Royal Households and senior peerage will be watching the day's events; on its right is a somewhat rickety three-storey pavilion for everyone else. Henry has asked for a further deep ditch to be dug in front of it to prevent incursions from the stands, but the soft earth and likelihood of rain mean that this would imperil the buildings rather shaky foundations. Instead an additional line of railings has been introduced.

In the very centre of the field are the cloth-draped wooden walls that make up THE TILT. Only introduced into jousting in the late fifteenth century, this allows much greater control and precision on their part of the knights, leading to fewer injuries. A second set of railings on either side of the tilt help to keep the horse running straight.

Around noon, the two queens – CLAUDE AND CATHERINE – will make their entrance, swiftly followed by Henry and Francis leading their teams of TENANS – the issuers of the chivalric challenge on which the tournament is based. They will be followed by two teams of VENANS or challengers led by DUC D'ALENCON and ADMIRAL BONNIVET. There will then follow a great deal of presentation, ceremony, doffing of lances and bowing. Finally THE JOUSTS will begin.

TUESDAY 13 TO SATURDAY 17 JUNE:
RAINY DAYS AND WRESTLING

The next five days of the tournament are going to be interrupted by squalls and sometimes heavy summer rain showers. TUESDAY 13TH will be rained off altogether and the field will become so sodden that the organisers will have to remove the counter-lists from the tilt; this will lead to much poor-quality jousting as riders are unable to keep their charges consistently close to the centre.

THE TOURNAMENT FIELD AND TREE OF HONOUR – YOU'LL BE SEATED ON THE LEFT.

WEDNESDAY 14TH will be equally dismal, but enlivened in the afternoon by a large WRESTLING COMPETITION in the mud between English guards and Breton wrestlers, as well as an ENGLISH ARCHERY DISPLAY.

Things will be dry enough on THURSDAY 15TH for JOUSTING to recommence with both Henry and Francis putting in an appearance. HENRY'S JOUST WITH MARSHALL LESCYN is the sporting highlight of the day and a sartorial triumph, with his cloak decorated with lozenges and eglantine flowers of gold. The following day it will rain again and, though a few jousts will be held, neither kings nor queens, nor anyone very special, will show up. However, on SATURDAY 17TH the sun will return and a decent day's jousting will commence. Both Henry and Francis will appear to be in particularly good fettle, breaking eighteen and fourteen lances respectively in their contest with a team led by the Earl of Devonshire.

SUNDAY 18 JUNE: BACK TO THE BANQUET

The camp will be thick with rumour and gossip today, as FRANCIS will be paying a surprise early morning visit to HENRY'S APARTMENTS, after which they will go to MASS together. Henry will then depart for Ardres and Francis will be relaxing in Queen Catherine's apartment before DINNER. Again the dining hall will be

GO EASY ON THE ROAST SWAN TO AVOID THE FATE OF THE POOR
UNFORTUNATE THROWING UP ON THE LEFT.

divided during the meal, with men and women on different sides, but afterwards the tapestries will be cleared and the DANCING will begin, led this time by Francis himself. He will be entering the hall with ten companions in long, velvet-hooded gowns adorned with plumes.

MONDAY 19 AND TUESDAY 20 JUNE: LAST JOUSTS, COSTUMES AND THE TOURNEY

The final days of the JOUST will be clear and dry. On the Monday the two kings will be present and will conduct an elaborate exchange of horses and gifts. On Tuesday they will return to the tilts.

Do try and look out for KING FRANCIS'S CLOTHING, which, on the days he jousts, have been designed to signal through a variety of symbols – brooches and embroidery – carefully calibrated chivalric phrases. Members of the French court will be on hand to help decode these, so feel free to ask. Tuesday's motto, for example, is 'Heart fastened in pain endless/when she/delivereth me not of bonds.'

Tuesday will also be the day of the TOURNEY in which combatants fight on horseback and in pairs, but in open space rather than across a barrier. Weapons include blunted swords, staves and clubs but much of the skill and excitement is in the quality of the HORSEMANSHIP as riders attempt tight turns and precise moments of ACCELERATION to ensure their blows have maximum force. The very best competitors will time their runs and blows in front of the Queen's pavilion.

WEDNESDAY 21 AND THURSDAY 22 JUNE: COMBAT ON FOOT

The FOOT COMBAT of these two days involves individual bouts fought across a central wooden barrier – thus preventing grappling and wrestling and keeping the emphasis on weapon skills. Combatants will use short swords, spears and pikes. It is particularly worth noting the quality of HENRY'S ARMOUR. Although unable to use his most modern and sophisticated armour, after lengthy and complex negotiations with the French Henry is able to wear a suit that displays many technical innovations of the royal armoury. Francis has insisted on the use of closed visors and the tonlet – a protective skirt of metal plates. To this Henry will have added cuisses – laminated steel breeches – and lames, which are the articulated steel plates bound to leather strips that provide unrivalled protection and freedom of movement at the joints.

FRIDAY 23 JUNE: MASS AT THE TILTYARD

Overnight, a huge workforce has been working furiously to repair the TILTYARD and build a vast public stage over it. On this they will have built a large chapel richly furnished with tapestries and bejewelled crucifixes (you may recognise them from the Royal Chapel back at the English camp). Amazingly the task will have been accomplished. You will find the CHAPEL positioned between the Queen's pavilion and the general viewing galleries.

MASS will begin at noon with Cardinal Wolsey leading proceedings, Note the relative height of the various clerics on the platform: Wolsey is positioned just above Cardinal de Boisy; both are higher than France's other cardinals, while the bishops of both nations are lower still. Music and singing come from the ROYAL CHOIRS of both nations and the organ from Henry's chapel. The French organist PIERRE MOUTON, accompanied by voice, sackbuts and coronets will play a particularly good rendition of the liturgical prayer *Kyrie*.

Look out for CARDINAL BOURBON, who will take the gospel to both Kings and both Queens for them to kiss. Henry and Francis will also embrace with the PAX – a holy kiss – while the Queens join arms. Just prior to the Elevation of the Host, the point at which the wafers and wine become the body of Christ, be sure to look up. You will see a DRAGON appear in the sky. As one contemporary would later report, 'Lo! Flying in great loops, a slender and hollow monster stretched out in the sky.' While later paintings will depict a great fire spitting beast, you will see that this is a large, if sturdy and highly decorated, FRENCH KITE. Cardinal Wolsey's face, upstaged by this event, is worth your consideration.

SATURDAY 24 JUNE: THE LAST SUPPER

Once again the two Kings will EXCHANGE CAMPS AND PALACES for a final FAREWELL BANQUET. On this occasion both will have dressed in their MASQUE OUTFITS before the meal. If you are alert you may be able to see Henry ride out dressed as Hercules in a woven gold lion's pelt carrying a great wooden club wrapped in green damask. His company are dressed as mixture of HEBREW KINGS and Christian warriors like KING ARTHUR and CHARLEMAGNE. Tonight's feast will be concluding with the presentation of jewels, gems and other prizes to the winners of the tournament. Drink up, but do return to the Fortescue pavilion for your DEPARTURE.

The Great Exhibition

THE GREAT EXHIBITION OF THE WORKS OF Industry of All Nations – to give it its full title – was a vast celebration of the wonders of human ingenuity, held in London in the summer of 1851. Housed in the biggest greenhouse in history, it featured over 100,000 exhibits and attracted 6,039,195 visitors – equivalent to two-sevenths of the population of Britain at the time. Attendances on most days hovered around the 50,000 mark. Despite the global scope of the event, around half the exhibits were from the host nation or its Empire, giving the show a pronounced flavour of Britain v The Rest of the World. As Britain was approaching the zenith of her power – in 1851 she produced half the world's iron, more than half its cotton cloth and the lion's share of its revenue – it was no great surprise that she came out rather well. The host nation also had the distinct advantage of organising the show.

Accustomed as we are to global trade fairs and expos, it would be easy to overlook the staggering novelty of the Great Exhibition.

ENLARGED FOLD-OUT FLOORPLANS OF THE EXHIBITION WILL BE
PROVIDED TO TRAVELLERS.

Never before had so many nations come together in one place, except to some extent on the battlefield. And never – at least in Britain – had the classes intermingled so freely. The authorities, still haunted by the spectre of the French Revolution, not to mention the wave of populist uprisings that had swept through continental Europe in 1848, had been terribly anxious in advance about what might happen when the barriers of social segregation were lifted. In the event, everyone rubbed along together very nicely, with dukes and yokels equally transfixed by the items on show, and by each other.

As far as the exhibits themselves are concerned, the time traveller cannot really lose. They are either remarkable in themselves or it is fascinating to observe how fascinating your fellow visitors find them. Many items that are unremarkable to twenty-first century eyes make the Victorians gaga with excitement. So erase any lingering painful memories of the Millennium Dome from your mind and visit the exhibition that really will change the world.

NOTE: this is a two-day trip that can be taken at any point during the Exhibition: see 'Tickets' for further information.

BRIEFING: INVENTING THE EXHIBITION

THE GREAT EXHIBITION owes its existence to two men: HENRY COLE, the co-inventor of the postage stamp, and Francis Albert Charles Augustus Emmanuel Saxe-Coburg Gotha, aka PRINCE ALBERT. Prior to his involvement in the project, Albert had been suffering acutely from what might be described as Prince Charles Syndrome: an urgent need to define a role for himself beyond accompanying the Queen on official functions. Through the Great Exhibition, he seems to have nailed the problem, and largely silenced the London smarties who have hitherto looked on him as an insufferably pushy and puritanical German arriviste.

In 1843, the Prince became President of the SOCIETY OF ARTS, an organisation which promoted useful inventions. Two years later, this august body held a small exhibition behind its headquarters near the Strand. One of the prize-winners was Felix Summerly, aka Henry Cole, for the design of an admirable tea set. Cole subsequently joined the Society and in 1848 approached Albert with a proposal for a national exhibition to be held three years later.

The Prince hummed and hawed a bit. Meanwhile, Cole travelled to Paris for the 1849 iteration of an exhibition the city had hosted every few years for half a century. While there, he learned that the French had been seriously thinking of opening up their show to international exhibitors. The idea had been rejected but it got Cole thinking. An international show in London would act as a major stimulus to trade. Other nations would inevitably want to exhibit, partly out of competitive spirit, partly from fear of missing out. Yet Britain was guaranteed to be the focus of attention. What wasn't to like?

When Cole went back to the Prince Consort with his proposal for an international show, Albert was immediately sold. Thereafter, things moved quickly. It was decided that the Exhibition should be financed by subscription rather than by Parliament, and in January 1850 the Queen appointed a Royal Commission to turn the dream into reality.

On 21 March, a sumptuous banquet was held in the Egyptian Hall at Mansion House in the City of London to spread the word and drum up support for the project. It was attended by almost 200 provincial mayors, foreign ambassadors, politicians and military top brass. At the end of dinner, Prince Albert addressed the assembled great and good with the following words:

'Gentlemen, the Exhibition of 1851 is to give us a true test of the point of development at which the whole of mankind has arrived in this great task, and a new starting point from which all nations will be able to direct their further exertions.'

What you are about to see is a vindication of these portentous words.

THE TRIP

The VENUE for the Great Exhibition occupies around eighteen acres of HYDE PARK, towards its southern edge. Not coincidentally, this is where the Albert Memorial will be erected twenty-one years hence, with the eponymous Prince holding a copy of the exhibition catalogue.

The choice of site has not gone down well in some circles. The upper-class residents of Kensington, terrified by the prospect of the lower orders descending on their patch, threatened

THE CRYSTAL PALACE, SHOWING THE SOUTH ENTRANCE. THINGS MAY BE A
LITTLE BUSIER THAN THIS POSTCARD SUGGESTS.

to go on strike at one stage. This would have taken the form of
them decamping to the country and cancelling 'the Season' (the
round of balls held in May and June each year). In the end, however, most of the toffs seem to have hung around. Even if they
hadn't, local businesses would have been cleaning up as a result
of the extra trade. One notable beneficiary is a certain CHARLES
HARROD. You might want to pick up some picnic materials at
his grocery store in Knightsbridge, a village a few hundred yards
south of the Park. In a few years he will be expanding it rather
dramatically.

THE CRYSTAL PALACE

The Royal Commission originally invited architects to tender designs for the proposed Exhibition but none of the 245 submissions was deemed sufficiently compelling. Instead, the Commission came up with a plan of its own, largely the work of ISAMBARD KINGDOM BRUNEL. On 22 June 1850, a drawing of the proposed edifice appeared in the *Illustrated London News*, to almost universal dismay. For one thing, it was unremittingly dull. For another, it was made of brick, and to produce the requisite 19 million bricks, every kiln in Britain would have to dedicate several months to the project to the exclusion of all else. It seemed unlikely the building would be finished on time.

At this worrying juncture, a saviour appeared in the form of the Duke of Devonshire's head gardener. JOSEPH PAXTON's previous project had been constructing a large greenhouse at Chatsworth dedicated to the Victoria regia lily, based on a prefabricated iron frame. He reasoned that the same cutting-edge technology could be used to build the gigantic structure required for the Great Exhibition, and in double quick time. Paxton was duly awarded the gig.

Although the critic John Ruskin has bitchily likened Paxton's handiwork to a cucumber frame, it is at least as impressive as anything it contains. The CRYSTAL PALACE is like a cross

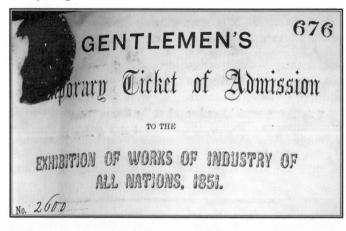

GENTLEMEN'S   676

...orary Ticket of Admission

TO THE

EXHIBITION OF WORKS OF INDUSTRY OF
ALL NATIONS, 1851.

No. 2600

between a medieval cathedral and a railway terminus. It is shaped like an elongated crucifix, nearly a third of a mile long and 408 feet wide. 330 enormous iron pillars, hundreds of smaller ones and more than 300,000 panes of glass have been used in its construction.

SOME PRACTICAL ISSUES

The Company has reserved ROOMS in MIVART'S HOTEL in Brook Street (soon to be purchased by Mr and Mrs Claridge). A dinner and bed-and-breakfast package is a surprisingly reasonable 15s (about £165 in today's money). However, if you would prefer a more communal experience, we can offer beds at THOMAS HARRISON'S FURNITURE DEPOSITORY on Ranelagh Road in Pimlico; this has been converted into a hostel with 1,000 dormitory beds for the duration of the Exhibition. Renamed 'The Mechanics Home', it features dining and smoking rooms, good washing facilities and a doctor. All for 1s 3d a night.

We can arrange for you to be SET DOWN at your London accommodation or, if you prefer, elsewhere in England, so you can travel to London by STEAM TRAIN. Your fellow passengers will be as thrilled as you just to be experiencing this novel form of transport, while their wild speculations about what they will be encountering in the capital will infect you with excitement. Once in London, transportation should be no problem, but beware of profiteering by local omnibus and cab drivers. If it rains, they will bump up their prices and not back down.

TICKETS

Your experience of the Great Exhibition will vary according to the stage of its run at which you visit. Tickets are more expensive for the early weeks, so if you come then you'll have more elbow room and perhaps see more celebrities. But you will miss the chance to mingle with the 'great unwashed', which will be a pity, as observing ordinary if rather gobsmacked Victorians in action is a fascinating sight in itself. On the celebrity front, you stand a reasonable chance of seeing QUEEN VICTORIA moseying about the place. She can't get enough of the Exhibition and will pay around thirty visits before heading for Balmoral in July. You'll need to arrive early, though, as her policy is to pitch up a couple of hours before opening time, lingering long enough to coincide with some of her subjects. Hint: she's the short dumpy chinless lady wearing a crown. You may also run into CHARLES DICKENS, CHARLES DARWIN, GEORGE ELIOT, LEWIS CARROLL, EMILY BRONTË or ALFRED, LORD TENNYSON.

The cost of tickets varies enormously. A SEASON TICKET is 3 guineas for men and 2 guineas for women (£346/£231 in equivalent modern prices). Purchasing one may seem unnecessary but it will allow you to attend the OPENING CEREMONY. The entrance charge on the second and third days is £1, falling to 5s for the next 18 days. Thereafter, the price is 1s from Monday to Thursday, 2s 6d on Fridays and 5s on Saturdays.

WHAT TO WEAR

The company offers a choice of costume, dependent on what class you wish to represent yourself as belonging to. For MEN, a top hat and a cane are de rigueur if you want to come across as reasonably posh, and some kind of headgear is essential whatever your social aspirations. The elaborate facial hair associated with the Victorian era has yet to become popular, and if you arrive with a beard or mutton chop whiskers, you will be presumed to be French. For WOMEN, flounced crinoline skirts are all the rage, but at this stage the underlying garments are made with linen stiffened with horsehair, rather than the hoops or cages which will be introduced in a few years' time. Pretty much all women of all classes wear bonnets.

WHAT TO EAT

Food on offer inside the palace is dismal. The two REFRESHMENT COURTS will sell you a plate of ham or a pork pie for 6d, with bread and butter 2d extra. Schweppes soda water (the 'official beverage' of the event) comes in at 6d a glass, while a small ice cream is 6d and a large one 1s. These are very high prices for the era and there have been numerous complaints about unwashed waitresses. Our advice is to bring a PICNIC. This will also allow you to beat the alcohol ban. Mivarts Hotel can arrange a packed lunch, or, as noted, you could visit CHARLES HARROD'S GROCERY SHOP on Knightsbridge.

Alternatively, those in the know make the brief stroll to THE SYMPOSIUM OF ALL NATIONS, an upmarket 1,500-seater pop-up restaurant situated where the Royal Albert Hall now stands. The proprietor is a Frenchman named Alexis Soyer, Britain's first ever celebrity chef. Prior to this venture, he displayed his philanthropic side by opening soup kitchens in Ireland during the potato famine. A slap-up Franco-English meal will cost you between 2s–10s (£22–£110).

EMERGENCIES

While you should always be aware of the presence of PICKPOCKETS – this is Fagin's London, after all – you should be pretty safe within the Palace. As a result of the ruling class's largely unfounded fears, the place is crawling with policemen, undercover and otherwise. There is a police-operated LOST CHILDREN AND PROPERTY desk near the crystal fountain.

If your emergency is in the bowel department, you can, for the first time in history, avail yourself of a PAY TOILET, courtesy of the pioneering sanitary engineer George Jennings. This will cost you 1d. If your needs are purely liquid, men can use the urinals for free, but women will have no option but to 'spend a penny'.

1 MAY: THE OPENING CEREMONY

If you have opted for a season ticket, you will be able to attend the OPENING CEREMONY on 1 May. The QUEEN AND PRINCE ALBERT will not arrive until shortly before noon but the doors to the Crystal Palace will open at 9am. You are well advised to get to the Palace considerably before then and to allow plenty of time for your journey. Hyde Park and the roads from Buckingham Palace will already be jammed by 6am. By mid-morning, as many as a million people will be lining the route, around a tenth of them foreigners.

THE OPENING CEREMONY FEATURING VICTORIA AND ALBERT. FORMALITY IS THE ORDER OF THE DAY. DON'T EXPECT BALLOONS.

Once inside the Palace, grab a seat as close as possible to the RAISED PLATFORM near the centre of the building. This is where the Queen will sit, on an elaborate chair borrowed from the Indian section of the Exhibition, covered in crimson velvet and shaded by a blue silk canopy adorned with fleur-de-lys symbols made from ostrich feathers. At 10am, the CELEBS will start to arrive. You may spot the DUKE OF WELLINGTON – 82 today – hobnobbing with the slightly older MARQUESS OF ANGLESEY. This is a touching moment. The two haven't got on since Wellington displayed a distinct lack of sympathy for the then Lord Uxbridge during the Battle of Waterloo. 'By God, I've lost a leg!' the immortal exchange had begun. 'By God, so you have!' had been its conclusion.

As noon approaches, anticipation will have reached fever pitch. The ARRIVAL OF THE ROYALS will be heralded by a fanfare of trumpets, a volley of cannon fire from the far side of the Serpentine and ear-splitting cheers echoing up and down the galleries. Then a vast organ near the southern entrance will strike up the national anthem. When the noise has died down, Prince Albert will deliver a rather self-congratulatory speech, the Queen will respond, the Archbishop of Canterbury will bless the Exhibition and the massed choirs of several cathedrals will belt out Handel's 'Hallelujah Chorus'. In a delightful departure from the script, a Chinaman will appear in front of the dais at this point, bowing repeatedly at the royal couple. Everyone will assume he is some kind of dignitary, but in fact he is the captain of a junk moored at Limehouse, overcome with emotion.

The Royal Party will then make its way up and down the length of the Palace, solemnly inspecting some of the exhibits. The Queen will then declare the Exhibition open, before descending the platform and leaving the building. Several excitable ladies will take turns to sit on the recently vacated throne, still warm from the monarch's behind.

You are now free to explore the Palace at your leisure.

THE EXHIBITS

It is a guidebook cliché to state how long it would take to see all the exhibits in a major museum but in this instance we're going to do it anyway: *The Times* has calculated that it would take about 200 hours to do the Great Exhibition justice. Roughly speaking, BRITISH AND IMPERIAL EXHIBITS occupy the western half of the Palace, while the REST OF THE WORLD is squeezed into the east. This applies to both ground level and the first floor galleries, but the items on display in the latter tend to be smaller and dinkier. This is where you will find much of the stuff at the quirky/bonkers/steampunk end of the spectrum.

The grandest and most popular aproach to the Palace is the SOUTH ENTRANCE, which leads in to the celebrated TRANSEPT. Here you will immediately see how Paxton dealt with the problem of ten elm trees that everyone assumed would have to be felled to make way for the building. He simply enclosed them. This gives an immediate sense of the scale of the Palace, which will be enhanced as you progress to the CRYSTAL FOUNTAIN at its very centre. Made by Follet Ostler, this is made of highly polished pink glass and is 27 feet high. As well as being awfully pretty, it is a valuable landmark and a favourite spot for picnickers.

BRITAIN AND THE EMPIRE

The western half of the GROUND FLOOR of the Palace is devoted to BRITISH AND IMPERIAL exhibits. Turning left from the North Transept, you pass through the less dramatic part of the INDIA SECTION (the good stuff is on the other side of the MAIN AVENUE, which bisects the Palace) and into the misleadingly named FINE ARTS COURT, an eclectic display ranging from flowers made from human hair to a vast oak sideboard carved from a tree in the grounds of Kenilworth Castle. Beyond this and stretching all the way to the western end of the Palace is the MACHINES IN MOTION area. This

HOWD'YA LIKE THAT? TRANSPORTATION FOR THE
MODERN MAHARAJAH IN THE INDIAN SECTION.

is perhaps the most popular section of the whole Exhibition, giving
a glimpse of the wondrous new technologies about to transform the
planet. Power is provided by steam, generated by a group of boilers
housed outside the building. One highlight is JAMES NASMYTH'S
STEAM HAMMER, powerful enough to flatten vast chunks of steel
but delicate enough to crack a boiled egg placed in a wine glass
without breaking the glass (a procedure you may get to witness).
Another is DE LA RUE'S PATENT ENVELOPE MACHINE, capable of
transforming ordinary sheets of paper into 2,700 perfectly folded,
gummed and stacked envelopes per hour. A machine that churns
out 100 fags a minute is also extremely popular.

Just the south of this section is a display of LOCOMOTIVES,
including the London and North Western's 1,140 horsepower

LIVERPOOL engine, and a prototype TRAM, or 'railway in the streets' as the manufacturer describes it, the latter term having yet to be coined. You will notice your fellow visitors reacting to such vehicles in much the same way as an early twenty-first-century audience might respond to a drone plane.

When you have sated your appetite for steam power, move south to the Main Avenue. If you look towards the western wall of the Palace, you will be confronted by your image reflected in the LARGEST MIRROR IN THE WORLD. Its effect is to double the size of the building, which was plenty big already. Turning round, you will find yourself looking down the entire length of the Palace, with the crystal fountain a small dot nearly a furlong and a half away. As you head towards it, the first thing you will come across is a forty-foot scale model of LIVERPOOL DOCKS, replete with 1,600 miniaturised ships. Next comes a succession of other models, including one of the recently opened BRITANNIA RAILWAY BRIDGE, an engineering marvel consisting of parallel tubes spanning the Menai Strait. After this, almost anything can and does pop up. Ostrich feathers vie for your attention alongside samples of EARLY PHOTOGRAPHY, a sperm whale's jawbone, a display of illumination systems for lighthouses and a huge ELECTROPLATED VASE depicting Prince Albert alongside the likes of William Shakespeare and Sir Isaac Newton.

After taking a well-earned breather at the crystal fountain, it is time to tackle the southern half of what might be termed the WESTERN NAVE. This begins with the second and more opulent area devoted to INDIA, the 'jewel in the crown' of the British Empire. The centrepieces are four spectacular gifts to Queen Victoria from the NAWAB OF BENGAL: a canopied velvet throne, two palanquins, one carved from ivory, and an elaborate howdah. If you are visiting during the early weeks, you are likely to be as puzzled as everyone else as to the purpose of the last object. Then a stuffed elephant will arrive from the museum of Saffron Walden in Essex and all will become clear: a howdah is a covered and canopied seat for placement on the back of such beasts.

Directly to the west of this section are areas devoted to Canada, the West Indies, South Africa and New South Wales. The most popular CANADIAN EXHIBITS are snowshoes, sleighs and other devices suggestive of extreme cold. The least charismatic are the various cod liver oil products displayed for NEWFOUNDLAND. The WEST INDIES area is dominated by a profusion of fruits and flowers, while the AUSTRALIAN and SOUTH AFRICAN zones major in exotic wildlife, including a stuffed platypus, a 103 lb tusk and several ostrich eggs.

Acting as a buffer between these colonial displays and more products from Britain are AUGUSTUS PUGIN'S MEDIEVAL COURT and the BRITISH SCULPTURE ROOM. Pugin's display is a deliberate attempt to counterbalance the largely industrial flavour of the British exhibits. One side of the room is devoted to ecclesiastical paraphernalia, the other to furniture, tapestries and the like. It is all very Victorian Gothic, a throwback to an idealised version of the 1450s. Although the craftsmanship is impressive, many visitors find it hard to see the point of the display in the context of the brave new world the Exhibition is celebrating

The sculpture room, on the other hand, tends to be heaving, despite – or more likely because of – the disapproving press reviews. Both phenomena can be explained by the abundance of NUDES on display, particularly female ones. Naked ladies, even in stone, have yet to become commonplace as of 1851.

Between here and the western end of the Palace, visitors are hurled back into the Industrial Revolution with a vengeance. The displays nearest to the Main Avenue are organised by city, successively BIRMINGHAM (gas fittings and other domestic items for the middle classes), SHEFFIELD (steel goods, including the mother of all penknives with eighty blades), YORKSHIRE (woollen fabrics) and MANCHESTER (cotton). Behind these is a long stretch of agricultural implements and machinery, acting as a magnet for besmocked country folk, who gaze on them wistfully dreaming of the easier future they portend.

It is now time to pop upstairs.

N 280.—HAMMOCK AND BED IN ONE.
Will sustain six persons in the water.

INGENIOUS INVENTIONS WERE BIG AT THE GREAT EXHIBITION. THIS
TYPICALLY BRITISH CONTRIBUTION – A HAMMOCK THAT CONVERTED INTO A
RESCUE DINGHY – WOWED THE CROWDS.

THE BRITISH GALLERIES

THE GALLERY hugs the perimeter of the Palace, leaving a huge cruciform space in the middle. Peer over the side rail to take in the magnitude of your surroundings with the tide of humanity slowly circulating down below and the soaring roof of the transept above. Then make your way to the south edge of the gallery, just above the main entrance. You will then be able to 'do' the whole western gallery, which is devoted to smaller British exhibits, in one extended anti-clockwise walk.

First, however, the BRITISH SECTION makes a slight incursion into the EASTERN GALLERY, in the form of a display of NOVEL ITEMS OF CLOTHING. They include a Wellington hat (as opposed to boot), garments employing elastic to free their wearers from the tyranny of lacing, and a pair of tartan socks studded with 1,300 diamonds. Moving into the WESTERN GALLERY, you will be inundated with silk from Spitalfields and Paisley, lacework, chemicals and pharmaceuticals, and GUNS, including a revolutionary telescopic sight.

As you enter the Western Gallery, look out for the display entitled 'PHILOSOPHICAL, MUSICAL, HOROLOGICAL AND SURGICAL INSTRUMENTS'. This is a showcase for the unparalleled Victorian talent for invention. Offerings include a waterproof timepiece ticking away merrily inside a glass of water, and clocks powered by electricity (whatever next?). Globes are also well represented, with one set made from inflatable tissue paper. The star attraction, however, has to be Dr Merryweather's Tempest Prognosticator. This is likely to be the first leech-powered weather forecasting device you have come across. It relies on the creatures' habit of leaving the water when they detect a fall in atmospheric pressure, suggesting that rain is imminent. In this instance, their exodus triggers an alarm bell.

If this item leaves you hungry for more leeches, you will find an extraordinary mechanical example in the surgical instruments display, along with a walking stick containing medicines, medical implements and an enema, and a bed designed to tip out its occupant at a predetermined hour. In the best tradition of British public events, there is a jolly Bobby available to act as a guinea pig. Another medical marvel is an adjustable human figure with 7,000 steel components.

You are now on the west side of the north transept, crammed with fine British porcelain from Staffordshire and Worcestershire. There is a staircase here, down which you should proceed. You may wish to 'spend a penny' (see EMERGENCIES); Ladies and Gents are available on either side of the refreshment court. You are advised to take advantage: you are about to tackle the rest of the world.

THE REST OF THE WORLD

The half of the Palace devoted to the portions of the planet outside the British Empire is arranged in such a way that the displays of the major exhibiting nations occupy both sides of the Main Avenue (the lesser nations are tucked in wherever there is space). This pattern is then repeated in the eastern half of the first floor gallery. The best way to approach the ground floor is to zigzag your way across the Main Avenue, allowing you to take in all of the exhibits from a given country. In the gallery area, this isn't possible – if you tried to look at all the Austrian exhibits, for example, you would fall to a grisly death – so you just have to make your way round, eventually saying to yourself, 'Oh look, it's Austria again'.

GROUND-FLOOR WORLD EXHIBITS

Before you plunge into the rest of the world, a peek at the legendary KOH-I-NOOR DIAMOND is mandatory. Weighing in at 191 carats, it fell into British hands two years ago with the annexation of the Punjab. It is housed in a sort of glorified birdcage on the Main Avenue just to the east of the crystal fountain. Unfortunately, once you have battled your way to the front of the crowd surrounding it, you are almost certain to be underwhelmed. Due to a combination of poor cut and uninspired lighting, the gem singularly fails to dazzle. This will be rectified next year, when it will be trimmed down to 109 carats, but for now you'll just have to enjoy complaining about it. Nearby, you will find a rather more sparkly assemblage of oversized gems known as the Hope Collection and a vast nugget from the Mariposa goldmine in California.

Your zigzagging can now commence in earnest, beginning with the area just to the northeast of the crystal fountain. This is shared by EGYPT, TURKEY, PERSIA AND GREECE, with hookah pipes and elaborately decorated weapons featuring prominently. The Greek offerings mainly consist of marble statues, while the Turks reveal their dedication to smoking with a crutch that can also be used as a pipe.

On the other side of the Main Avenue is the CHINESE SECTION, largely furnished by London merchants rather than the Eastern Empire herself. As might be expected, there is a great deal of fine porcelain, lacquer ware, silk and bamboo. The exhibits that most capture the visitors' imaginations, however, are grotesque carvings made from tree roots and examples of the edible birds' nests that are the main ingredient of the barely conceivable soup of that name. Made by swiftlets from their own saliva, they do little to dispel the European conviction that the Orientals are a rum lot.

To the east of the Chinese section are the SWISS displays. There are plenty of cleverly carved toys and furniture but it is the WATCHES that make the big impression. They come in every conceivable form and setting – on bracelets, embedded in rings, attached to compasses, you name it. Queen Victoria is particularly enamoured of this part of the Exhibition. Crossing the Main Avenue again will lead you to SPAIN, PORTUGAL AND THEIR COLONIES. Tobacco products loom large, from Havana cigars to Manila cheroots, and the whole section is perfumed by several barrels of snuff. You will also find a wall from the Alhambra in Granada and a marvellous carving of a bullfighting ring.

Immediately to the east is an area devoted to parts of what will eventually become ITALY, specifically Rome, Tuscany and the Kingdom of Sardinia, which at this stage in history includes Piedmont and Savoy. The keynotes of this section are mosaics, exquisitely engraved seashells and miniaturisation of one kind or another. The ultimate example of the latter is a CARVED CHERRY STONE featuring Saint George, his dragon and twenty-four tiny human heads.

Further to the east, on either side of the Main Avenue, are the FRENCH displays. With 1,740 exhibitors, France has the biggest presence in the Palace after Britain. To the gall of the hosts, the old enemy seems to do everything with more style, the Sèvres porcelain and Gobelin tapestries easily surpassing their British equivalents. Luckily, the agricultural and other machinery from across the Channel is generally agreed to be clunky and second-rate. The French section also boasts a controversial eighteen-foot sculpture of Queen Victoria rendered in zinc, not a metal she is accustomed to.

ONE OF THE ENCLOSED ELMS PROVIDES A STUNNING BACKDROP TO THE
CRYSTAL FOUNTAIN, AND TOWERS ABOVE THE GALLERIES.

BELGIUM and HOLLAND come next, with displays on either side of the main thoroughfare. The Dutch exhibits vary from a selection of the world's most powerful magnets to the Kniphausen hawk, a life-sized representation of the bird encrusted with rubies, carbuncles and amethysts. The Belgians major in sculpture, notably the largest example of the genre in the whole Exhibition, an eleventh-century Crusader mounted on horseback.

Moving ever eastwards, we come to AUSTRIA, at this stage an empire encompassing much of central Europe, the Balkans and parts of northern Italy. The latter provides the Exhibition with exquisite Venetian glass and a collection of MILANESE SCULPTURE so popular that the authorities have had to institute a one-way system. From Budapest come spectacular embossed silver and copper reliefs of victorious battles of Alexander the Great, while Vienna dishes up a clock with seventy-two dials. The Austrian capital is also big on PERFUME – a big draw for the ladies is the first of two eau de cologne fountains in this part of the Palace.

Beyond Austria is the GERMAN section, although technically there will be no such country for another twenty years. Consequently, this area is divided into areas representing Saxony, Prussia, 'Northern Hanseatic Towns' and the Zollverein, a customs union of several Germanic states. Highlights include another eau de cologne fountain, this time actually from Cologne, and a fruit dish as tall as a ten-year-old, decorated with figures representing the progress of humanity from nomadism via agriculture to science and the arts. At the apex a modern man (presumably a German) stands atop a palm tree brandishing a flaming torch at a serpent. The most popular German exhibit, though, is August Kiss's sculpture of an Amazon on horseback being attacked by a tiger. It stands on the Main Avenue, just to the west of BRAZIL's sole contribution to the Exhibition, a pair of bouquets of flowers that turn out on close inspection to be made from feathers.

The penultimate section of the eastern stretch of the Main Avenue belongs to RUSSIA. Tsar Nicholas I has sent over a stunning collection of jewellery, but the exhibit that will blow your socks off is an entire room made of Siberian malachite, from the twelve-foot-high doors to the tables and chairs. Opposite is a rather small SCANDINAVIAN section, which is frankly missable unless you are a big fan of Swedish steel.

At last, no doubt feeling that you have actually walked round the world, you come to the last exhibiting nation on the ground floor, the USA, heralded by a large model of the Niagara Falls and a seven-ton chunk of zinc. Mining is a cornerstone of the American economy and there are enough mineral samples dotted around this section to satisfy the most ardent geologist. Indeed, for the first few weeks of the Exhibition there isn't a lot else. Much to the pleasure of many Brits, who regard their transatlantic cousins with a mixture of derision and trepidation, many of the US exhibits are held up due to transportation problems.

However, when they do arrive, the hosts are forced to concede that the young nation has put on an impressive show. Agricultural implements feature prominently and are lighter, quicker and cheaper than their British equivalents, outperforming them in a series of tests conducted in the late summer. The USA also emerges triumphant in the BATTLE OF THE LOCKSMITHS, with New Englander Alfred Charles Hobbs claiming a £200 prize for successfully picking a pair of locks manufactured by the British firm Chubb and Bramah. Noone is able to crack his company's Parautopic Lock.

Other American exhibits that make a splash are Samuel Colt's revolutionary REVOLVER, a coffin that can preserve a body in a vacuum (right up the street of the death-obsessed Victorians) and a tiny portable SEWING MACHINE. The latter offers the British their first glimpse of a technology that will transform the lives of millions of women. In a few years Isaac Singer will unleash his version on the market.

If you are suffering from the industrial equivalent of Stendhal Syndrome at this point, more dubious refreshments are available in the northeast corner of the Palace, with Ladies and Gents facilities close at hand. Thus fortified, you are ready to head upstairs for the final leg of your Palace tour.

EASTERN GALLERY WORLD EXHIBITS

Perhaps mercifully, the Eastern Gallery contains fewer must-sees than other parts of the Exhibition. We suggest you make your way to the southwestern part, where you will be comforted to see those diamond-studded tartan socks again. Proceeding east, you will initially find yourself back in France, this time in the realm of CLOTHES AND TEXTILES. One of the more striking exhibits is a portrait of Queen Victoria executed in human hair.

The southern stretch of the Eastern Gallery is devoted to products from the ZOLLVEREIN. Amid an array of Prusso-Bavarian pianos and related instruments is an extraordinary bellows-operated device called an AEOLODICON. There are also wooden and tin toys of every conceivable variety, plus an illuminated Christmas tree – still a novelty to the British despite the best efforts of Prince Albert. But the stand-out exhibits here are the über-kitsch 'COMICALITIES' produced by Hermann Ploucquet from Stuttgart. These consist of hundreds of stuffed animals arranged in anthropomorphic tableaux. Frogs receive shaves, hedgehogs ice-skate and a pine marten schoolmaster chastises a group of naughty bunny pupils.

OUTSIDE – AND DEPARTURE

A few items too bulky for display inside the Palace are dotted around outside its extremities. At the eastern end you will find a lifeboat and CAST-IRON FOUNTAIN from France, a vast GRANITE CROSS from Sweden, a WEEPING CYPRESS TREE from China and a large INDIAN TENT. To the west are several enormous lumps of coal, three battleship-sized ANCHORS and a prototype LEVEL CROSSING, which looks a bit forlorn in the absence of a train track. Nearby is Marochetti's celebrated statue of RICHARD THE LIONHEART, which will later find a permanent home outside the Houses of Parliament. You will DEPART from here.

VE Day

7–8 MAY 1945 ✳ LONDON

LONDON COULD TAKE IT. AFTER NEARLY six years of total war, rationing and living in shelters, having endured the Blitz and the V2 rocket bombs, it really was all over; and on 8 May 1945 the city came out to play and put on the biggest party it had ever seen. You'll arrive just in time to hear VE DAY declared and DRINK CHURCHILL'S HEALTH in the bohemian shadows of SOHO. On the day itself, you'll wake to the newspaper headlines at Piccadilly Circus, take VICTORY LUNCH AT THE SAVOY and watch TRAFALGAR SQUARE fill to bursting before breaking out into drunken reverie and celebration. You'll hear CHURCHILL ADDRESS THE CROWD on Whitehall, watch KING GEORGE VI experiment with the royal wave from the balcony of Buckingham Palace amongst a crowd of 50,000, dance the conga all night, kiss a GI or two, and roll out the barrel.

> **NOTE:** WAG will shortly be offering a bespoke journey to New York for VJ Day on 14 August 1945. With the war in the Pacific over at last, this was the big one in the Big Apple. Join the crowds in Times Square and stand beneath the greatest wave of ticker tape the city has ever seen.

....

BRIEFING: PARTY LIKE IT'S 1945

....

It wasn't as if the country hadn't seen it coming. Germany's total defeat had been certain since the early months of 1945. The UK Board of Trade, ever cautious with frivolous consumption, had taken red, white and blue bunting off the cotton ration. The Ministry of Works had announced – in advance of the end of the war and the anticipated celebrations – that 'bonfires will be allowed, but the government trusts that only material with no salvage value will be used'. While bunting and bonfires will be much in evidence on the night of 7 May, London still fretted as it waited for the final official signal that Germany had surrendered and that the War in Europe was over. Churchill had planned to announce this on the morning of 7 May but was forced to wait by the Soviets, who insisted that the surrender actually be signed and then the news embargoed before a simultaneous announcement was made. However, all of this was short-circuited by the release of the news of the surrender by the Associated Press in New York. With over a million people streaming onto the streets of Manhattan, it didn't make much sense to wait any longer and Churchill authorised a BBC broadcast, announcing that the next day, 8 May, would be VICTORY IN EUROPE DAY.

THE TRIP

You will be arriving at 6.00pm on the evening of 7 MAY 1945 in GLASSHOUSE STREET, a narrow passage that opens out onto the north side of Piccadilly Circus; please return here by 9am on the morning of 9 May for your DEPARTURE.

As you walk out into Piccadilly Circus it will be clear that London is still in wartime mode: the many neon and illuminated signs remain turned off and you will see the statue of Eros is boarded up and covered with adverts for war bonds. You may also sense the anticipation and excitement that is breaking out. Fighter planes have been executing outrageous loops and manoeuvres over the city centre all afternoon and the newspaper sellers have started shouting 'War is over!' Note, too, that toilet rolls have begun to fly out of office windows in central London; you may well see more.

V FOR VICTORY. THE SIGN CHURCHILL TAUGHT A NATION. IF YOU WANT TO
JOIN IN, TAKE YOUR CUE FROM THE LADY IN THE TWEED JACKET.

MONDAY 7 MAY: EVE OF VE DAY

Take your time to explore the Piccadilly Circus area, but do try
and be near a wireless in any one of the area's MILK BARS or CAFES
for 7.40pm, when the OFFICIAL ANNOUNCEMENT OF VE DAY will
be made. The BBC presenter will read the words: 'in accordance
with the arrangement made between the three great powers, tomorrow, Tuesday, will be treated as Victory in Europe Day and
will be regarded as a holiday'. You should then be able to hear
the sound of thousands of TUGBOATS and SHIPS moored on the
Thames blasting their horns.

As the news sinks across the country, PICCADILLY CIRCUS will
be the place where the party begins. Over the next three hours
around 10,000 people will gather here and in the nearby streets.

A BONFIRE will actually be assembled and lit on SHAFTESBURY AVENUE. A walk through Soho to the north will lead you to small fires set up in the ruined basements of bombed-out houses. This is a good chance, while there is still some breathing room, to join a CONGA LINE, do the HOKEY-COKEY or dance with a range of servicemen. However, the party will be abruptly terminated by the weather. Around midnight a sharp summer THUNDERSTORM will break, lightning sheets will rent the sky and the rain will fall for a couple of hours. Fortunately this is the last time you'll need to run for cover on this trip. The rest of your stay will be dry and 8 May will be a warm spring day. When you are ready for bed, head to the corner of Piccadilly Circus and Regent Street. A room has been booked in your name at the very respectable REGENT PALACE HO-TEL (Piccadilly Circus, W1; Telephone – Regent 7000), reached across a courtyard graced by an Art Deco cut-glass dome.

EATING AND DRINKING

Britain has been on rations for nearly six years and they are not about to be lifted any time soon. Even in the West End of London, where restaurants, hotels and cafés remain in operation, food can be hard to come by and is of the most variable quality. With this in mind we have taken the liberty of making a booking in your name for both lunch and dinner at the SAVOY HOTEL (90 The Strand, WC1; Telephone – Temple Bar 4343). It's a bit of a bargain. Despite its very well-heeled clientele, wartime restrictions mean both meals are a very reasonable five shillings (plus, for non-residents, a 3s 6d 'house charge' sting). You will spot senior members of the allied military command and members of the Cabinet here and can enjoy the laid-back swing of American pianist Carroll Gibbons and the Savoy Hotel Orpheans. VICTORY LUNCH will be a three course affair with wine: La Tasse de Consommé Niçoise de la Victoire, La Volaille des Iles Britanniques, La Citronette Joyeuse Deliverance, La Coupe Glacee des Allies and Le Médaillon du Soldat. The VICTORY DINNER is less elaborate: soup, chicken and iced peaches.

More modest fare is available at the LYONS CORNER HOUSES dotted across the West End. These are palatial, too, in their own way and cater for everyone. Those of you who have chosen to go in uniform may well be offered a free tea and a bun, but there is plenty to suit the most modest budgets. You will find a FOOD HALL on the ground floor and themed restaurants on the next three (or four in larger branches). You can use the phone, send a telegram, or get your hair and laundry done while you eat. The interiors are richly decorated with a kind of popular Art Nouveau swank that made them the people's palaces of the era. The waiting staff, all female, are dressed in identical black and white uniforms and are known as NIPPIES. Gay travellers will be pleased to find that an informal camp corner, orchestrated by the nippies, is available in these establishments. The classic corner houses are located on the Strand, Coventry Street and Tottenham Court Road.

Hotel restaurants, with which the company has an arrangement, include the STRAND PALACE, the REGENT PALACE and the CUMBER-LAND. They are open twenty-four hours a day. For those with more contemporary tastes, some of London's first INDIAN RESTAURANTS can be found just a stone's throw from the main VE day parties in Soho. Establishments include the DUR-BAR and the BENGAL INDIAN on Percy Street, the DILKUSH on Windmill Street, and the SHALIMAR on Wardour Street.

STREET PARTIES are another option for the peckish. Larders will have been raided, pantries emptied and ingredients pooled by neighbours and families. There will be cakes and scones and things made of egg powder and grey pastry that only the brave will contemplate. Either way, go easy; people have been saving up for this for years.

More pressing may be the issue of ALCOHOL. Many establishments in central London will run out of beer relatively early on in the evening. We suggest you take the opportunity to drink up early and spend some of Friday evening exploring takeouts from the pubs and grocers in Soho.

TUESDAY 8 MAY: VE DAY

The morning of 8 May will begin brightly. Perhaps the first thing you will note is the sound of CHURCH BELLS ringing. They will be a ubiquitous background to most of the rest of the day. Piccadilly Circus is again a good place to begin and take in the moment. Newspaper sellers will be plentiful, passers-by will want to take a look at your copy and start up a conversation. The *Daily Mail* headline is 'It's All Over', the *Daily Express* opts for 'This is VE Day' and the US forces paper, *Stars and Stripes*, opts for the robust 'Nazis Quit'. The *Daily Mirror* has been teasing its readers with the prospect of cartoon starlet Jane appearing in the buff on the day the war was won. Pick up a copy and see how they handle that promise.

Alternatively you might like to take the chance of a moment's peace and reflection before the party gets going. A SERVICE OF REMEMBRANCE will be held at ST PAUL'S CATHEDRAL at noon, but do try and get there in good time, as it's going to be completely packed. (Take the tube: eastbound Central Line from Oxford Circus to St Paul's.)

VE DAY AFTERNOON

BUCKINGHAM PALACE – which is best approached from the Mall or Birdcage Walk – is not looking at its best. The stone is filthy and many of its windows are either blacked out or bricked up. The central balcony, which has been wreathed in crimson and gold velvet drapes, makes it look even worse. It's been a long war.

People will be gathering here from around 10am, their numbers growing steadily through the day, but there won't be much to see till gone 11am when various convoys of worthies, including the ROYAL FAMILY in OPEN HORSE-DRAWN CARRIAGES, make their way in and out of the Palace gates. The biggest crowds will be present for the appearances of CHURCHILL WITH THE ROYAL FAMILY at around 5.30pm and again at 9.30pm. The royals – KING GEORGE, QUEEN ELIZABETH and the PRINCESSES ELIZABETH AND MARGARET – will make six other balcony appearances during the day. The King is in full naval officer gear, the Queen has a terribly large hat on, which she will exchange for a diamond tiara for the late-night appearances. Elizabeth is the one wearing WVS khaki, Princess Margaret is in blue and exhibiting a nervous hair-touching tic. The princesses are going to be allowed out of the palace in the company of two Guards officers later this evening. If you do spot them, be cautious about following.

Just a few minutes' walk away along the Mall is TRAFALGAR SQUARE, which will be full by 1.00pm and remain that way into the small hours of 9 May. Of particular note are the HAWKERS working the crowd outside the National Gallery selling victory rosettes in red, white and blue, Union Jacks on sticks, cardboard party hats and Churchill badges. Listen out for the pitch, 'Churchill for sixpence: Worth more!' In the afternoon a small ensemble will be performing selections from the best of GILBERT AND SULLIVAN OPERETTAS here. Look out later on tonight for the GIRL IN THE RED DRESS with white polka dots, who will be carried to the top of one of the fountains by two British army officers as the crowd applauds.

DANCING IN THE STREETS: WAR OFFICE GIRLS GET TO GRIPS WITH GIS.

If what you want are SPEECHES and moments of collective triumph, then you need to head for WHITEHALL, which leads off Trafalgar Square through Admiralty Arch, and PARLIAMENT SQUARE, which lies at the far end of Whitehall just beyond the Cenotaph. Along the way you will note the MINISTRY OF HEALTH, whose balcony will already decked in Union Jacks, and which will be used throughout the day. Note also, two-thirds of the way down Whitehall on your right, the CABINET OFFICE and the rooms from where CHURCHILL will make his key 3pm broadcast. Finally, walk past the Cenotaph and you will see the HOUSES OF PARLIAMENT on your left. These locations will be jam-packed from about 1.30pm and if you are to get a good vantage point we suggest you get down there well before 1pm. The crowd will be well ordered and there is no worry of crushes, but it is not for the claustrophobic. Do note the bus inching through the crowd which has the words 'Hitler missed the bus' chalked on it. A small cameo will occur at 2.40pm, when a naval officer will appear on the balcony opposite the Ministry of Works dressed as a PANTOMIME HITLER and proceed to impersonate him to much applause.

Then at 3.00pm Big Ben will strike the hour and the crowd will fall silent. You will finally hear CHURCHILL SPEAK through one of the many megaphones set up on Whitehall's lampposts: 'Yesterday at 2.41am at Headquarters, General Jodl, the representative of the German High Command, and Grand Admiral Donitz, the designated head of the German state, signed the unconditional surrender.' The crowd will cheer especially on the announcement of the ceasefire, the relief of the Channel Islands, and the shout-outs for Eisenhower and the Russians. Churchill will wind up with a reminder about the Pacific War, still in progress, and end with: 'Advance Britannia! Long live the cause of freedom. God save the King!' Then the OFFICIAL CEASEFIRE will be heralded by the bugles of the Royal Horse Guards, followed by a mass rendition of the National Anthem. Depending on where you are at this point it might be possible to edge towards PARLIAMENT SQUARE, where at around 3.30pm you will see Churchill standing in the back of an open-top car which will be creeping through the ecstatic crowd, making the short journey from the Cabinet Rooms to the Houses of Parliament.

The BUSINESS OF THE HOUSE will take another hour or so with MPs gathering to hear Churchill, then attending a joint service of remembrance with the Lords and a late departure for the Prime Minister after he forgets his cigars. CHURCHILL will reappear around 5pm puffing heartily on an absolute stonker as he is driven towards Buckingham Palace. Keep an eye on the skies (though you will hear the noise long beforehand) as a flight of Lancaster bombers will pass overhead to great acclaim, letting off enormous plumes of green and red smoke.

THE GANG'S ALL HERE – FAVOURITE SONGS

The soundtrack of 1945, especially on the dance floors, has been overwhelmingly American – with the big band and swing sounds of Glenn Miller, Benny Goodman and Andrews Sisters commanding the airwaves. However, in the crowd tonight it is the old sing-along favourites that have the floor. Expect to hear all of the these at some point on your trip. You might want to join in (song sheets can be found in your pocket or handbag).

Land of Hope and Glory

Roll Out the Barrel

Knees Up Mother Brown

We Going to Hang up the Washing on the Siegfried Line

The Lambeth Walk

White Cliffs of Dover

We'll Meet Again

Pack Up Your Troubles

It's a Long Way to Tipperary

Kiss Me Goodnight, Sergeant Major

ROLL OUT THE BARREL. A WAGON LOAD OF BEER ON ITS WAY THROUGH PICCADILLY CIRCUS (WITH EROS STILL UNDER WRAPS).

VE DAY NIGHT

One of the most exciting elements of the evening for Londoners is that the city will turn on its ILLUMINATIONS for the first time since the outbreak of the war. You may have noticed blackout curtains and papers being ripped from windows all day. This evening street lighting will be in operation, public buildings of all kinds will be specially lit, and shops, theatres and cinemas will turn on their neon signs. One particular moment of illuminated streetlife can be seen mid-evening on Haymarket, where the TIVOLI CINEMA's red signage bathes the street. You may see an ample woman in a Union Jack apron dancing with a middle-aged gent as an accordionist plays 'South of the Border'.

Though there is still much speech-making and balcony-appearing by the great and the good to come, the heart of the party is in PICCADILLY CIRCUS and the focus of the action is at RAINBOW CORNER. Previously the TROCADERO, a Lyons Corner House, this was taken over by the US armed forces in 1942 and has served as the centre of GI social life in London for three years. Indeed it has proved a magnet for locals entranced by the Americans' music, style and demeanour. Today it will be party central as great waves of people move in and out of its bars and ballroom and back onto the street. From mid-afternoon, the club band will relocate to the balcony just above the entrance and provide an all-day soundtrack for dancers and revellers. GIs will be creating impromptu TICKER-TAPE PARADES from the windows in the upper floors, with toilet paper, files, phone books, apple cores and shredded newsprint.

No traffic has been able to get through here since before 3pm and from early evening the pace and the crush will be stepping up. Look out for the NORWEGIAN SAILOR stripped off at the top of a lamppost and a variety of British and American soldiers scaling EROS. Occasionally jeeps and taxis loaded with merrymakers, often piled onto the roof and the bonnets of the vehicles, will inch their way through. We do advise you not to join them. One

American soldier, already plastered in lipstick, will be calling out for volunteers to join his collection. Both sexes can expect the offer of a quick kiss and a cuddle to come from a variety of quarters.

If you want a break from the crowds on Piccadilly Circus, take a short walk to LEICESTER SQUARE. Its many trees will be beautifully lit and it is a good place to go for fireworks, flares and a more raucous edge to proceedings. The streets of SOHO next door are even better. The FRENCH HOUSE on Dean Street is the place to get a glass of wine with London's FREE FRENCH, while Soho's émigré HUNGARIANS will also be partying. The WINDMILL THEATRE on Great Windmill Street, whose risqué nude revue has been running since the 1930s, is always a place to go and see what's up and who is around. For those seeking something a bit jazzier and smokier, try the SHIM SHAM CLUB on Wardour Street.

BUCKINGHAM PALACE, too, will continue to be a focus for crowds during the evening, and as they get larger and larger ST JAMES'S PARK next door will become full to overflowing. For those who like a spot of celebrity-watching, keep in mind that NOËL COWARD will be putting in an appearance near the gates around 8.30pm. He will be accompanied by the entire cast of *Blithe Spirit* – his play running to packed audiences in the West End. The stars of the show include CECIL PARKER, FAY COMPTON and MARGARET RUTHERFORD. The noted popular composer IVOR NOVELLO will also be with them.

At 9pm KING GEORGE VI will be broadcasting his address to the nation live from the Palace and will then make a final BALCONY APPEARANCE WITH CHURCHILL and his family. You will find that by this hour things have got altogether more raucous in front of the Palace gates. Look out for the young trumpeter HUMPHREY LYTTELTON, who will be exuberantly playing on the Victoria Monument in front of the main entrance to the Palace. He will be joined by a man with a large bass drum strapped to his stomach, an American sailor with a trombone and an old lag blowing a single but effective bass note from the horn of a gramophone. After twenty minutes dancing and playing Lyttelton will strike up 'High

'WERE WE DOWNHEARTED?' CHURCHILL SOAKS UP THE
ADULATION, ALONGSIDE THE DUO – BEVIN (RIGHT) AND ATTLEE (FAR
RIGHT) – WHO WILL SOON REPLACE HIM.

Society' and be lifted onto a handcart. The whole ensemble will
then make its way over the next couple of hours down St James's
Street to Piccadilly Circus, then to Trafalgar Square and back again
to the Palace. ST JAMES'S PARK is also worth a wander at this hour,
The trees and paths will all have all been lit, one of the city's largest
bonfires is roaring, while in the park's darker corners you will find
the atmosphere amongst couples unrestrained to say the least.

The final balcony appearance of the night will be CHURCHILL
AT THE MINISTRY OF HEALTH on Whitehall. He will be preceded
by members of the cabinet including Deputy Prime Minister and
leader of the Labour Party, CLEMENT ATTLEE, and the president
of the Board of Trade, ERNEST BEVIN. Listen out for the drunken
Tories and aristocrats who will be giving them some stick and
calling out for Churchill. When he does arrive, Churchill will
conduct more of a call-and-response dialogue with the crowd

rather than give a speech: 'We were all alone for a whole year. There we stood. Did anyone want to give in?' The crowd will roar back, 'No!' 'Were we downhearted?' will be met by the call, 'No fear!' The whole thing will wrap up about 10.30pm with the Prime Minister leading the crowd in singing 'Land of Hope and Glory'.

AWAY FROM THE WEST END

Although the West End is the heart of the action, there are many smaller and more intimate celebrations going on in the suburbs, which might be worth your time.

NORWOOD The bonfires and effigies at street parties in this south London suburb are particularly good. Apsley Road boasts a Hitler swinging from a gallows so large that it effectively blocks the road. Nearby Balfour Road has Hitler dressed up with a swastika flag and a sign reading 'I have no further territorial claims in Europe'. 'No' has been crossed out and 'Hell' painted over 'Europe'. They'll be BURNING THE FÜHRER around 8pm.

London and Croydon Railways train to South Norwood.

RAVENSCOURT PARK There will a huge bonfire in this small park, between Hammersmith and Chiswick. A sizable band will also be playing throughout the evening and you can enjoy the bizarre sight of the massed ranks of uniformed nurses from the nearby Queen Charlotte's Hospital dancing on the lawns.

Piccadilly line to Hammersmith then District line to Ravenscourt Park.

ST PAUL'S Although it is not the centre of festivities, the great dome of Wren's cathedral is a focus of the city's best illuminations. The crossed searchlights over the golden cross on top of the dome are particularly striking. Later in the evening a spectacular 'V for Victory' illumination will be created over the dome.

Central line to St Paul's or Bank.

WILLESDEN The teenagers of Hanover Road in Willesden have been particular active building their bonfire. You will see handwritten bills on the lampposts of the surrounding roads as you walk towards the party. A bombed-out plot, strung with Union Jacks and bunting, has been piled high with salvaged wood, while a remarkably life-like Hitler swings above the pyre on a set of gallows. A stuffed model of Goering with two iron crosses on his uniform sits on a chair at its foot. At 9.15pm a crowd of 100 teens will have gathered and a gramophone will have been brought outside. At 9.30pm the bonfire will be lit, to cries of 'Don't let him end too soon, let him linger'; some of the kids will douse Hitler with a hose to prolong his agony. Expect a lot of old fireworks and home-made flares. Then a piano will appear in the street and you will get all the classics. The dancing will be shy to begin with, but by 11pm the place will be roaring.

Bakerloo line to Queens Park.

MIDNIGHT AT BIG BEN

As the evening inches towards midnight and the official end of the War in Europe, you might like to think about getting to WESTMINSTER, where BIG BEN will be striking the hour and an enormous Union Jack flying above the House of Lords will be dramatically picked out by multiple spotlights.

The best vantage point is probably in the middle of Westminster Bridge, which lies on the south side of Parliament Square. From here you will be able to see not only Big Ben and Parliament, with its river terrace garlanded by lights, but the south bank of the river. Here you will see rotating searching lights, the seat of the London County Council, COUNTY HALL, picked out in red, white and blue lights, while the boats and ships on the Thames will all be strung with coloured bulbs.

As midnight approaches, silence will fall over the considerable crowd, broken only by the final bong of the midnight chimes. Expect cheering, fireworks going off all over the place, searchlights whirling, and every boat on the Thames blasting its horn. If you do find yourself in a quieter spot at midnight, the radio will certainly be on. Listen out for the BBC's Stuart Hibberd announcing: 'As these words are being spoken, the official end of the war in Europe is taking place.'

At this point you may wish to just carry on and party through the night, rather than making use of your hotel. You will have no shortage of fellow revellers. For those who need a brief lie-down, GREEN PARK, HYDE PARK and ST JAMES'S PARK will also be available. The evening will stay dry, the temperature will be cool but not cold. There will plenty of fires to keep you warm and it will be safe. Police reports confirm almost zero crime in the city today.

Woodstock

15–18 AUGUST 1969

WOODSTOCK WAS THE EXCLAMATION point at the end of the 1960s, a defining moment when many strands of the American counterculture fused together. 'The Woodstock Music and Art Fair: An Aquarian Exposition', as it was billed, was a three-day music festival held on Max Yasgur's farm in Bethel, New York State in the summer of 1969. But, as you will see, the music was merely the setting for a cultural, perhaps even spiritual transformation.

Planned with 100,000 people in mind, half a million showed up and walked across the woefully incomplete fencing that the organisers had failed to erect. At 4pm on Friday, as they surveyed the great mass of humanity that had gathered before the main stage, the management declared it a free festival. Not long after, New York State governor Nelson Rockefeller designated it a disaster zone.

The latter is pretty descriptive. The event is absurdly undercatered and underprovisioned, a state compounded by the roads being blocked for miles around and by squalls and storms turning much of the site into a MUDBATH. The musicians arrive late, the schedules are chaotic and drugs of all kinds are plentiful. But something even more powerful than the blue sunshine acid doing the rounds is at work: a massive outbreak of spontaneous sharing, giving and caring breaks out.

And through it all the most fabulous array of the era's musicians perform: from the Latino rock of SANTANA to the multicultural funk of SLY AND THE FAMILY STONE, from the protest songs of JOAN BAEZ and JOHN SEBASTIAN to the laments and sweet harmonies of CROSBY, STILLS, NASH AND YOUNG. And, of course, the showstopping finale from JIMI HENDRIX. The organisers had promised three days of music and love, and though things didn't pan out quite as they had intended, that is what the 'half a million strong' Woodstock nation got.

....

BRIEFING: WHY WOODSTOCK?

....

Woodstock was the brainchild of four twentysomethings: the enigmatic MICHAEL LANG, an über-cool head-shop owner and small-time music promoter; the maniacal ARTIE KORNFELD, who was vice president of Capitol Records; and two very straight Manhattan flatmates playing venture capitalists, JOEL ROSENMAN and JOHN ROBERTS.

The quartet's initial encounters turned on the idea of establishing a hip new recording studio in the town of Woodstock in upstate New York, which many of the era's leading musicians – like Bob Dylan and The Band – had made their base. The never built studio was to be funded and promoted by a big music festival. Building on the success of San Francisco's huge human BE-INS and the MONTEREY POP FESTIVAL, both held in the 1967 SUMMER OF LOVE, the project soon mutated into something much bigger and acquired a roster of musicians that was truly extraordinary.

PLAN A had been to hold the event on an old industrial park in the town of Wallkill, about thirty five miles from Woodstock. Just weeks before the opening day, however, with many tickets already sold, local protests forced the land owner to withdraw his offer. A series of chance encounters led the organisers to the hamlet of WHITE LAKE near Bethel, New York, and an unlikely saviour in the form of dairy farmer MAX YASGUR, renowned for his sour cream, yoghurt and chocolate milk. A deal was struck and in a mad flurry of activity in late July and early August 1969 Yasgur's farm was converted into a huge festival site.

It was staffed by the HOG FARM, a hippie commune from New Mexico who would run the kitchens and freak-out tents and, together with a bunch of off-duty New York police officers, provide the PLEASE FORCE, Woodstock's very own security force trained to say 'Please don't do this, do something else'.

By opening day Friday 15 August 1969, the stage was built, the sound system was just about working, and 50,000 people had already turned up, most of them without tickets. They just pitched their tents and sat waiting for the music to begin. Meanwhile, the festival audience continued to grow.

THE DUDES WHO MAKE WOODSTOCK: MICHAEL LANG AND ARTIE KORNFELD. THEY LOSE THEIR SHIRTS BUT IT ALL TURNS OUT COOL.

THE TRIP

Your point of arrival and departure is the inside of a green and white 1963 VOLKSWAGEN CAMPER VAN, parked on the north verge of Route 17 about half a mile from BETHEL. As you will see as you get out of the van, it is just one of thousands of vehicles parked up on this narrow stretch of road that curves through the low hills and woods of the Catskills. The centre of the road will be filled by a steady stream of festival-goers abandoning their cars and walking west. Take a breath and enjoy the sweet smells of fresh cow manure and Colombian Gold that fill the air. The first major turning on your right takes you up into Bethel proper and to the hamlets that cluster around WHITE LAKE. You will see that cars have begun to pile up here too, and the traffic is blocked to the north. The locals' attitudes towards 'the kids' are very variable. Some have created impromptu stores in their front gardens; others will offer you a cup of coffee and something to eat, particularly once the event has been declared a disaster zone and is all over national TV.

For those who like to plan ahead, take the short walk up Route 14 to Kauneonga Lake, then left onto Broadway, where you will find a considerable crowd around VASSMER'S GENERAL STORE. Featured in the movie *Woodstock*, this shop is run by the genial Arthur and Marian Vassmer. While many local stores have closed, Vassmer's will serve thousands over the long weekend. This is your best chance to stock up on chocolate, cookies, wine, cigarettes, Rizlas and toilet paper – the standard fare of today's festivals, but lamentably absent from Woodstock.

THE FESTIVAL SITE

'By the time we got to Woodstock, we were half a million strong', Joni Mitchell will sing in her famous paean to the festival. Now it's time to join them. Keep heading west on Route 17 and go

PERRY ROAD

NORTH

WEST SHORE ROAD

CAMPER &
TRAILER PARKING

HAY
FIELD

CRYSTAL
POND

THE WOODS

GROOVY WAY

HIGH WAY

FREE
STAGE

PUPPET THEATER

PORT-O-SANS

HOG
FARM

FREE
KITCHEN

PORT
-O-SANS

MESSAGE &
COMMUNICATIONS
AREA

MAIN
GATE

HOSPITAL
TENT

PLAYGROUND

MEDICAL
TRAILERS

INDIAN
PAVILION

HURD ROAD

PORT-O-SANS

STAGE
AREA

FOOD
FOR
LOVE

AMPHITHEATER

PERFORMERS'
PAVILION

MUDSLIDES

WEST SHORE ROAD

GETTING TO WOODSTOCK

SITE

HAPPY AVENUE

55

VASSMER'S
GENERAL
STORE

17B

NORTH

0   1 MILE

round the south end of White Lake. There won't be any doubt as to where everyone's going. Your only decision is when to cut off to your right towards the festival. We recommend that you head down to the valley about two miles out of town, just before the road crosses a stream. Then, keeping the wooded area to your left, it's a ten-minute stroll across the hayfields. Try to remember where you've turned off. Fix it in your mind. Really. You have to get back to this road and then to the VW camper on Monday morning and you may not be in peak condition when the time comes.

THE CAMPSITE

You should now be looking down on the main designated CAMP-SITE. This lies outside the main festival arena and what remains of the fence surrounding it, but with 50,000 people estimated to have arrived by Thursday night, the campsite will already be spilling over into the woods. Grab what space you can and look to see if there are still any piles of cut logs around. The Hog Farm left them out for campers to take and the organisers encouraged people to make fires and get cosy. Feel free to do so.

TOILETS AND WASHING FACILITIES are thin on the ground and not for the faint of heart. If you are wise, you will have picked up a stash of tissues at Vassmer's. In addition to the Port-O-San at the bottom of the hill, there are also toilet blocks behind the Indian Pavilion in the festival arena and at the top of the hill in front of the main stage, next to the food concessions. For the hygienically minded the best bet is the large and relatively clean FILIPPINI POND, a fifteen minute amble due north of the Free Stage. Skinny-dipping, diving and frolicking are highly recommended, though not compulsory.

Depending on how long it has taken you to get this far, you may find that an area in front of the main gate has started to become the INFORMATION AND COMMUNICATION ZONE – an improvised necessity in a world without the mobile phone. It is a cluster of notice boards, messages on totem poles and tents with helpful people in them. You many not find who you are looking for but you are bound to run into someone or something interesting here all weekend.

ABBIE HOFFMAN, the notorious and theatrical political activist, has persuaded the organisers to let him have his own tent in the communication zone. From here, he and other Yippie (Youth International Party) activists will be issuing hastily typed INFORMATION SHEETS to the bamboozled crowd. The Saturday-morning edition, for example, will read as follows: 'Everything might seem groovy now. But think about tomorrow. Life could get hard. If you're hip to the facts below, pull together in the spirit of the Catskill mountain guerilla and share everything. Dig It!' There really isn't enough food at Woodstock, so take your cue from the man: share what you have and receive gifts graciously. Water is not in short supply, with standpipes widely available, though the functioning of the system is at best erratic. Contrary to the rumours you will be hearing, neither the tap water nor the bottled stuff flown in by the National Guard is laced with LSD.

WEATHER REPORT

Your walk to the festival site will be in very pleasant late summer sunshine with just a hint of cloud. But don't kid yourself: this is Woodstock. It's going to rain and you've got to love it. Richie Havens, who opens the show on Friday, will later say, 'The rain made the people interact with each other ... to share whatever we had ... so I balance it out as a cosmic accident.' Many of your fellow festival-goers will be in JEANS AND T-SHIRTS or less. While this is perfectly permissible, the agency does recommend some kind of period-appropriate RAINWEAR (or make use of the raincoats and micro-tent stashed in the camper van, next to the cooker).

On FRIDAY the delightful mix of sun and scurrying clouds will turn blustery later in the evening. At around 10pm, during Ravi Shankar's set, it will start raining heavily. Lighter showers will persist through the night, turning to steady drizzle early on SATURDAY morning. Things will dry for out for the first few acts but another rain storm after lunch will continue until after 4pm. When the music resumes, temperatures will be a warm but damp 70°F. Rain returns for an hour or so later in the evening, peaking during the

Grateful Dead's set. This will be cut short for various reasons, including the risk of the band getting electrocuted as they play in puddles of water.

SUNDAY will begin sunny, warm and breezy, but storm clouds will start to gather at around 2pm. Joe Cocker will have just completed his set at around 4.30pm when the final thunderstorm will break, drenching the festival for an hour. The rest of the day will be dry and, for those that have the stamina to stay, MONDAY MORNING, post-Hendrix, will be sunny and golden.

'WHAT WE HAVE IN MIND IS BREAKFAST IN BED FOR 400,000. KEEP FEEDING EACH OTHER ... AND IF YOU'RE TOO TIRED TO CHEW, PASS IT ON.'

EATING AND DRINKING

The food concession arrangements at Woodstock are unsatisfactory, to say the least. Unable to secure the services of established caterers, the organisers have gone with an outfit called FOOD FOR LOVE, long on promises but short on capital. Despite having been loaned $65,000 and had their stands built for them at the top of the hill overlooking the the main stage, Food for Love will run out of supplies – a basic range of burgers, hot dogs and sodas – within a few hours.

If you do want get a burger, get there on Friday late afternoon, after Woodstock has been declared a free festival, when a group of leftist activists from Greenwich Village will put in an appearance, chanting 'Free food for the people' and looking threatening. A squad from the Hog Farm/Please Force will appear (note their motley red armbands), giving out large burning incense sticks to calm everybody down. You will then see that most of the people at the concession stands are exchanging joints for burgers and the entire kitchen crew are smoking them at a lick. For the next hour or so they will just hand out food for free. But get in line pronto, for soon it will all be gone.

Your most reliable food source for the weekend is the FREE KITCHEN, located just to the west of the Information and Communication area. They will serve up three meals a day all through the festival. Breakfast is a muesli mix of rolled oats, sesame seeds, honey, raisins and wheatgerm. Lunch and dinner consist of great vats of bulgur wheat and brown rice served up with whatever locally sourced vegetables can be found. There are some mighty soy sauce dispensers, too. The queues are long but brisk.

Woodstock's greatest eating pleasures, however, are the RANDOM OFFERINGS that will come your way. From Saturday onwards the helicopters of the National Guard and medical services will be introducing a strange array of canned goods into the mix, including thousands of one-ounce cans of olives and tins of tuna. Good luck with the can opener. Saturday afternoon will see packages of baloney sandwiches, Hershey bars, Melba toast and plastic bottles of cola thrown down to the crowd. Locals in Bethel and Monticello will also take it upon themselves to bus in loads of homemade sandwiches and trays of hard-boiled eggs.

THE ARTS FESTIVAL

Everyone will remember Woodstock for the music, but it was always intended to be a wider arts festival. Not much of it has survived the late changes of plan, but the best of what remains can be found to the east of the main campsite in and beyond the woods.

Nestled in the trees near the West Shore Road is the FREE STAGE, built and vaguely curated by the MERRY PRANKSTERS, a troupe of California acid-head situationists given to impromptu happenings and drug-fuelled partying. The Pranksters' fabulous painted school buses can be seen parked up behind the Free Stage. Performances include yoga sessions, a late-night appearance on

Friday by Joan Baez, and spiritual and meditative performances with a massed array of Tibetan gongs. This is the best part of the festival for joining improvised groups of drummers – still very much a novelty. You also stand a good chance of being offered hallucinogens.

Additional entertainment is available about 200 yards up the slope, where the PUPPET THEATER is putting on shows all day. Push on through the trees from the Free Stage and you will come to what was intended to be the car park. You will also find it functioning as an overspill campsite and general hangout, especially the HAY FIELD up the hill and the shady areas around CRYSTAL POND. However, the most interesting part of the site is THE WOODS. Covering about four acres, this delightful strip of woodland is criss-crossed by two main paths, signed as THE HIGH WAY and THE GROOVY WAY, and lit by long strings of fairy lights. Along the paths you will find an eclectic assortment of tarot readers, troubadours, meditators, frolicking couples, bead sellers and dope dealers.

Most of the crowd will be heading east towards the main stage. As you follow through the main gate or over the now-trodden-down fencing, take note of the cluster of tents and the large white trailer parked at the bottom of the hill. The HOSPITAL TENT is the main place to seek medical care. You may have noticed that many of your fellow festival-goers are barefoot and quite a few of them are pitching up here with glass and metal cuts. There will also be thousands of bad-trip casualties to be attended to over the course of the weekend. A similar 'talking down' service is also available at Hog Farm from late on Friday evening (see TURNING ON, TUNING IN AND FREAKING OUT, overpage).

Two special attractions in this area are the INDIAN PAVILION and the PLAYGROUND. The former is a collection of tents and tepees exhibiting the best in contemporary Native American art, with many artists from New Mexico and California in residence. The Playground consists of a selection of wood and rope structures dotted around the field and designed to be played on. Look

out for the large stone-on-a-rope swing and the maze. Best of all,
ascend the tree trunk climbing frame and throw yourself onto the
fabulous mountains of hay bales below.

TURNING ON, TUNING IN AND FREAKING OUT

Given the sharing ethos of the festival, you should have no problem getting yourself just as stoned as you want to be. Expect joints and pipes to be passed your way and feel free to make polite inquiries. Possession of a cigarette lighter, useful during key moments of the music, is invaluable as your way to the REEFER: most will have forgotten or lost theirs. For those of you who would like to secure your own supply, we believe the going rate is around $5 for a bag of something nice from Colombia.

There is no shortage of LSD at Woodstock, either, most of it in pill form. The Pranksters, who are running the Free Stage in the main campsite, will be doling it out for free through most of the weekend. The famous announcement from the main stage warning about the brown acid being 'not specifically too good' has some truth, but as the man says, 'It's your trip.' Reports of green, blues and red acid abound. Casual inquiries of those not too far gone will get you to them. Usual rules apply: just take half a tab and see how it goes; you can always go back for seconds.

A range of strong prescription drugs, amphetamines, Valium and other benzodiazepines, magic mushrooms and psychoactive cacti will be in circulation. The MESCALINE going round appears to be particularly rough – if swirling Aztec imagery and icons is not your thing, it is perhaps best avoided. ALCOHOL is available, and wine bottles will be coming your way pretty often, but if this is your drug of choice we suggest you make sure you visit the liquor stores in Bethel early on during your stay.

On Friday afternoon you will find MEDICAL FACILITIES at Woodstock rather thin on the ground. At the north end of the main festival area there are a cluster of first aid tents, and the small medical trailer parked alongside them houses trained medical staff. As the number of psychedelic freakouts rises sharply over the weekend, CHILL-OUT TENTS will be established alongside the original hospital tents and then around the festival. Many of these will have characteristic pink and yellow stripes, which may or may not be soothing to the target market. Others will be obvious from their clientele. The regular medical staff on site will be reinforced by new arrivals from New York helicoptered in on Saturday morning. If you go to them on an acid bummer, they will give you a big shot of Thorazine. This will stop the trip, but send you into something close to a vegetative state.

For those who prefer talking cures, there is an alternative. Most of the chilling out and calming down work will be done by members of the Hog Farm, supplemented by people they have brought down from their own bad trips who have become impromptu psychedelic paramedics. Here the advice is to ride the thing out and enjoy the beauty. Saturday evening is a particularly good time to have your freakout as John Sebastian (who will have played a set on the main stage by this point) will come with the members of The Lovin' Spoonful to play a soothing acoustic set to the assembled acid casualties.

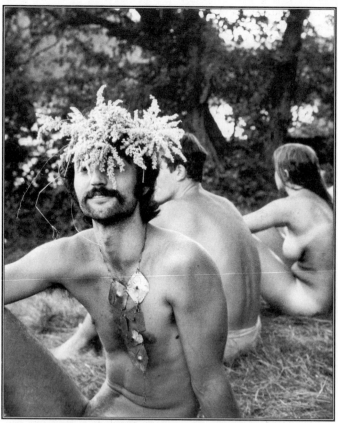

THE UNDRESS CODE. THIS IS PERFECTLY ACCEPTABLE, BUT THE COMPANY DOES RECOMMEND SOME KIND OF FOOTWEAR.

DAY BY DAY: THE MUSIC

The main stage is situated in a naturally shaped amphitheater, surrounded by a huge crowd. To see this at its best, approach over the brow of the hill by the service road. At the foot of the hill you will see the MAIN STAGE, 30 yards wide but tiny from this distance. Around it is a high wooden garden fence, and behind it is the performers' backstage zone. It's worth dwelling for a moment on this city of tents and tepees and the fantastic curving wooden bridge that carries the musicians and crew to and from the stage. Note also the sixteen loudspeaker arrays on 70-foot-high towers that snake up the hill. You will see that many people have climbed them for a better view of the stage. There will be no reports of casualties, but we do not recommend joining them.

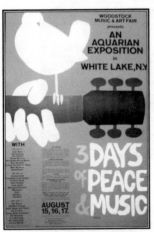

This is the moment to take in the sheer scale of the crowd. There will be anything up to 300,000 people in front of you. Of course, the demographic is mainly white and middle class, with a heavy bias towards New York, but watch the passing throng and you will see all manner of young folk: African, Native and Asian Americans, college students and dropouts, hippies, Yippies and folkies, politicos and preppies and Hari Krishna monks.

This is also the time to think about where you want to sit to watch the music: close up to the fence, mid-distance or way at the back? Wherever you choose, the sound quality will be remarkably good given the conditions. And, to hear the bands, you will need to stick with your choice for the day. While the music is on and the sun is out, there won't be room to swing a cat. If you need to, now is the time to head for the concession stands at the top of the hill and the nearby Port-O-Sans. This area is also where you will also find some of the best MUDSLIDES and puddles once the rain arrives.

FRIDAY, 15 AUGUST

On Friday, the crowd will have been gathering in front of the main stage since morning, waiting for the concert to begin just after lunch. You may well feel a certain restiveness as the hours slip by without any musicians appearing, but rest assured the show will go on.

At just gone five o'clock, CHIP MONCK, your MC for most of the next three days, will make the announcement everyone has been waiting for: 'Sit down! Stand up! Do whatever you wish to do but we're ready to start now and I bet you're pleased with that. Ladies and gentlemen, please, Mister Richie Havens.' RICHIE HAVENS and those members of his band who have been able to get to the gig are being literally pushed onto the stage as the only outfit even close to being ready. Note the bass player arriving just after Havens; he has just finished an epic twenty-mile walk through the traffic jams carrying his guitar. Havens will hold himself and the crowd together with a two-hour performance of improvised hard-edged folk and protest tunes, including an incomparable rendition of "Freedom".

Behind the scenes, the producers are desperately searching for acts that are both physically and mentally present. Serendipitously, they have found the Indian yogi and guru SWAMI SATCHIDANANDA hanging out backstage. He is up next, sent on to play for time. Around seven o'clock you should hear his steady high-pitched voice even if you can't see this tiny figure in saffron robes with exuberant long ringlets and a magnificent white beard and moustache. Sitting cross-legged on a small podium and surrounded by his monkish devotees, Satchidananda will declare, 'Through music we can work wonders. Music is the celestial sound, and it is sound that controls the whole universe, not atomic vibrations. Sound energy, sound power is much, much greater than any other power in this world.' Right on, brother! His set will conclude with a collective chant of 'Hari-Om'.

Just after half past seven the show proper will finally be ready to roll. SWEETWATER, originally booked to open the day, are first up,

LEVITATION IS ALL YOU NEED. SWAMI SATCHIDANANDA OPENS
PROCEEDINGS ON FRIDAY AFTERNOON.

mixing folk rock with cello and flute. At 8.20pm the frizzy haired BERT SOMMER is the first of a pair of solo folk-guitar boys, his current hit "Jennifer" and a brilliant version of Simon and Garfunkel's' "America" evoking the biggest responses. He is followed an hour later by the willowy TIM HARDIN, a rising star of the folk circuit. According to witnesses backstage, Hardin has been 'completely blitzed' for the last twenty-four hours and is in profound dread of the enormous crowd. But, despite his shakiness, he will manage to take things up a notch with his version of "Simple Song of Freedom" and his current hit "If I Were a Carpenter".

Things will be taking a sharp turn, musically and climatically, around ten o'clock. RAVI SHANKAR, the great Indian sitar player, will take the stage and rip through three standards from the Indian classical repertoire before the heavens open and the first of many short, sharp downpours begins. Once the shower stops at around 11 o'clock it will be time for the recently launched New York folkie MELANIE to play. Just prior to her set, the stage announcer will say, 'This is the largest crowd of people ever assembled for a concert in history, but it's so dark out there we can't see and you can't see each other. So when I say three I want every one of you to light a match.' Everybody who can get it together will do so, though you stand less chance of getting your fingers burned if you've taken our advice and brought along a lighter. Melanie will be sufficiently inspired by the illuminations to write the hit song "Lay Down (Candles in the Rain)".

At five minutes to midnight a very young and very stoned ARLO GUTHRIE will take to the stage. The son of American folk hero and protest-song pioneer Woody Guthrie, Arlo has spent the last five hours hanging out in the crowd, having a smoke and expecting to play tomorrow. The fact that he is on now has thrown him somewhat. There will be some sticky moments and lapses of memory during his set but the stoner paranoia of "Coming into Los Angeles" and the optimistic resilience of "Amazing Grace" should make a lot of sense. Finally, at just after one o'clock in the morning, the last act of the night will be tuning up: the queen of the American folk scene, JOAN BAEZ, six months pregnant at the time. With the weather alternating between drizzle and showers, Baez's rendition of "We Shall Overcome" may feel particularly pertinent.

SATURDAY, 16 AUGUST

First up on the main stage is Tom Law from the Hog Farm, enjoining you and everyone else to take part in a vast meditation and yoga session. Muesli, served from huge plastic vats, will be available at the left-hand side of the stage from about 11am. Saturday's music will begin quietly with the little-known QUILL playing a short set from about 12.30pm, enhanced by the many maracas and other percussive instruments that they will be handing out to the crowd. Feel free to grab yourself one, but do remember not to bring it home lest it should interfere with the time–space continuum.

The failure of a number of artists to have shown up even by this advanced stage will ensure a special treat for early risers. At 1pm COUNTRY JOE MCDONALD will be performing solo. The high point will come at the end of the set when McDonald will orchestrate the Fish Cheer: 'Give me an F! Give me a U! Give me a C! Give me a K! What have you got?' Feel free to join in. This will segue into the fabulously upbeat "I-Feel-Like-I'm-Fixin-to Die-Rag"; a song that combines the sardonic black humour of Tom Lehrer with the politics of the anti-war movement. This will be the first major collective act of singing.

You may wish, like many in the audience, to time your recreational activities so you peak at around 2pm today, when SANTANA will be playing. One of the musical highlights of the weekend, the band's blend of raging rock guitar, keyboards and percussive Latino rhythms make for an ecstatic performance, with a matching response from the crowd. "Soul Sacrifice" is perhaps the first amongst equals. Of special interest, dancing close to the stage, is the naked man with the sheep in his arms. He has been walking around the festival with the said animal in his arms for most of the last thirty-six hours.

The light rain will cool you down after Santana, but the sun will return as JOHN B. SEBASTIAN takes to the stage in his wire-rim glasses and paisley shirt at around half-past three. Previously the lead singer of The Lovin' Spoonful and currently beginning an ill-fated solo career, John B's set will capture the moment perfectly. As Woodstock producer John Morris will later recall, 'Something magical transformed the stage when John Sebastian ambled out.' His short, gentle acoustic set will lift you and the crowd, your clothes will be drying out and Sebastian, as stoned as his audience, will forget the lyrics to a number of his tunes but find the words that are needed. When he looks out, in real awe, at the scale of the crowd and says, 'Wow, We really are a whole *city*,' the crowd will rise as one. Then it will be onto the blues rock of the KEEF

'HOW DO YOU EXPECT TO STOP THE WAR IF YOU CAN'T SING LOUDER THAN THAT?' COUNTRY JOE HAS A POINT. FEEL FREE TO JOIN IN.

HARTLEY BAND, followed by the Indian-folk-jazz fusion of THE INCREDIBLE STRING BAND. Most of the crowd seem confused by the cult British hippies' modal improvisation and unusual tunings.

More mainstream service will be resumed at half past seven, with a solid set of foot-tapping boogie provided by CANNED HEAT, enlivened by the high falsetto blues of lead singer Bob Hite on "Going Up the Country" and "On the Road Again". Midway through the set a rogue member of the audience will clamber up on the stage and embrace him, before the pair share a cigarette and dance together. MOUNTAIN, on at nine, will be offering straight-ahead rock. You, like the band, will be beginning to battle the drizzle that is turning into rain, but hang in there: at half past ten THE GRATEFUL DEAD are coming on. The band have spent the last two hours embroiled in a gigantic row over getting paid in cash upfront, during which time the stage has morphed into one vast puddle. Certainly when recollecting the night the group will not claim it to have been their finest hour, but for many the oddball noodling, jamming and riffling amongst short-circuiting electrical equipment seems a pretty standard night out with The Dead. Things will come to an abrupt halt during their fifth song, "Turn on Your Love Light" when the amps will overload and switch off.

The rain will calm down for the rest of the night, allowing an amazing succession of artists to take the stage in the early hours of Sunday morning. Do not miss CREEDENCE CLEARWATER REVIVAL performing a storming set of their Louisiana swamp blues – it won't feature on the movie of the festival, as the band refuse to be filmed. JANIS JOPLIN AND THE KOZMIC BLUES BAND will be clearly the worse for wear, having consumed an enormous quantity of champagne, but Janis's slurred blues howl on the encore "Ball and Chain" will be electrifying. Half-past-three brings SLY AND THE FAMILY STONE, California's freewheeling multi-ethnic alchemists of soul, psychedelic rock and funk. You will notice by now that the vast majority of the crowd have curled up, flaked out and gone to sleep, in their sleeping bags, if they have them.

However, the band's ecstatic and literal performance of "Gonna Take You Higher" will get even the most comatose on their feet and dancing. THE WHO are up next at 5am, as ostentatious, bombastic and loud as befits a set built on their rock opera *Tommy*. Look out for Abbie Hoffman, who will take the stage just after "Pinball Wizard". He will grab a stage mike and deliver a rambling speech about the imprisoned leader of the White Panthers. Pete Townshend, The Who's guitarist, will smack him with the back of his guitar and knock him off the stage.

The dawn will break to the accompaniment of the eerie, eclectic sound of San Francisco's trippy-dippy JEFFERSON AIRPLANE. Guitarist Paul Kantner will recall, 'The crowd was into it once they were awake. There were just a lot of people sleeping-bagged out. People were crashing and burning.' So do try and wake up before their closing number "White Rabbit" sends you off into a surreal wonderland of half-sleep and dreams.

SUNDAY, 17 AUGUST

On Sunday morning you may find yourself and your neighbours a little slow to get going. The stage will follow suit, with nothing until 2pm when JOE COCKER AND THE GREASE BAND will appear. First the band, all tripping on LSD, will be loosening up with a few instrumentals and then the stuttering shambling Cocker will join them. They will amble through Dylan's "Just Like a Woman" and "I Shall be Released" but hit their peak with a sensational heartfelt take on "With a Little Help From My Friends". You should probably stay right to the end of the set, but be alert: slate-grey storm clouds will be gathering behind the stage. As the applause rings out, the winds and the rain will arrive. They are going to lash you and everyone else for the next hour or so. If you do stick around, you can enjoy the forlorn attempts of the MC and the crowd to turn back the elements chanting, 'No Rain, No Rain'. There is also the opportunity of some serious mudslide lunacy at the top of the hill.

The rains will let up after five o'clock. By six the sun will be shining again, and if you are hawk-eyed you will see a small bespectacled figure, pipe in hand, walking up to the microphone. MAX YASGUR'S SPEECH is one of the highlights of the day. The assembled multitudes will feel an immense wave of good vibrations and love as his voice rings out with the words 'I think you have proven something to the world – that half a million kids can get together have three days of fun and music and nothing but fun and music. And God bless you for it.' Then it's back to the music, with COUNTRY JOE AND THE FISH rehashing Joe's set from Saturday lunchtime, this time as a band. Just after eight o'clock

REMEMBER WHAT WE SAID ABOUT NOTING JUST WHERE YOU LEFT YOUR CAR? YOU DON'T WANT TO RELIVE THE WHOLE '70S, DO YOU?.

the pace will be cranked up by British blues rockers TEN YEARS AFTER, with a pumping version of Sonny Boy Williamson's "Good Morning Little School Girl", and the manic but articulate guitar of Alvin Lee on "I'm Going Home".

You may well be flagging at this point, so it is good to know that the mood is about to become more sedate and reflective. THE BAND, who have recently made their first album without Bob Dylan, put in a strong folk-rock set, notable for "The Weight" which everyone knows from the *Easy Rider* movie. JOHNNY WINTER's blues-rock guitar starts on the midnight hour and this albino Texan axeman should carry you through to the spacey jazz rock of BLOOD, SWEAT & TEARS at half past one on Monday morning. Stamina will be further rewarded when at three o'clock the recently formed CROSBY, STILLS AND NASH sit gingerly on their high stools and open with an immaculate version of "Suite: Judy Blue Eyes" with soaring pitch-perfect harmonies and sweet and melancholy melody. After their own acoustic set they will be joined by the enigmatic, bad-tempered but extraordinary NEIL YOUNG, first playing a duet with Stephen Stills before they all play a short electric set including the haunting "Long Time Gone".

Dawn is coming. You have been lulled into an ethereal dream by the plaintive harmonies of Crosby, Stills and Nash. You may be simply mud-caked, rain-battered and exhausted, but there are still five hours to go and the PAUL BUTTERFIELD BLUES BAND is going to get you there. Starting at six in the morning they will be serving up a set of uptempo Chicago white-boy blues, with talking guitars and wailing harmonica. If that isn't enough musical caffeine for you SHA-NA-NA's maniacal set of retro pop classics should be. Their all-singing all-dancing covers of "Jail House Rock" and "At the Hop" are unfeasibly upbeat for eight o'clock in the morning.

There is then an hour's pause – for whatever you want man – before the finale. At just after 9am JIMI HENDRIX and a five-piece band will open with "Getting My Heart Back Together Again". Two hours of wild psychedelic rock later, the amphitheater will feel like an abandoned battlefield. The crowd will have shrunk to less than 50,000, leaving a landscape of abandoned possessions, piles of rubbish and smouldering fires. In the midst of this Hendrix will announce that he is 'just jamming' before unleashing his extraordinary version of the "Star-Spangled Banner" and closing with a spine-tingling rendition of "Hey Joe". You are witnessing musical history.

PART TWO

MOMENTS THAT MADE HISTORY

The Execution of Charles I

THE DAY KING CHARLES I WALKED TO THE scaffold and put his neck on the chopping block was a truly momentous one. For centuries, a monarch's claim to absolute power had rested on the Divine Right of Kings – their authority rubber-stamped by the Almighty, placing them just below God and making them untouchable by their subjects. Charles's execution definitively demonstrated that this was no more than a spurious excuse for an individual to lord it over everybody else purely because of their genetic inheritance.

Of course, Charles was not the first monarch to meet a violent end; sibling rivalries, dynastic feuds, foreign interlopers, warfare and plain old *coups d'état* accounted for many a royal. But he was the first since ancient Rome to be killed in defence of a political principle – that principle being the sovereignty of Parliament and, by extension, the people who elected it. So began a process that would lead inexorably to the American Revolution of 1776 and the French Revolution soon after, shattering the illusion of monarchical power and bequeathing a world where kings no longer rule the roost.

On this 24-HOUR TRIP you will join the crowds at the place of execution and witness a moment that sent shock waves through European society. You will also get to sample the charged atmosphere of a city on the edge of the unknown; some dreaming of the end of this world and of a new improved one, others fearful of what was to come.

BRIEFING: THE ENGLISH CIVIL WARS

Early on the morning of 6 December 1649, COLONEL PRIDE and a regiment of foot soldiers congregated around the HOUSE OF COMMONS in Westminster. Pride held in his hand a list of parliamentary MPs who were to be barred from entering the building. He and his men excluded around 180 MPs (100 had already fled the capital) and arrested 45 of them.

Eighteen months previously England's first Civil War had ended in victory for Parliament's New Model Army. However, King Charles, despite being their prisoner, had not given up hope of regaining his power and nor had his supporters, who engineered a series of regional revolts, known to later historians as the SECOND CIVIL WAR; this lasted from May 1648 until the end of August when Colchester, the last Royalist outpost, fell after a long siege. Nevertheless, Charles still believed he could come out on

top, encouraged by the fact that a majority of MPs favoured a compromise settlement.

But THE ARMY had other ideas. Some 40,000 strong, it was the most radical force in the country and saw itself as the guarantor of the revolution. It also viewed Charles as a criminal, responsible for the 200,000–300,000 lives lost in the wars. When Parliament refused to discuss its bill of rights, the GRAND REMONSTRANCE, 7,000 troops marched on London and occupied it on 2nd December.

Parliament refused to be bullied and on 4 December, after an all-night session, it voted to continue negotiations with the King. The next day, a meeting of senior army figures led by HENRY IRETON, Oliver Cromwell's son-in-law, decreed that Charles had 'betrayed the trust reposed in him and raised war against the nation to enslave it'. To enforce their will, they decided to remove the MPs that stood in their way. PRIDE'S PURGE, as it became known, left only 80 MPs – THE RUMP – in the House of Commons. They could be trusted to toe the party line over the King's fate.

CHARLES IN THE DOCK, FACING THE HIGH COURT OF JUSTICE, WESTMINSTER PALACE, JANUARY 1649.

From then on, things moved fast. On 13 December, negotiations with the King were abandoned. On 2 January, after the House of Lords had rejected Charles's impeachment, the Army padlocked the Lords' Chamber and proceeded without them. The Rump then voted for the King's trial to proceed.

The trail began on 20 January. Charles's defence rested entirely on the DIVINE RIGHT OF KINGS: 'no earthly power can justly call me, who am your King, in question as a delinquent ... on the contrary, the authority of obedience unto Kings is clearly commanded in both the Old and New Testament'. After three days during which he persistently refused to plead or recognise the legitimacy of the court, Charles was removed. There followed two days of witness testimony – thirty individuals who all attested to the King's direct involvement in the bloodshed of the Civil Wars.

After further deliberation, the verdict came on 27 January: Charles was found 'guilty of all treasons, murders, rapines, burnings, spoils, desolations, damages and mischiefs to this nation, acted and committed in the said wars', and sentenced to death 'as a tyrant, traitor, murderer and public enemy to the good people of this nation'.

THE TRIP

You will arrive at 2pm on Monday 29 January 1649 at your lodgings on ST MARTIN'S LANE, about half a mile from the Parliament building. You'll have a few hours of daylight to explore your surroundings.

MONDAY 29 JANUARY

Apart from the execution, there will be not be much in the way of entertainment to be found. The theatres have been shut for seven years and, even though four reopened briefly at the New Year, they were quickly shut down again by the Army, who arrested any actors that resisted. Other common recreational pastimes – wrestling, archery, shooting and animal baiting – are all proscribed, too.

Walking the city streets, you will notice the effects of the precipitous decline in living standards caused by the war; prices are

OFF WITH HIS HEADS! CHARLES IN TRIPLICATE BY ANTHONY VAN DYCK.

sky-high and wages are low. The exodus of Charles's court, his Royalist followers and the nobility in general, is reflected in the lack of luxury items in the denuded shops – gold and silver jewellery, ornate clocks, silk and satin garments have disappeared from view – and the barren state of the usually bustling markets. The disruption of food supplies is currently chronic; much of the countryside is laid to waste and there are shortages of beef, fish and dairy products.

These deprivations will add an edge to a city gripped by feverish political and theological debate over the King and what the future will be like without him. Walk into any TAVERN and you will be entering a hotbed of argument and discussion. Before you do, we suggest to get right up to date with the issues and how they are being perceived. The easiest way to do this is to buy a NEWSPAPER. There are six established licenced weeklies, plus three new pro-Army papers – *A Perfect Summary*, *The Army's Modest Intelligencer* and *The Kingdom's Faithful Servant* – which have been rushed into print in the last few weeks to meet the public's insatiable appetite for news. The mostly widely read rag is *A Perfect Diurnall*, out today. It is cautiously pro-Parliament, with a circulation of around 3,000 copies.

To get a more radical perspective, look out for the latest edition of *The Moderate*, edited by GILBERT MABBOT, who was appointed chief censor by the Army in 1647; it supports THE LEVELLERS, a loose conglomeration of agitators demanding a thorough *levelling* of society that will eradicate inequality and give everybody the vote. Their ideas are popular with soldiers, craftsmen, artisans, apprentices and London's labouring poor. *The Moderate* also contains the most detailed reporting of the King's trial. You may also find yourself being handed a copy of one of the three illegal ROYALIST PAPERS – *Mercurius Melancolicus*, *Mercurius Elemticus* and *Mercurius Pragmaticus* – whose editors are all fugitives. Each copy is secretly printed on small, movable presses and distributed by a network of hawkers who risk being whipped if caught.

To hear these views expressed out loud, make your way to ST PAUL'S CATHEDRAL, where the Presbyterian preacher OBADIAH SEDGEWICK will be delivering passionate sermons in defence of Charles. Alternatively, over in Whitehall, you will see HUGH PETER, the populist Army chaplain, promoting the Republican cause. On most street corners you will also find PAMPHLETS expressing both sides of the argument; two of the most representative are John Goodwin's pro-Army *Right and Might Well Met*, and the Royalist *Might Overcoming Right*.

Everywhere you go, it will be hard to avoid the BEGGARS clogging up the streets – destitute rural workers who have flocked to the city in search of sustenance, limbless veterans, and war widows with their starving orphans. Also hard to miss will be signs of the Army's presence; COVENT GARDEN PIAZZA, home to exclusive mansions that were built for the elite during the 1630s, is now being used as an open-air stable for the cavalry's horses, all tethered up to 'the doors of noblemen's, Knights' and gentlemen's houses'.

CLOTHING, ROOMS AND FOOD

Your choice of clothes is political. CAVALIER FASHIONS – elaborate ruffs, extravagantly designed satin tunics, expensive accessories and flowing locks – are a no-no, unless you want to be labelled an ungodly Royalist. To fit in with the crowd, you will be dressed in the simple, plain outfits associated with the PURITAN MOVEMENT (contrary to received wisdom, black is not the predominant look: black dyes were prohibitively expensive and faded quickly). WOMEN TRAVELLERS, your hair cut short and covered by a linen cap, will wear a MURREY (mulberry) coloured high-necked woollen smock, a wide white collar with a subtle hint of lace embroidery and Dutch-style wooden clogs. MEN will wear a dull-green, ankle-length thick wool jacket, a black top hat to conceal your cropped hair, and suitably worn-in brown leather boots.

ROOMS

We have rented you a room in a lodging house at CECIL COURT off St Martin's Lane, and a *tabling* contract has been signed which obliges the resident servants to prepare you at least one meal a day. To keep your room warm and the winter chill at bay (it's so cold the Thames is frozen over), we have managed to get some highly sought-after coal; due to the war it is a rare commodity. Most folks are relying on wood to keep the home fires burning, but even though the Royal Forests have been stripped bare, there is not enough to go around. People are so desperate they are taking timber from wherever they can find it; you will notice missing doors, posts, seats, benches and railings.

DINNER

DINNER is at 6pm. Given the food shortages, don't expect anything fancy. You will be served POTTAGE, a primitive stew that is the main source of nourishment in these difficult times. Made by boiling grain in water to create a thick gruel, your pottage will include a small amount of beef, acquired with some difficulty, and some root vegetables that may well have seen better days. A loaf of bread – supplies are currently adequate, though fear of famine is mounting after a series of bad harvests and an exceptionally wet summer – will help mop it all up.

As imports of French wine have collapsed, the best we can offer is a sweet Spanish variety. Beer, the staple drink of the day, is also available, despite being heavily taxed and its production restricted to keep the price of grain down. Fruit, the key ingredient in most contemporary DESSERTS, is nowhere to be found. Instead, the cook will rustle up some curd-cakes for you, fritters made from a pint of curd, four eggs, with two of the whites removed, sugar and nutmeg, all stirred together with a sprinkling of flour and fried with a little butter until golden brown.

If you'd rather go out to eat, we suggest you visit a local inn called, appropriately enough, THE KING'S HEAD, on the corner of Chancery Lane and Fleet Street. Again the fare on offer will be simple. The owner, like all tavern-keepers, is suffering hard times. He is selling less wine in a week than he used to shift in a day, while demand for the meals cooked in his kitchen has fallen by 75 percent. But tonight the King's Head is full, jammed with ordinary Londoners engaged in intense conversation about tomorrow's big event. Take a pew and listen in or, if you're bold enough, dive into the heated arguments raging over this Great Matter.

TUESDAY 30 JANUARY

You will rise at dawn. BREAKFAST will consist of beer and the remains of last night's loaf. Before you set off on this bitter, gloomy morning, you will be provided with a packed lunch and a bottle of beer to wash it down with; the cook has managed to find a hunk of scarce Cheddar cheese to accompany whatever's left of the bread. We suggest you go to the TOILET now – there is a chamberpot in your room – as there are no public lavatories near the execution site. If you have to find somewhere to relieve yourself, you will almost certainly lose your place in the crowd; every second you are absent will put you further and further away from the action.

It will take you about 20 minutes to reach ST JAMES'S PARK, established in 1532 by Henry VIII and landscaped by James I. Today, the lake is frozen solid, the trees bare, plants and wildlife nowhere to be seen. Here you will join a smattering of onlookers waiting to catch a glimpse of the King leaving ST JAMES'S PALACE, an imposing red-brick, twin-towered Tudor structure built on the site of a leper hospital. At about 10am, KING CHARLES, looking older than his 48 years, his hair and beard grey, skin sallow and with deep rings under his eyes, will emerge escorted by the Bishop of London, WILLIAM JUXON, his guardian THOMAS HERBERT, and COLONEL MATTHEW TOMLINSON, leading two companies of helmeted infantry in crimson-red tunics with pikes raised, and with drummers out front beating a steady march.

You will see some spectators hurling abuse at Charles and an old man – a former servant of the King – weeping copiously as Charles and company trudge grimly across the park to an open wooden staircase that leads directly into WHITEHALL PALACE. The King will then proceed to his old room – now completely stripped of all the splendid fineries that used to fill it – where he will wait to be called to the scaffold.

GETTING INTO POSITION

It is a short stroll from the park to KING STREET, a broad thoroughfare that links Westminster to Charing Cross. This runs directly through Whitehall Palace, which extends about two hundred yards inland from its gardens and frontage on the river. Take up a viewing position in front of the BANQUETING HOUSE that stands at right angles to the red-and-black-chequered brick of HOLBEIN GATE, built by Henry VIII to create a corridor joining the residential section of Whitehall Palace to The Tilt Yard (the blank wall a bit further up on the opposite side of King Street), the galleried Cock-Pit and other outbuildings on the St James's Park side, all of them currently occupied by the Army, who have mounted a battery of guns on a platform nearby.

Though King Street will already be filling up with people of all classes and descriptions, there will be none of the festivities normally associated with a public execution: no street sellers or performers, no jugglers or minstrels, no drunken high spirits. This will be a sombre occasion. Adding to the oppressive mood are two TROOPS OF CAVALRY, each rider armed with two pistols and a sword, wearing their distinctive Roundhead uniform – custard-yellow tunic, silver breastplate, and helmet with a curved lip to protect the neck and visor to shield the face – stationed at the north and south end of the street.

The SCAFFOLD, draped completely in black, has been erected to stand firm against the stone façade of the Banqueting House, which is all classical Roman motifs, columns and arches. Three or four *staples* (wooden pins with pulleys attached) have been driven into the scaffold so that Charles can be restrained if he tries to resist his fate. Also note the extremely low CHOPPING BLOCK; normally it would be two feet high, allowing a victim to kneel, comfortably place his neck down and insert his chin in the special groove hollowed out of its flat surface. Today, the block is only ten inches off the ground and Charles will have to stoop awkwardly to get his head onto it.

By lunchtime the crowd will have grown to occupy every available space. People are hanging out of windows, cramming balconies and standing on rooftops. As you munch your cheese and sip your beer, spare a thought for the King, who will be eating his last meal on earth – white bread and a glass of claret.

THE EXECUTION

At around 1.30pm, people will start appearing on the scaffold. You will see BISHOP JUXON, COLONEL TOMLINSON, COLONEL FRANCIS HACKER, some guards (including the *Leveller* journalist JOHN HARRIS) and several shorthand writers with notebooks and ink horns, ready to note down everything that happens. Centre of attention are the EXECUTIONER AND HIS ASSISTANT, both dressed in black tight-fitting coats, their faces disguised by masks, false wigs and fake beards.

Not surprisingly, the identity of the executioner is a matter of some dispute. The most likely candidate is RICHARD BRANDON, chief *headsman*. Known as 'Young Gregory' – his father was also in the execution game – Brandon has a good eye, steady nerves and hands and the necessary experience; he has already dispatched the Archbishop of Canterbury, an earl and several other nobles in his short career. In June, stricken down by a terminal fever, Brandon will make a deathbed confession and admit that he was paid £30 to wield the axe. His assistant is probably a volunteer from a staunchly Republican regiment.

At 2.00pm the King makes his appearance, stepping straight out of one of the Banqueting House's eight large windows and onto the scaffold, wearing two heavy shirts so he won't shiver in the cold and give the impression that he is scared. Though every word Charles speaks will be recorded for posterity by the reporters near the block, you will not be able to hear a thing. Lip-readers will be at an advantage. However, if you monitor his expressions and his body language, you'll be able to work out who Charles is talking to and how long each exchange lasts.

First, Charles will unfold a small piece of paper on which he has scribbled a few words that he will now address to the crowd, his voice so quiet that every syllable will be lost before it reaches you. During his BRIEF ORATION, Charles will call himself 'the martyr of the people', and accuse those who condemned him of exercising 'an arbitrary power' and ruling by 'the power of the sword'. Rather than rousing the crowd, his speech is met by deathly silence. The wind momentarily knocked out of his sails, Charles hesitantly asks Colonel Hacker to 'take care to put me not in pain'; if Brandon botches the first stroke it could take a number of swings of the axe to dislodge the head, a prolonged, messy and excruciatingly painful business.

Next, Charles speaks to Bishop Juxon, confirming that he will 'die a Christian according to the profession of the Church of England'. Juxon tries to comfort Charles by reminding him that he is bound for Heaven, where he will 'find a crown of glory'. Charles nods appreciatively and replies: 'I go from a corruptible to an incorruptible crown; where no disturbance can be, no disturbance in the world.' The Bishop (like many in his profession, he is keen to have the last word) agrees that it's 'a good exchange'.

Then there is a bit of stage theatrics. Brandon tucks his victim's hair neatly under his cap, Charles removes his cloak, decorated with the jewelled pendant of the Order of the Garter that bears the figure of Saint George, hands it to the Bishop, removes his doublet and puts his cloak back on. This ritual complete, Charles draws an icy breath and looks down at the low chopping block. Perturbed, he turns to his executioner; 'You must set it fast.' Brandon is unmoved: 'It is.' Charles, still not happy, tries again: 'It might have been a little higher.' Brandon remains firm: 'It can be no higher, sir.'

Frustrated, but realising the futility of continuing, Charles mutters to himself, stands, hands and eyes lifted up, and bends sharply down to put his head on the block. While Brandon ensures that all Charles's hair is firmly inside his cap, Charles stretches out his arms and makes one final request: 'Stay for the sign' (wait until I'm ready). Brandon, perhaps for the first time comprehending

CHARLES I ON THE SCAFFOLD, IN FRONT OF THE CROWDS, WITH A RATHER
FANCIFUL BANQUETING HOUSE BEHIND. THE PRINT IS CONTEMPORARY.

the enormity of what he is about to do, softly and humbly agrees,
addressing Charles as 'Your Majesty'.

An expectant hush falls over King Street as Charles stretches
out both his arms. Brandon raises the mighty axe – supplied by the
Tower of London, it is thirty-six inches long, weighs over seven
pounds, and has a sixteen-inch blade with an especially bright
(sharp) ten-inch cutting edge – and brings it hurtling down onto
Charles's neck, hitting the third and fourth vertebrae and cleanly
severing his head. The terminal blow is greeted by an eerie moan
from the crowd, so unnerving that an observer remembered it
being 'such a groan as I never heard before and desire I may never
hear again'. You may find yourself joining in.

Brandon will briefly wave Charles's head at the crowd, before it, and the rest of him, is swiftly placed in a coffin covered with black velvet and carried inside. While it is customary to put the severed heads of traitors on public display, in this case the regicides decide not to go that far; they are worried about arousing sympathy for the departed monarch and sparking a backlash. Instead, Charles's head will be sewn back onto his body, and then his corpse will be embalmed and placed in a lead coffin. Despite showing the royal personage due respect, the regicides don't want Charles resting in Westminster Abbey, so the body will be conveyed to Windsor on the night of 7 February. Two days later, Charles will be buried in the Henry VIII vault in Saint George's Chapel.

DEPARTURE

In the seconds after the fatal blow is struck, a few spectators will be able to dip their handkerchiefs in the royal blood spilled on the cobblestones beneath the scaffold – as a memento or good luck charm. However, the troops quickly assert their authority and disperse the shell-shocked crowd, numbed by the cold and what they have just witnessed, sending it and you streaming away from the scene into back alleys and winding lanes. Half an hour later the place is deserted.

Those hoping to linger a little longer on the streets will be deterred by a show of strength from the cavalry. COLONEL JOHN HEWSON and his squadron will ride through the centre of town, sweeping from Charing Cross to the Royal Exchange, ensuring that Londoners return directly to their homes, rather than hanging around for hours as they normally would after a major public ceremony, leaving the city silent and empty, winter darkness fast approaching. It is clearly time to leave. Make way back to your LODGINGS as quickly as you can, from where you will DEPART.

The Women's March on Versailles

4–5 OCTOBER 1789 ✳ PARIS/VERSAILLES

THE FRENCH REVOLUTION WAS ONE OF the greatest upheavals in history: its defining feature was chaos; its outcome anything but inevitable. At various crucial moments the people of Paris made decisive interventions, each time pushing the Revolution in a more radical direction. THE WOMEN'S MARCH ON VERSAILLES established the template for these mini-insurrections. Its display of strength emboldened the people, giving them the confidence to take control of events and bend them to their will.

Over forty-eight hours a group of tough working-class Parisian women – their contemporaries called them Amazons – ransacked the PALACE AT VERSAILLES and forced KING LOUIS XVI and QUEEN MARIE ANTOINETTE to up sticks and relocate to Paris, where they became virtual prisoners. Their stunningly opulent palace was left abandoned, its sumptuously decorated rooms and mirrored halls deserted, the doors shut, the gates locked, the glorious gardens patrolled by armed guards. A few years later, both the King and Queen would go to the guillotine, a journey that began on the day the women came to town.

On this trip, you will spend a NIGHT OUT IN PARIS, enjoying the pleasure gardens of the PALAIS ROYAL, where the whole city goes to play. Next day (5 October 1789), you will join the women on their march for bread and storm the Palace at Versailles, returning in triumph to Paris to party a second night away.

BRIEFING: REVOLUTION AND THE 'AUSTRIAN WHORE'

Earlier in the year (14 July), Paris rose up to LIBERATE THE BASTILLE, the most loathed and notorious prison in France. It was the symbol of everything rotten about the *ancien régime* – a system that the delegates of the newly convened NATIONAL ASSEMBLY are determined to dismantle – and a cause for much celebration. However, the euphoria has not lasted for long. While the National Assembly has spent August consigning feudalism to the trashcan of history and framing the DECLARATION OF THE RIGHTS OF MAN, the citizens of Paris increasingly fear a counter-attack from the forces of reaction, either a direct intervention by a foreign power or an aristocratic plot. Adding to the mounting tension are severe bread shortages; though this summer France has had the first decent harvest in years, a drought has meant that millers did not have enough water to grind the corn.

The price of a standard four-pound loaf has risen over the year by sixty per cent Throughout September, bakers have been attacked for overcharging and grain carts have been randomly seized.

By October, Paris is on a knife edge. And on 2 October there is a perfect provocation when a lavish banquet, attended by Marie Antoinette, is held in honour of the King's Flanders Regiment (the Black Musketeers), who have been called to Versailles to bolster the royal defences. Over the course of a debauched evening the soldiers sing monarchist songs; they wear hats emblazoned with cockades in black (the Queen's colour) or white (the King's) rather than the TRICOLOUR that is an essential item for all true supporters of the Revolution. Worse still, they allegedly cursed and trampled on the Revolution's tricolour cockade. When news of these outrages

MARIE ANTOINETTE PLAYING AT BEING A PEASANT.

reaches Paris, it is swiftly inflated. Indeed, the gossip is that Marie Antoinette participated in an orgy with members of the regiment. These rumours lead inevitably to the Women's March on Versailles.

On the march, you may be shocked by the women's intense hatred of MARIE ANTOINETTE and the savagery of the abuse they hurl at her, often sexual in nature. Married at fifteen, queen at nineteen, Marie Antoinette secured a bad reputation by dressing inappropriately and attending Parisian theatres and decadent social gatherings without her husband. In 1777, *Anandria*, the first of what became a steady stream of pornographic novels about her, was published. It included generic elements – lesbianism, nymphomania and masturbation – that would be recycled in songs, satirical verses and other books. The most widely read is *Essai Historique sur la Vie de Marie Antoinette*, first published in 1781, reprinted in 1783 and then updated on a yearly basis until her death a decade later.

More firmly based in fact is the belief that the Queen is as profligate with money as she is in the bedroom. While ordinary people starve, she spends like there is no tomorrow and has a particular weakness for diamonds. This toxic combination of material and moral depravity, both real and imagined, will account for much of what you see and hear over the next few days. If, however, you are expecting to hear her say 'Let them eat cake,' or something similar, you have been woefully misled; she never said any such thing. As you will see, it would have been most unwise.

THE TRIP

You will arrive at 3.30pm on SUNDAY 4 OCTOBER 1789 in the courtyard of the HÔTEL DE SOUBISE, 60 Rue des Francs-Bourgeois, in the heart of Paris. The Soubise is what is known as a *hôtel particulier* – a very posh B&B – one of the grand mansions of the super-rich that stand empty most of the time, as their owners spend no more than a few days a year in Paris. Our choice belongs to the Prince de Soubise – who is characteristically absent – and has dozens of rooms decorated in a rococo style. It has a small army of servants and is lavishly appointed with exquisite furnishings, fine art on the walls, marbled baths, bidets and king-size beds. Both sexes will have their own upholstered POTTY CHAIRS with a hole in the seat and a chamberpot underneath, the men's receptacle purely functional, the women's an ornamented bourdaloue, which looks like a gravyboat. The servants will be on hand to empty them.

Your clothes for your night out in Paris will be typical of the city's professional middle classes. Men will be wearing a wig, dark green jacket (open at the front with tails), white leggings, calf-length leather boots and a top hat. Women will have their hair up in a bunch, a shawl and a relatively plain low-cut dress with a voluminous floor-length skirt and lace frills. Men may carry a silver-topped cane, women a parasol.

SUNDAY NIGHT AT THE PALAIS ROYAL

THE PALAIS ROYAL is the place to be after nightfall. Open to all and sundry, it belongs to the Duc d'Orléans, who inherited it in 1776 and decided to transform it into a pleasure palace. Its three-tiered arcades run in galleries round the perimeter of the site and contain sixty pavilions, all enclosed by trees which line a large promenade. Though the SHOPS will be closed – it is Sunday, after all – you can gaze at the fashionable clothes, designer wigs and exquisite lace garments displayed in their windows.

On the PROMENADE, there will be hawkers selling all manner of items and you will be able to select from the plethora of publications that have been released since the Revolution did away with censorship; newspapers like *Révolutions de Paris*, with its racy prose, eyewitness reporting and captioned illustrations, or Marat's incendiary *L'Ami du Peuple*, which urges readers to 'sweep away the corrupt, the royal pensioners and the devious aristocrats'. Also on offer will be SATIRICAL PAMPHLETS, political tracts and ballad sheets. Cheap FIREWORKS – for twelve sous you can buy squibs, rockets and serpents – are on sale everywhere and provide a constant backdrop of noise and colour, adding to the carnival atmosphere.

As you wander round you will see LIMONADIERS (lemonade sellers) plying their wares, and we suggest you try some: *limonade* is France's favourite soft drink and a source of national pride, considered the best in Europe. This is not surprising given the care that goes into its preparation. The yellow rind from three or four lemons is sprinkled into a jug filled with clean spring water, covered and left to stand for a few hours. Next, the juice from the lemons is added and, after 30 minutes' waiting time, filtered

CAMILLE DESMOULINS ADDRESSING A CROWD AT THE
PALAIS ROYAL, OUTSIDE THE CAFÉ DE FOY.

eight times through a coarse linen cloth. After adding sugar the whole mixture is run through the cloth two more times, resulting in an extremely refreshing and thirst-quenching beverage. After drinking a glass or two, you may need to empty your bladder; if so, there are public latrines – enclosed rooms with rows of wooden seats and a lunette (cover) over each hole.

For contemporary popular entertainment, the Palais offers the THÉÂTRE BEAUJOLAIS, featuring three-foot-tall marionettes and child actors, and the VARIÉTÉS AMUSANTES, which stages music-hall-style farces and melodramas to packed houses. Novelty attractions – MAGIC LANTERN and SHADOW-LIGHT SHOWS – can be found in the wooden galley running along the Palais, alongside a kind of FREAK SHOW; one of the biggest draws is Paul Butterboldt, the FOUR-HUNDRED-POUND MAN; also look out for a DEFROCKED PRIEST singing obscene songs while strumming his guitar.

A must-see for all visitors are the WAX-WORKS DISPLAYS at Salon No. 7, mounted by Philippe Curtius, a pioneer of this form of spectacle and owner of Paris's first waxwork museum, *Le Grand Couvert*. At the Palais you will pay twelve sous to sit up close, or two sous at the back. In front of you will be waxwork tableaux featuring various royal families, cultural and intellectual giants like Voltaire, and military heroes.

For those of a sporting disposition, there are BILLIARD TABLES and GAMBLING DENS on the upper floors. After 10pm, flocks of PROSTITUTES will gather by a colonnaded area known as the Camp des Tartares.

EATING AND DRINKING

There is no need to leave the Palais for dinner. Its RESTAURANTS are the finest in Paris. The best, and most expensive, is the CAFÉ DE CHARTRES, where you can enjoy *plats bourgeois* (the general term for haute cuisine) such as fried mutton feet, rabbit steaks with cucumber, roast veal in pastry and vine-leaf fritters. Slightly cheaper, but no less excellent, is LES TROIS FRÈRES PROVENCAUX, run by three brothers from Marseille who serve regional speci-alities; *bouillabaisse* (fish soup) and *brandade* (puréed salt cod). Normally with your meal you'd expect a top-quality *pain mollet* (soft bread) like the elaborate *pain de fantaisie*, however, in times of need, when BREAD is scarce, it is customary not to bake such fancy loaves and the owners will respect this tradition; to ignore it is to invite trouble.

For coffee, a dessert of sorbet or ice cream, and a liqueur to finish, the Palais also has plenty of CAFÉS to choose from. The current hotspot is the CAFÉ DE FOY, frequented by leading rev-olutionaries like Georges Danton and Camille Desmoulins. The COFFEE comes from Santo Domingo in the Caribbean and you can have it strong and black, or with milk (*café au lait*); you can even get a *mocha*. Take a seat at one of the outside tables under the chestnut trees and you will be surrounded by all manner of Parisians passionately debating politics. Games of CHESS are also available at a number of tables: chess is a common feature of café culture and standards are high, competition fierce. So if you are an enthusiast, pull up a chair and test your moves against the best in revolutionary Paris. For a more refined atmosphere visit the CAFÉ DE LA RÉGENCE, with its marbled tables, mirrored walls and chandeliers.

FRENCH BREAD

The role of BREAD in the events you are about to witness is critical –and symptomatic of its importance to eighteenth-century French society. Available in a range of shapes and sizes, from round to long and thin (don't call them *baguettes* as the word doesn't appear until 1920), their unique flavour and texture is largely due to their ingredients: salt, either grey from the salt marshes or white from the Normandy seaside; water drawn from rivers, fountains, wells, or directly from rainfall; butter; sometimes milk and sugar; occasionally egg, for a glazed effect. White stone-ground flour is sifted through cloth to create three main types of dough: *ferme* (hard), *molle* (soft) and *bâtard* (bastard), which is somewhere in-between the two and is overtaking *ferme* as the standard variety.

Bread also denotes social class. The elite will mostly eat *pain mollet* (soft, crusty, savoury bread); the bourgeoisie, *bâtard* breads like the aptly named *pain bourgeois*; and the vast majority *pain du commun* (hard crustless bread). Over the course of this trip, you will sample a range of these loaves and get a taste of what the Women's March is all about.

LOWER ORDERS

If you want to be better acquainted with the lives of the working women and men who will lead you to Versailles tomorrow, we suggest you walk the short distance to the less affluent neighbourhoods near LES HALLES (Paris's main market) and go into any busy TAVERN, where you will be able to get reasonable wine from Bordeaux and Burgundy, and a hearty bowl of soup. The bread, if there is any, will either be *pain à soupe*, which is a very flat loaf made entirely from crusts and *bâtard* dough, or a *pain du commun* (hard) like the local staple, *gros pain de Paris*. For a more downmarket experience, check out one of the many street-corner

WINE SHOPS, where you can buy a bottle to take-away or stay and drink standing up (there are no chairs) and mix with labourers on a daily wage – market porters, chimney sweeps, coachmen – as well as criminals and hookers.

In all these venues, you will hear the clientele speaking POISSARD, the favoured slang of the market women and fishwives. Derived from the word *poix* (pitch), it is a crude but vibrant patois featuring heavy elision, fractured syntax and grammar, plus rudimentary rhyme, perfect for jokes and ribald songs. It has quickly become fashionable, taken up by the bourgeoisie and the aristos, who get a kick out of dropping it into polite conversation.

MONDAY 5 OCTOBER 1789

After your late night – Paris does not sleep until about 4am – you will need to ready for BREAKFAST by 7am, dressed in your PROLE-TARIAN OUTFIT. Women should be wearing a white bonnet, loose white blouse and a white apron over a billowing pleated skirt. Men should wear a red cap, white shirt with a sleeveless brown leather jacket and blue *culottes* (knee-breeches). Both sexes will have a TRICOLOUR COCKADE, best worn as a sash, either wrapped round your waist or across your torso.

At your local patisserie try a *pain à café*, which is a rich break-fast roll. Obviously it goes well with coffee, but we recommend you order a *chocolat chaud* instead: either a dark chocolate brew – vanilla and sugar mixed with cocoa paste – or a creamier version with milk. Since its arrival in France in the seventeenth century, HOT CHOCOLATE has been growing in popularity, and these days it's all the rage – Marie Antoinette has her very own *chocolatier* working on new recipes – and spices like cinnamon, nutmeg and clove are common additions. If you are fed up with bread and would like something different, try a *choux* bun; made by mixing butter, water, flour and eggs to create a light choux dough, this type of bun was recently invented by the *pâtissier* Avice.

While you are eating you will hear the Toscin sound from the Church of Sainte-Marguérite, followed by the BELLS of dozens of others summoning the citizens of Paris onto the streets to answer the call of a young woman who is banging a drum and yelling, 'When will we have bread?' As their numbers swell to nearly 7,000, THE WOMEN – mostly fishwives, shopkeepers, market traders and pedlars from the Faubourg Saint-Antoine, armed with cudgels, knives and sticks – are joined by men from the surrounding districts. Together the angry mob will proceed to the HÔTEL DE VILLE, Paris's town hall and the focal point of mass protest.

AT THE HÔTEL DE VILLE

You should be in the PLACE DE GRÈVE, outside the Hôtel de Ville, by 8am. On arrival, you will see the women, and some men, breaking down its locked doors. The more adventurous may want to follow them as they burst in, tearing up documents and ledgers as they search for weapons; however, this is not an occasion for wholesale looting; a wad of a hundred 1,000 livres notes goes missing but it will be returned a few weeks later, while 3.5 million livres in cash will be left untouched. This does not mean you will leave empty-handed; 700 rifles and muskets, plus two cannons, are seized and carried outside, where the increasingly restive crowd is busy denouncing the Mayor – JEAN-SYLVAIN BAILLY, an astronomer whose speciality is the moons of Jupiter – along with the Flanders Regiment and the King.

By 11am, the mood will be turning increasingly ugly, the women chanting, 'A Versailles, ou à la lanterne'. This is no idle threat. It has become customary to hang enemies of the people from lampposts (*lanternes*) before chopping off their heads. On hand to help is Mathieu Jouve Jourdan, better known as JOURDAN COUPE-TÊTE (Jourdan the Head-Cutter). Dressed all in black, carrying an array of hatchets and cleavers, Jourdan is a former butcher who gained his fearsome reputation thanks to his involvement in the murder of the financier Joseph-François de Foulon.

WOMEN ON THE MARCH. TWELVE MILES IS A LONG WAY
TO DRAG A CANNON IN THE RAIN.

Jourdan removed his head after his corpse had been dragged naked through the streets, then turned his attention to Foulon's hapless son-in-law, Bertier. Having shown Bertier his grisly handiwork, Jourdan proceeded to carve him into little pieces.

As the women string up ABBÉ LEFÈBVRE, the Hôtel de Ville's quartermaster, and Jourdan sharpens his blades, STANISLAS MAILLARD, a hero of the Sacking of the Bastille, intervenes and persuades them to cut Lefèbvre loose. Thanks to his standing with the crowd, Maillard is able to convince them that the time has come to march on Versailles.

THE MARCH

With Maillard and a group of drummers leading the way, you and the women begin the TWELVE-MILE MARCH in pouring rain that will persist throughout the day. You will cross the River Seine at the

Cité, follow the Quai des Orfèvres to Pont Neuf, cross over again to the Louvre, pass the Tuileries Garden, halt briefly at the Place Louis XV, then continue along the Champs-Elysées and the Right Bank until you reach Chaillot, then Sèvres (about halfway), and finally VIROFLAY, the last stop before Versailles. En route you will sing POISSARD SONGS about getting your hands on *bon papa* (the King), and watch gobsmacked onlookers being corralled into joining you, while shopkeepers hurriedly board up their premises.

AT VERSAILLES

After six hours on the road you will reach the town of VERSAILLES and proceed down its main boulevard, the AVENUE DE PARIS, where you will be met by local officials who greet you with fine words and barrels of wine. You will also notice the dramatic appearance of THÉROIGNE DE MÉRICOURT, a strikingly beautiful young woman astride a jet-black horse, wearing a plumed hat, crimson riding coat, and brandishing a pistol and sabre; this former courtesan will soon become a totemic figure, embodying the spirit of women's liberation.

While most of you will mill about drinking, a detachment of women, supported by men dragging one of the cannons, will continue down the Avenue to the PLACE D'ARMES, directly in front of the Palace, only to find the iron grille gates of the COUR ROYALE (Royal Courtyard) firmly shut and protected by the Gare du Corps (Royal Bodyguard), the Cent-Suisses (Hundred Swiss) and members of the detested Flanders Regiment. Undeterred, the women will threaten to open fire and insult the King for refusing to sign the Declaration of the Rights of Man.

LOUIS XVI, who has rushed back from hunting at Meudon, agrees to receive a small group of you. Once in his presence, one of the women, a seventeen-year-old flower girl, PIERRETTE CHABRY, will be so overawed that she faints; the King will rouse her with smelling salts and promise that any grain currently en route to Paris will be delivered immediately.

THÉROIGNE DE MÉRICOURT WAS THE MODEL FOR THE FIGURE OF LIBERTY
IN DELACROIX'S REVOLUTIONARY PAINTING, LIBERTY LEADING THE PEOPLE.

His offer will be met with healthy scepticism by the women outside and, as time passes, tempers fray after repeated attempts to force
the gates are thwarted by the FLANDERS REGIMENT. The King, un-
derstandably worried about further enflaming the women, has the
PALACE BAKERY emptied and its contents distributed among you
– tuck in to their excellent bread, as this may be all you get to eat
for a while. Around 6pm, the King will declare that he is ready to
SIGN THE DECLARATION OF THE RIGHTS OF MAN and ratify the
AUGUST DECREES that dismantled feudalism. For the moment,
these concessions will mollify the crowd, and for the next few hours a
sort of calm will prevail, broken only by the odd exchange of gunfire.

THE SALLE DES MENUS PLAISIRS

While you may be content to loiter outside the gates, there will
be plenty to see at the SALLES DES MENUS PLAISIRS, a complex
of buildings with huge rooms reserved for public functions and

ceremonies, located at 22 Avenue de Paris, not far from the Palace. The Salle you are heading for was expanded to accommodate the Estates General when it opened here on 5 May 1789, but soon became home to the National Assembly. 150-foot long, 75-foot wide, and thirty-foot high, its domed roof, painted ceilings, Grecian pillars and racked circular seating that surrounds the vast debating floor, take your breath away.

At first only a few of you will accompany MAILLARD into the Salle, where he will present your demands to the bemused delegates. But then hundreds of marchers – stinking of mud and dripping wet from the long march – enter the auditorium, some with hunting knives and swords dangling menacingly from their skirts. Pandemonium ensues. Deputies are elbowed aside to make room for everyone on the benches, one woman will occupy the President's chair and issue decrees on his behalf, others will fire their muskets into the air, the shots booming round the cavernous hall. You will see a young cleric trying to stop a fishwife from further insulting an archbishop by bending and kissing her hand; she dismisses his goodwill gesture and, instead of responding in kind, tells him she will not 'kiss the paws of a dog'.

Not all the assembly are treated with the same contempt. The women will happily mingle with MIRABEAU, the corpulent pockmarked revolutionary whose thunderous oratory and quicksilver mind have already made him famous, while ROBESPIERRE, a thin, stiff-backed provincial lawyer who will later gain notoriety as the architect of the Terror, exchanges pleasantries and makes encouraging noises.

OUTSIDE THE PALACE: MIDNIGHT

Towards midnight you will hear the tramping of massed boots and see thousands of torches approaching through the darkness. It's the NATIONAL GUARD, nearly 20,000 of them, marching six abreast down the Avenue de Paris, wearing their red-trimmed uniforms with blue coats, white lapels and leggings, the colours matching their cockades. This semi-professional militia, formed to defend the Revolution, is led by LAFAYETTE, a French hero of the American War of Independence and the nearest thing France has to a Commander-in-Chief, mounted on his white horse. Following in their train are thousands of armed civilians. The whole cavalcade left Paris at 4pm, delayed by Lafayette, who eventually gave up trying to persuade his men not to march on Versailles when a few of his officers suggested he might like the view from the top of a lamppost.

On arrival, Lafayette quickly secures an audience with the King, leaving you to wait impatiently for his return. When he finally reappears outside, he brings good news: the Flanders Regiment will be dismissed. The majority, by now a little weary, will be content with this, and by 3am Lafayette, sufficiently reassured that the worst is over, will head to his grandfather's house nearby to get some shut-eye. However, almost as soon as he is gone, a seventeen-year-old apprentice cabinetmaker, JÉRÔME HÉRITIER, will be shot dead by a Black Musketeer firing from a Palace window.

BACK AT THE NATIONAL ASSEMBLY

As the night wears on, you will receive regular UPDATES FROM THE PALACE, each concession by the King met with wild applause, and be treated to a brief visit from Lafayette. However, the excitement will start to fade as exhaustion takes hold. Many women will simply crash out where they sit; some will even fall asleep standing up. You may also be ready to curl up somewhere and take a nap. But, whatever you do, don't oversleep. Make sure you are BACK AT THE PALACE BY 4AM, for things are about to kick off.

INSIDE THE PALACE

For some reason, in the middle of the night a large detachment of Royal troops will be sent to the far end of the Palace Gardens, leaving the COUR DES MINISTRES lightly patrolled. The women seize their chance, breaching the gates and flooding into the COUR DE MARBRE, the Palace's innermost marbled courtyard, with direct access to the ROYAL APARTMENTS. These are located on the first floor of the immense Pavilion Block – the wings alone are half a mile wide – which also includes the private apartments of courtiers and government officials, their rooms enfilading off each other.

At this point, at around 4.40am, a few women will leave the main pack and set off HUNTING FOR MARIE ANTOINETTE; some are intent on using their aprons to carry her bowels, while one woman threatens to tear out her heart, cut off her head and fricassee her liver. Others will roam through the rooms of France's wealthiest individuals, stealing valuable items – tapestries, candlesticks, gold trinkets, porcelain figures. Look out for the DUC D'ORLÉANS, owner of the Palais Royal, leaning on the main stairway wearing a grey frock coat and slouched hat, riding whip in hand, pointing you in the direction of the Royal bedrooms. As you stream towards them, you may spot terrified courtiers hiding under chairs and diving behind sofas.

Approaching the QUEEN'S CHAMBERS, you will see the way barred by two bodyguards, TARDIVET and MIOMANDRE DE SAINTE-MARIE. Tardivet makes the fatal error of opening fire and hitting somebody; he is instantly seized and decapitated. Try not to be distracted by this gory scene; instead keep your eyes on Miomandre, who is backed up against the entrance to the Queen's antechambers. You will see him momentarily open the door a crack to speak to one of Marie Antoinette's maids, telling her to 'Save the Queen, they are here to assassinate her!' Then, seconds after he pushes the door shut again, he will be overwhelmed by the mob, who cave in his skull with their rifle butts.

A gang of women will now rush into Marie Antoinette's private rooms. Finding them empty – the Austrian Whore, wearing only her petticoat, has already slipped away and made it safely to the OEIL DE BOEUF (Bull's Eye), a locked chamber lit by a circular window, to be reunited with the King and her two children – they will vent their rage on her bed, puncturing it with their blades.

The majority of you will maraud through the magnificent HALL OF MIRRORS – seventeen arches, each with twenty-one mirrors – in search of your prey, until your progress is blocked by National Guardsmen led by LAZARE HOCHE, who form defensive ranks, some barricaded behind upturned tables, muskets at the ready. This show of force will bring you all to a standstill.

THE PALACE GARDENS

If this level of violence and mayhem is too much to stomach, we suggest you take a tour of the comparatively deserted PALACE GARDENS. Stroll past the geometrically perfect flowerbeds, cross the Allée d'Apollon, with its fountain, and you will reach the centrepiece of the park, the GRAND CANAL, a massive elongated pond in the shape of a cross, a mile long long and 200-foot wide. The right arm is called the BRAS DE LA MÉNAGERIE and points towards the King's collection of wild and exotic animals, the left one is the BRAS DE TRIANON, aiming in the direction of the Grand and Petit Trianons – neoclassical chateaux – that dominate this side of the park. Marie Antoinette keeps her special commode, a state-of-the-art flushing toilet, in the Petit Trianon.

Wander in any direction through the wooded areas and you will encounter remarkable constructions: the GROTTE DE THÉTYS, a grotto dedicated to the sea nymph decorated with shells to resemble an underwater cave; a secluded grove housing the BOSQUET DES SOURCES, a circular edifice with thirty-two arches and twenty-eight fountains; the secluded SALLE DE BALLE, an amphitheatre with a mini-waterfall; and the GALERIE DES ANTIQUES, a monumental array of ancient sculptures imported from Rome. However, don't wander too far afield; you'll want to be back in front of the Palace by 9.30am for the dramatic finale.

THE BALCONY SCENE

While the situation inside the Palace is at a stalemate, outside the cheering crowd has grabbed a couple of Black Musketeers and are preparing to disembowel them, with Jourdan Coupe-Tête directing operations. The HEADS OF THE BODYGUARDS Tardivet and Miomandre are, meantime, being paraded round on pikes, Miomandre's carried by an artist's model who is dressed in pseudo-Roman robes. The fun and games will be interrupted by LAFAYETTE on his white charger. Furious, he

LAFAYETTE PREVENTS POSSIBLE REGICIDE BY KISSING
THE HAND OF MARIE ANTOINETTE.

dives into the melee, frees the Black Musketeers and restores some kind of order.

Taking command, Lafayette instructs the National Guard to occupy the Place d'Armes, the Palace courtyards and the entrance to the Avenue de Paris, then heads inside the Palace where he is admitted into the sanctuary of the Oeil de Boeuf. Here, he tries to convince the King and Queen to return to Paris. Reluctant at first, they eventually bow to the inevitable. Nevertheless, it still takes Lafayette nearly two hours to get an agreement, leaving you and the vast mob gathered in the Cour de Marbre anxiously awaiting the outcome, fearful that the morning will end in a blood-soaked confrontation with the National Guard.

THE UNFORTUNATE TARDIVET AND MIOMANDRE RETURN ALOFT TO PARIS.

But thankfully, at 10am, Lafayette will walk out on the balcony above you, accompanied by the King. Here LOUIS promises to come back to Paris and take up his responsibilities – and the crowd bursts into spontaneous applause. Next, Lafayette will go some way to redeeming the royal bodyguard by pinning the tricolour cockade to one of their hats; again the crowd will respond positively. Then comes the trickiest part of the performance as MARIE ANTOINETTE comes out to face the music. Hoping to win your hearts, she brings her children with her, but at the sight of them everyone will roar 'Pas enfants!' ('No children!').

Earlier this year, on 27 June, Marie Antoinette had stood on the same balcony and introduced her children to a similarly huge gathering of citizens who were celebrating the birth of the National Assembly, and the crowd responded with genuine affection. But not today. An awkward, tense silence fills the courtyard. Lafayette, realising that one more false move will trigger a riot that will be impossible to stop, bows theatrically before his Queen and kisses her hand. Disaster is averted, and you and the mob will once again signal your approval.

RETURN TO PARIS – AND DEPARTURE

You and 60,000 other people will leave Versailles at 1pm. At the front and rear of this snaking, unwieldy procession will be the National Guard; at its centre, the solid gold ROYAL CARRIAGE carrying the King, the Queen (who has brought a casket of diamonds with her) and their children, escorted by Lafayette; behind it are coaches filled with courtiers, ministers and National Assembly delegates. The rest of you, a seething multitude, will ebb and flow around this parade of notables, offering protection to the train of wagons and carts filled with precious flour from the Palace stores.

The mood will be buoyant. Women are holding their swords aloft and heartily declaring that they are 'bringing the baker, the baker's wife and the baker's boy', while National Guardsmen, entering into the spirit of things, put loaves of bread on the ends of their raised pikes. Also being transported to Paris on the end of pikes are the heads of the two unfortunate bodyguards, Tardivet and Miomandre, now sporting powdered wigs supplied by a wigmaker from Sèvres; they will both end up on display at the Palais Royal. As the huge throng passes through villages on the outskirts of Paris, some locals think it best to remain behind locked doors, while others come out to watch. You will notice groups of irate peasants throwing clods of mud at the Royal Carriage.

By 6pm you are back in the PLACE DE GRÈVE, by now jam-packed with people, where you will watch the royal couple enter the Hôtel de Ville, wait while they are received by Mayor Bailly and representatives from all of Paris's sixty districts, and then see them make another balcony appearance, inspiring yet more jubilation and cries of 'Vive le Roi!' The Roi in question, and his bedraggled wife, will leave soon after for their new home in the Tuileries.

By now an immense street party is in full swing; Paris is literally jumping for joy. Plunge into the ecstatic festivities that will last until dawn, then make your way back to your HOTEL, from where you will DEPART.

The Assassination of Archduke Ferdinand

28 JUNE 1914 ✳ SARAJEVO

THE ASSASSINATION OF THE ARCHDUKE Franz Ferdinand and his wife Sophie, Duchess of Hohenberg, is a defining historical moment. The gunshots that end their lives set in motion a train of events that led to the outbreak of the First World War, the deaths of millions of people, the fall of three empires, the reconfiguration of the map of Eastern Europe and the Middle East, and numerous other consequences that would shape the twentieth century. Whether or not some kind of European conflict was inevitable, it would not have happened when it did and in the way that it did without the murder of the heir to the Habsburg throne.

The assassination itself was governed by the whims of fate: chance and coincidence determined the outcome. Given the acutely fine margins and random decisions that lead to the death of the Archduke, any alteration to the exact chain of events could seriously damage the time–space continuum. Travellers must, therefore, treat this journey with great seriousness, sticking rigorously to our guidelines.

BRIEFING: SERBIANS AND HABSBURGS

The forced withdrawal of the OTTOMAN EMPIRE from the BALKANS during the nineteenth century left a power vacuum that was filled by independent states with ambitions to extend their borders and claim territory they felt was rightfully theirs. The most aggressive of these was SERBIA; its nationalists dreamed of a Greater Serbia that included within it the Slav diaspora scattered across the AUSTRO-HUNGARIAN EMPIRE. Of particular interest was BOSNIA. At the Treaty of Berlin, 1878, Bosnia was placed under the informal control of the Austro-Hungarian Habsburgs, much to the annoyance of the newly liberated Serbs.

The formal absorption of Bosnia within the Habsburg realm, in 1908, was a provocation too far for ardent Serbian idealists, many of whom were linked to secret

ARCHDUKE FRANZ FERDINAND OF AUSTRIA.

societies plotting to undermine Austro-Hungarian control of the region. Among them was the teenager who pulled the trigger – GAVRILO PRINCIP. Born in July 1894 in the village of Obljag, a poor rural enclave near the Croatian border, Princip was a restless youth who opted out of both Military School and Merchant's School. By 1914, he had imbibed a heady cocktail of anarchism, revolutionary social-ism and Serbian nationalism, and was ready to give his life for the cause. With the help of THE BLACK HAND, a shadowy cabal with links to Serbian military intelligence, Princip and his fellow conspirators decided to kill Archduke Ferdinand on his state visit to the capital.

Sunday 28 June was a significant day for a number of reasons: it was the royal couple's wedding anniver-sary, it was St Vitus Day, a saint's day festival, and, more ominously, it was the day of the infamous BATTLE OF KOSOVO in 1389, during which a Ser-bian army fought an Ottoman one to decide the fate of their country. Despite a Serb assassin managing to kill the Ottoman Sultan, the battle ended in disastrous defeat for the Serbs, leading to nearly 500 years of Ottoman rule. Over time, the battle has become a cornerstone of Ser-bian national pride and it is zealously commemorated every year. To have the Archduke parade on Kosovo Day around Sarajevo was madness, like a red rag to a bull.

THE TRIP

Our Sarajevo assassination trip is designed to get you as close to the action as possible without jeopardising your security or the delicate balance of history. It is best to imagine you are on a covert mission, shadowing the assassins every step of their way, feeling what it was like to walk in their shoes. Your aim is to stay as invis-ible as possible, while adhering to a strict timetable; the success of the operation, and your safe extraction, depend on it.

All visitors to Sarajevo are required to register with the local police. Obviously this is not an option for time travellers. Instead, you will arrive at a safehouse shortly after dawn on the 28th. Men should WEAR PLAIN JACKETS, TIES, WHITE SHIRTS, and either a FEZ or a FEDORA. False moustaches will be provided where neces-sary. Women should wear FLOOR-LENGTH DRESSES, GLOVES and appropriate HATS.

In case you happen to be stopped by the police, you will be furnished with FALSE PAPERS and a cover story. You will also get a small MAP of your zone of operations, drawn on rice paper. If you are arrested, eat it.

BREAKFAST MEETING

At 7.30am you will leave the safehouse and walk to VLAJNIC'S PASTRY SHOP on Cumurija Street. Almost immediately, you will get a sense of what a multicultural city Sarajevo is. You will see mosques and synagogues rubbing shoulders with Serbian Orthodox and Croatian Catholic churches. No wonder the city is known as the 'Jerusalem of Europe'. You will also notice both the HABSBURG FLAG (black and yellow with an Imperial eagle) and the red and yellow BOSNIAN FLAG flying from many of the buildings to celebrate the royal visit.

At approximately 7.44am, enter Vlajnic's. Order a coffee and something to eat: their PASTRIES are highly recommended. Try either a *burek*, filo pastry filled with ricotta cheese, or, for those with a sweet tooth, *jabukovaca*, which is stuffed with apples. Take a seat a discreet distance from the entrance. A few moments later, one of the assassins, TRIFKO GRABEZ, a slight man with a large head and pencil moustache, wearing a black jacket and collarless white top, will enter the shop with DANILO ILIC, who was involved in organising the assassination; he is almost identically dressed except for his striped tie, with remarkably similar features to Grabez but a slightly different hairstyle (short with a side parting). The two young men will approach the counter and engage in jolly banter with the owner, DJURO VLAJNIC, and his assistant, Erna Atias.

Next to arrive is Nedeljko Cabrinovic, better known as NEDJO, slightly more distinguished-looking in a better-quality suit. Nedjo greets his colleagues, orders three cakes and a coffee, and then the three of them will walk right past you to a table at the back of the room.

At 8am precisely, GAVRILO PRINCIP will come in. He will be easy to recognise. Wearing an ill-fitting black jacket and white shirt, he has short cropped hair, a thick, broad nose and a thin moustache above his lip; his dark, intense eyes and haunted expression will stay with you forever. He will join his fellow conspirators, staying only a few minutes, just long enough to give them each a cyanide pill, and Nedjo a bomb.

Do not look directly at them. They are twitchy and easily spooked, ready to abort their mission at the merest sign of anything suspicious. After they are gone, wait at least ten minutes before leaving the cafe.

GETTING INTO POSITION

Now you will have time for a spot of reconnaissance. Once out of the pastry shop, head south for 100 yards to reach CUMURIJA

BRIDGE on APPEL QUAY, the riverside road down which the royal convoy will be driving. It is here, by the bridge, that the first attempt on the Archduke's life will take place. Notice the LAMPPOST next to it; this is where the assassin will be standing when he throws his bomb. Looking eastwards you will see a series of other bridges over the Miljacka River. The next one along is the LATIN BRIDGE, the oldest in the city. This is where Princip will be waiting.

Alternatively, you may prefer to locate yourself on the other side of the street. Here you will get the best view of the Archduke's car and the aftermath of the explosion. Lined with trees that provide plenty of shade, and tall, imposing residences built in a Viennese style, it will be more crowded than the riverside. There is, however, the risk of getting hit by shrapnel.

Once you have picked your spot, move swiftly on; you might attract the wrong sort of attention if you loiter here. Take the turning opposite the Latin Bridge and you will almost immediately be at the junction of Franz Josef Street, which runs parallel to Appel Quay. On the corner you will see MORITZ SCHILLER'S JEWISH DELI and general store, identifiable by the sign above it, the produce filling the windows, and a floor-to-ceiling hoarding in the shape of a German sparkling-wine bottle. The second assassination attempt will take place directly in front of the deli. When it does, there will be clusters of people lining Franz Josef Street, so wherever you choose to stand you will not look conspicuous.

Recce complete, you will have roughly an hour to kill before you need to be back at the first location. Be there no later than 9.45am; by then crowds of spectators will be lining the pavement and you want to ensure your view isn't obscured.

Given the tight schedule, we suggest you return to the Latin Bridge and cross over to the other side of the river. Here you will find a delightful PARK where you can sit beneath the trees and relax, taking in stunning views of the hills, over 5,000 feet high, that surround the city, decorated with orchards and splendid villas.

Alternatively, walk a short distance eastwards along Franz Josef Street and you will find yourself in a large TURKISH BAZAAR.

THREE OF THE ASSASSINS IN BELGRADE IN MAY 1914: TRIFKO GRABEZ, NEDELJKO CABRINOVIC (NEDJO) AND GAVRILO PRINCIP.

the quarter is known as BASCARSIJA and it is home to the GAZI HUSREV-BEG MOSQUE, the grandest in the city, flanked by a spectacular 140-foot-tall minaret. Named after the Ottoman governor of Bosnia who oversaw its construction, the mosque was built in the mid-sixteenth century and stands at the heart of a bustling market, with a myriad covered stalls occupied by carpet salesmen, craftsmen, greengrocers, saddlers and coppersmiths. It is quite a sight with the men in fezes, waistcoats and baggy trousers, the veiled women in brightly coloured traditional clothes.

THE FIRST ATTEMPT

At 9.50am you will need to be in position near CUMURIJA BRIDGE. The weather is warm and sunny. The crowd is in good spirits. Given the potential for trouble, you may well be surprised by the minimal police presence. By 10am all SIX ASSASSINS will also be in place, spaced at regular intervals along both sides of Appel Quay. The first in line is MEHMED MEHMEDBASIC, then NEDJO, who is close to you and Cumurija Bridge. VASO CUBRILOVIC is near to him, as is CVJETKO POPOVIC, positioned on the corner of

Cumurija Street. PRINCIP is next, lurking by the Latin Bridge, and finally TRIFKO GRABEZ, further along by Emperor's Bridge. Four of them, including Princip, are armed with Belgian-made FN Model Browning revolvers with .380 ACP ammunition; all of them are carrying bombs.

Your first sighting of the seven-car ROYAL CONVOY – which had left Sarajevo station at 9.45am and briefly visited a military barracks before driving to Appel Quay – will be at 10.08am. The first car you will see is full of local police, who have taken the place of the Archduke's own private security team after they were mistakenly left behind at the station. In the second car are the Lord Mayor and the Chief of Police.

The THIRD VEHICLE, a Gräf & Stift black convertible sports car, contains the ROYAL COUPLE. The ARCHDUKE is wearing a hat with an extravagant plume of light-green peacock feathers, a hussar's uniform with a blue serge tunic, a row of medals emblazoned across his chest, and white gloves. The DUCHESS, next to him on the back seat, is in a full-length white dress with a red sash at the

THE ARCHDUKE AND DUCHESS EMERGE FROM THE SARAJEVO TOWN HALL
TO BOARD THEIR CAR, FIVE MINUTES BEFORE THE ASSASSINATION.

waist, sporting a wide-brimmed hat with dark ostrich feathers over a white veil, a fur of ermine tails and, to keep cool, a white parasol and a dark fan. She is holding a posy of flowers. Facing them on a pull-down seat is Governor OSKAR POTIOREK. On the front two bench seats are the chauffeur, LEOPOLD LOJKA, who will play a decisive if misguided role in events, and COUNT FRANZ VON HAR-RACH, who purchased the car in 1910. Coming up behind are the other four cars, transporting assorted officials and aides.

At 10.12 am, the cars pass the first assassin, MEHMEDBASIC, but he fails to act. As the convoy reaches Cumurija Bridge, NEDJO steps up. After leaving the pastry shop, Nedjo had spent the intervening period getting his photo taken for posterity at Josef Shrei's studio, collecting six copies from the photographer before heading to Appel Quay. At 10.15am, if you are close enough, you will observe Nedjo take his bomb from his jacket and strike it against the lamppost, thereby priming it. However, instead of factoring in the twelve seconds it will take to ignite the fuse, he immediately throws it at the Archduke's car.

As it spins through the air, the Archduke's chauffeur, hearing the sound of the bomb being bashed against the lamp post, and thinking it is a gunshot, pulls the car a few inches forward, which means the bomb fails to land inside the automobile. Instead it hits the drawn-back roof and bounces off, landing in front of the fourth car, where it explodes, leaving a small crater in the road.

Once the bomb goes off, you have a choice of what to watch: either the chaotic scenes round the car or Nedjo's farcical attempt to kill himself. The sharp-eyed will see Nedjo first swallow his cyanide, which is insufficiently strong to do the job, and then try to drown himself by jumping off the wall into the Miljacka River. Unfortunately for him, the river, known for its peculiar smell and brown water, runs very low in summer – only an inch or so deep – and after dropping fifteen feet Nedjo lands on its banks. He is quickly pursued by four men, including a gendarme brandishing a sabre and a Muslim detective with a gun at the ready. Together they easily take him prisoner.

On the other side of the road, as the smoke clears, there is panic and confusion. The Governor's assistant has a head wound, an Austrian officer is slightly injured, seven spectators are suffering from shrapnel, and a woman watching from her balcony has a perforated eardrum. The Duchess has a slight graze on her shoulder.

After a short delay, the convoy sets off again in the direction of the TOWN HALL, its next designated stop, passing the other assassins, all of whom remain immobile, while the crowds hang around the scene, taking photos, gossiping excitedly, wondering what to do next.

THE SECOND ATTEMPT

Do not dawdle. Head straight for SCHILLER'S as casually as possible. News of the bombing has already reached the deli, and several customers, plus Schiller's wife, are gathered outside, discussing the attack in animated tones. You, on the other hand, might want to nip inside for a stiff drink to steady the nerves. A shot of the local *rajika* brandy, made from plums, should do the trick. Be out front again by 10.43am, where you will see PRINCIP standing about six feet from the entrance. After Nedjo's failure, Princip has the presence of mind to recall that the planned route for the royal convoy involved driving down Franz Josef Street, so he decides to try his luck there.

While you are waiting, spare a thought for the royal couple who will be carrying out their official duties at the TOWN HALL regardless of the traumatic experience they have just been through. Only once does the Archduke lose control of his emotions. The hapless Mayor, without time to alter his welcoming speech, is uttering the usual platitudes when the Archduke angrily interrupts him with a furious outburst: 'What good are your speeches? I come to Sarajevo on a friendly visit and someone throws a bomb at me!'

By 10.38am, the Archduke and Duchess will be ready to leave. Though the rest of their official itinerary has been cancelled, and

PRINCIP STEPS UP TO THE MARK. AN ARTIST'S IMPRESSION OF THE SCENE FOR THE COVER OF THE ITALIAN PAPER, LA DOMENICA DEL CORRIERE.

the Archduke's advisors are begging him to leave the city without further delay, he insists on visiting the hospital to check on the wounded.

Fearing that there may be more assassins waiting to strike, they decide to avoid Franz Josef Street altogether and stick to APPEL QUAY. Tragically, nobody bothers to tell the drivers about this change of route; so when the first car reaches the Latin Bridge it turns right into FRANZ JOSEF STREET, followed by the Archduke's automobile, arriving at the junction by SCHILLER'S at 10.45am.

Governor Potiorek, still in the car with the royal couple, suddenly realises they are going the wrong way and orders the chauffeur to turn round. Lojka stops and reverses the car, halting directly in front of PRINCIP. Barely able to believe his good fortune, Princip raises his gun, turns his head and fires twice. One of the bullets goes straight through the side of the car where the DUCHESS is sitting. It enters her right groin and lodges in her abdomen. The other bullet hits the ARCHDUKE in the neck, severs his jugular vein and wedges itself in his spine. (Both entry wounds are tiny, so don't expect to see much in the way of blood or any other visible signs of injury.)

For a moment, the couple remain motionless, then their heads drop slightly before they slowly slump forward in their seats as their car gets moving again, heading towards the river. At the same time, Princip swallows his defective cyanide and turns the gun on himself, but a nearby spectator swiftly snatches it away from him, and Princip is instantly set upon by enraged policemen, soldiers and civilians, who pummel him to the ground.

As one of the most important crime scenes in history, you will naturally want to get close to the action. But beware: there are photographers in the crowd taking shots of the immediate aftermath. To avoid getting CAUGHT ON CAMERA, move well away from Princip as soon as he has discharged his weapon. To avoid getting mistaken for an accomplice, clear the area within ten minutes of the shooting.

DEPARTURE

You will depart at precisely 11.45am. If you are in a group, split up and take separate routes back to the safe house. At 11.30am, the city's church bells will ring out, announcing to the world that the royal couple are dead. The streets will fill with angry, distressed people joining together for a spontaneous PROTEST, marching through town chanting anti-Serbian slogans. By then, you will be long gone, mission successfully accomplished.

However, if you wish to EXTEND YOUR TRIP and sample the charged atmosphere of a city entering crisis mode, there is a LATER DEPARTURE TIME available at 9.30pm. If you opt for this, you will probably want some refreshment after the morning's action, so head to the TURKISH BAZAAR and treat yourself to a MEZE at a cafe, or try the delicious street food, which includes *cevapi*, a kind of kebab with sausages and onions in pitta bread, or, for the vegetarians, *pita di spinaku*, with spinach, cottage cheese and feta. During the afternoon you will inevitably be caught up in the DEMONSTRATIONS gripping Sarajevo; you may well share the crowd's righteous indignation after what you have just witnessed.

By early evening, no doubt footsore and hungry, you will be after a proper SIT-DOWN MEAL. There are many decent restaurants offering regional specialities. Bosnian soups are particularly satisfying and filling. *Beya* is a chicken soup with carrots, okra, beans, potato, celery and parsley, while Sarajevo soup uses similar vegetables combined with veal and sour cream. Both are a meal on their own. The local BEERS are good and strong. BOSNIAN WINE packs quite a punch: a mix of sugar, water, yeast, alcohol and a shot of rum fermented for two weeks in a sealed container. Gentler on the palette and the head are the more refined *Zilvakra* (white) and *Blatini* (red).

The finest cuisine in town is served at the *Hotel Austria*, where visiting dignitaries stay. However, it will be in lockdown after the assassination. It could be more interesting to take a table at the Serbian-owned HOTEL EUROPE – which, next day, will be overrun and ransacked by angry mobs as an orgy of rioting is unleashed across the city.

Avoid the BARS, which will be crawling with secret police, spies and informers ready to snatch anybody who seems to be at all out of place. If that were to happen, you could find yourself lost in the black hole of the Habsburg criminal justice system – corrupt, venal and Byzantine – from which you might never reappear.

The Fall of the Berlin Wall

9–11 NOVEMBER 1989 ✳ BERLIN

'WHAT HAPPENED IN BERLIN LAST WEEK was a combination of the Fall of the Bastille and a New Year's Eve blowout of revolution and celebration'. That was the verdict of *Time* magazine in the immediate aftermath of the Fall of the Berlin Wall. In three extraordinary days the entire postwar history of Europe was rewritten and the Cold War in effect brought to an end. After nearly thirty years of longing, over a million East Germans poured through the Wall into West Berlin, turning the city into a vast street party of reunification, joy and wonder. You really have to be there.

....

BRIEFING: COLD WAR

....

At the end of the SECOND WORLD WAR Germany was divided into four sectors – one for each of the occupying powers (the United States, Soviet Union, Britain and France). BERLIN, lying deep inside the Soviet sector, was divided in a similar manner. Then, as Cold War

THE WALL'S 'DEATH STRIP', VIEWED FROM WEST BERLIN IN 1986.
GRAFFITI ON THE WESTERN SIDE IS BY THE ARTIST THIERRY NOIR.

tensions turned to active hostility, the US, British and French sectors combined to form the FEDERAL REPUBLIC OF GERMANY (FRG), or WEST GERMANY. Simultaneously the Soviet Sector become the GERMAN DEMOCRATIC REPUBLIC (GDR) or EAST GERMANY. The old German capital of Berlin went the same way, creating the tiny enclave of WEST BERLIN inside communist East Germany.

Over the next few years a steady stream of migrants from East Germany – above all, the young, skilled and ambitious – headed for West Berlin and never left the FRG, thus placing an intolerable strain on the economic and political stability of the GDR. The State responded at midnight on 13 August 1961 by building the BERLIN WALL, known to the communist regime as the ANTI-FASCIST PROTECTION RAMPART. The wall, nearly 200km long, would eventually encircle West Berlin, combining a wall on the border itself and an inner set of barriers within East Germany, fortified and patrolled with minefields, guard dogs and a shoot-to-kill policy. Nonetheless many would attempt to escape across the wall, and over a hundred East German citizens would pay with their lives.

Twenty-eight years later the Wall still stood, but the regime that maintained it was faltering, its citizens' loyalty exhausted by state tyranny, its economy a pale shadow of what was clearly visible on television beaming in from the West. The arrival of the reforming President Gorbachev in the Soviet Union had seen a wave of reforms begin across Eastern Europe. In early 1989, the opposition trade union Solidarity formed a government in Poland, while in Hungary the Communist Party initiated a massive series of reforms, opening its borders with Austria and refusing to police East German and Romanians who attempted to cross it. Over half a million East Germans would use this escape route, until the GDR responded by barring travel to Hungary. This encouraged another exodus of its citizens to the West German embassies in Prague, Warsaw and East Berlin, where they demanded asylum. In early October, sealed trains carried thousands of East Germans to the West and in desperation the East Germans closed their borders entirely. Its citizens were left with the choice between loyalty and voice – and over the next month, despite decades of morale-sapping surveillance and repression, they chose voice.

The protests began in Dresden, where a demonstration around the railway station turned into a full scale riot. In Leipzig, on 4 November, the Monday Marches, organised by tiny opposition groups and the Lutheran Church, swelled into a gathering of 100,000 led by Kurt Masur, the city's orchestra conductor. The determined and sombre Leipzigers marched the entire length of the city's ring road in a display of oppositional resolve.

Two days later in East Berlin, while an increasingly panicky Communist Party met in conference to discuss regulations on movement, over half a million citizens flooded into the centre of East Berlin to oppose them. In a complex series of events guided by misunderstanding, incompetence and panic, it was left to the hapless GDR minister GÜNTER SCHABOWSKI to give a press conference on the regime's response, live on television in both East and West. This took place at 6.53pm on 9 November. Unable to formulate the precise nature of the regime's policy, he blurted out that the new regulations (intended to be introduced very gradually) would begin immediately and be applicable to East–West Berlin crossings (also not planned in the original documents).

It no longer mattered. The people heard that the borders were open – and they acted upon the news.

THE EVENT

You will be arriving in EAST BERLIN at 6.00pm on 9 November 1989 in the hallway of 15 Finlandstrasse. The building is part of a whole street of empty houses cleared by the East German authorities after the Wall was built. You will find yourself about two hundred yards from the BORNHOLMERSTRASSE CHECKPOINT: step out onto the street, turn right and you will see the neon-lit watchtower and high wire fences of the border crossing. Please return to the hallway of 15 Finlandstrasse by midnight on the evening of 11 November. All three days of your trip will be bright, sunny and cold, with temperatures close to zero at night. Do wrap up, and stout footwear is recommended.

ROOMS, FOOD AND COUNTERCULTURE

A room in East Berlin has been booked for you at the HOTEL METROPOL on Friedrichstrasse, just north of the city's most famous boulevard, Unten den Linden. Opened in 1977 as the modernist flag ship of *Interhotel* (the East German state tourist agency), the hotel is reserved exclusively for Western visitors and accepts only hard foreign currency. Its 1970s decor – orange plastic fascias and brown-patterned wallpapers – are a bit tired, but it remains a pleasant and tranquil oasis for this tumultuous weekend. Do note that the all rooms are extensively bugged, so be discreet in any reference to the agency, or indeed time travel, or events as-yet-unfolded. For the more adventurous, a roof over your head is also available amongst the SQUATS of PRENZLAUER BERG, heartland of East German counterculture; try the crowd at 61 Lychenerstrasse or 7 Beherferlinerstrasse.

While in East Berlin, we strongly advise travellers to sample local food and drink. Nothing will taste the same again in post-Wall Germany. The hot dogs, in particular, have a sinister colour and consistency; the fizzy drinks are weird chemical conconctions; even the schnapps ain't right.

We expect most visitors to focus on the action near the Wall, but if you want to take in a little of WEST BERLIN'S COUNTERCULTURE we suggest you make for the PIKE CLUB, in a back courtyard on Heinrich-Heine-Strasse, in the Kreuzberg quarter, just south of Checkpoint Charlie. On the night of the 9th, East German punk outfit DIE ANDEREN (The Others) are playing; oddly, a number of East German bands – even punks – have had permits recently. By the time you arrive it will be a beer-soaked, pogoing, manic punk party. Also well worth a visit over the weekend is DSCHUNGEL, a modernist 1920s café that pulls in the most louche cocktail drinkers in the city; recently guests include David Bowie and Iggy Pop.

THURSDAY 9 NOVEMBER: DIVIDED BERLIN

Having located the BORNHOLMER STRASSE CHECKPOINT, take a little time to wander the streets of the MITTE quarter with its fabulous crumbling architecture. Since the building of the Wall, the area has steadily emptied of its original working-class population and become a magnet for the most disaffected of the

GDR's citizens. In the many small bars and drinking holes in the streets around the checkpoint you will hear the locals discussing the meaning of the Schabowski press conference and wondering if the border really might be opened this evening.

Do not linger too long. From around 7.20pm onwards you will find a crowd beginning to gather at the Eastern entrance to the Bornholmerstrasse checkpoint. Two particularly vociferous young men – ARAM RADOMSKI and SIGGI SCHEFKE – will be shouting out questions to the perplexed-looking border guards, asking whether they can cross over to the West. The guards will be joined by a senior officer, more discussion will ensue, but no permissions to cross will be given at this point. If you can, try and look up into the brightly lit offices of the checkpoint where the figure of LIEUTENANT COLONEL HARALD JÄGER, the senior officer on duty this evening, will occasionally appear. He is square-faced with a side parting and, as you wait at the gate, he will be furiously phoning his superiors for advice on what to do as the crowd grows in size and in its sense of anticipation.

By 8.00pm the crowd will have swelled to a few hundred and will be joined by an increasingly long line of vehicles full of people seeking to cross. At 8.30pm a police car will works its way to the front of the crowd. The officer in that car will address the crowd by megaphone, instructing them to go to a nearby police station to gain an exit visa. You should ignore this instruction, as will most of the locals. At 9.00pm the border guards will re-appear and take the loudest and most persistent members of the crowd into the CHECKPOINT OFFICE. Following orders from an increasingly befuddled Stasi HQ, the plan at this point is to stamp their passports, show them the way to the West and expel them permanently from the country. Around thirty or so people will be let through on this basis; you should not try and join them. Stay with the crowd, now many thousands strong, reaching back down Bornholmerstrasse and spilling into the side streets. Listen out for the regular chants of 'Open the gates!'

At approximately 11.30pm Harald Jäger, on his own initiative, will give the order to OPEN THE GATES. Two of his subordinates, Helmut Stoss and Lutz Wasnick, will appear by the main barriers and begin pulling them open by hand. Immediately the huge crowd behind the gate will start pushing forwards and force the gates open themselves. A great surge of humanity will follow as thousands of laughing, crying, shouting and jubilant East Berliners head through the gate and into the West. As you go, it is worth pausing to catch the looks of weary incomprehension on the faces of the border guards.

ROOM FOR ONE MORE. THE BRANDENBURG GATE, 9 NOVEMBER. THE TEXT
ON THE SIGN, 'NOTICE! YOU ARE NOW LEAVING WEST BERLIN', HAS BEEN
MODIFIED WITH THE WORDS 'WIE DENN?' ('HOW, THEN?').

INTO THE WEST

Once you have passed through the Bornholmerstrasse checkpoint, cross the BÖSEBRÜCKE BRIDGE and you have arrived in West Berlin. You can stop here and watch the extraordinary lava flow of East Germans coming through all night. Some West Berliners will be gathering to watch and to greet their fellow countrymen, but we suggest at some point in the evening you take a stroll to see the action at other points along the Wall.

Approximately fifteen minutes' walk southwest is the CHECKPOINT ON INVALIDENSTRASSE. You will find that the Stasi and the East German border guards here are taking a much stiffer line with East Germans trying to cross over, as indicated by the large, noisy and agitated crowd that are stuck on the other side of the border. West Berliners will also be gathering here. Around 1.00am, look out for the arrival of WALTER MOMPER, the Social Democratic mayor of West Berlin. He is easily recognisable – a bald man with a very bright-red scarf and a megaphone – and will be addressing both the crowd and the West and East German border guards, calling for calm and for the East Berliners to be let through. By 1.30am it is pretty clear to all that no one will be passing across here this evening, so take the first left off Invalidenstrasse and head into the TIERGARTEN, West Berlin's large park. You can't miss UNTER DEN LINDEN, the large road that runs east–west through the park. Follow the crowds east and after 400 yards the Wall should come back into view. Behind it you will see the great neoclassical columns of the BRANDENBURG GATE.

Although there is no checkpoint at the Brandenburg Gate, which is inaccessible from both East and West Berlin, lying in no-man's land between the two parts of the Berlin Wall, Berliners from both sides of the divide have been drawn to the gate all evening. The scene will be all the more dramatic as American television companies have established themselves here and installed floodlights to illuminate both the wall and their own broadcasts. On the Western side the Wall is unusually low and has, for some of its length, a flat top. If you arrive early you will find a crowd just milling around, but from 9.00pm onwards individuals will begin climbing up to the Wall. We advise that you not to join them at this point as the East German border guards will be using water hoses for the next couple of hours in an effort to knock people off. Look out, though, for one young man who will be braving the water cannon, shielding himself using an umbrella given to him by one of the crowd. Later in the evening the hoses will be turned off and the Western side of the Wall will make an excellent vantage point from which to view a steady stream of East Berliners walking across the eerily lit plaza that the Brandenburg Gate stands in.

Your final stop on the evening's itinerary is CHECKPOINT CHARLIE, the most famous of the border crossings, located in the US zone of West Berlin, south and east of the Brandenburg Gate. Just follow the line of the Wall until you reach Friedrichstrasse. Here you will see the small metal hut that serves as the checkpoint office on the Western side and the famous CAFÉ ADLER, a regular haunt of spies and military officials during the Cold War. Should you choose to come early in the evening, café owner Albrecht Rau can be seen making his way to the East with a tray laden with glasses, sparkling wine and hot coffee for the border guards. They will refuse the drinks, but Albrecht will be celebrating anyway. The border guards will then attempt to seal the border by putting a variety of additional barriers in place, but by a quarter past midnight the crowds will start tumbling over them.

FRIDAY 10 NOVEMBER: CENTRAL BERLIN

Today is a day to just wander around central Berlin. Over half a million people will be making the journey through the Wall today. The vast majority will do so on foot, but some 26,000 vehicles will cross the border, nearly all of them East Germany's characteristic TRABANTS and WARTBURGS. You will soon become accustomed to the unique sound of the Trabant's sclerotic two-stroke engine and the peculiar fumes and billowing toxic smoke generated by the ersatz mixture of petrol and oil that they run on. Some cars will be flying the East German flag but with the hammer and sickle emblem at the centre cut out, leaving it remarkably similar to the West German flag.

You will also note the sharp differences in attire between East and West Berliners. VISITORS FROM THE EAST have unsurprisingly drab wardrobes and thin coats; economic inequalities that will persist for the next three decades. This will all be nicely summed up in POTSDAMER PLATZ mid-morning when the West German president, RICHARD VON WEIZSÄCKER, will arrive, shake a few hands, and then head off in his gleaming black Mercedes followed by a dirty-khaki Wartburg and a filthy-green Trabant. Meantime, take in the sweet sounds of a hundred HAMMERS AND CHISELS at work taking souvenirs of the Wall – in the West, the most covetable areas are those covered in graffiti. This is also a moment to appreciate the speed at which the commercial impulse can work: much of the new chippings and rubble will soon be turned into souvenirs, while *T*-shirts with the legend *Ich war dabei: November 9* (I was there: November 9) will already be on sale near the Wall.

But today is about unity. Everyone is a Berliner and everyone is a German, including the enormous number of people flooding into the city from all over Western Europe. One example not to miss is the Amsterdamer in Postdamerplatz who will be parking up with a van full of 10,000 roses straight from the Dutch city's famous flower market. He will proceed to give them to the new arrivals. Flowers are not the only gifts on offer. Public transport is effectively free today and tomorrow, with bus drivers refusing fares and the underground system full to bursting. A special edition of the local newspaper, *Berliner Morgenpost*, will be given away free on the streets, and throughout the day many individual Berliners, and some cafés and restaurants, will be offering free drinks, snacks, teas and coffees. Near the checkpoints there are trucks doling out bags of free fruit, chewing gum and Western cigarettes – another treat that will be spontaneously passed around. For those that are partial, the Kreuzberg district around Checkpoint Charlie also offers plenty of welcoming joints. Follow your nose and look interested.

On their first visit to the West, East Germans are entitled to a welcoming gift from the West German government of 100 Deutschmarks, available on presentation of ID at any bank or post office. The BERLINER BANK on West Berlin's fanciest shopping street KURFÜRSTENDAMM is worth looking in on to see this in action – expect a queue five deep and a quarter of a mile long. While the street's enormous and opulent department stores will be drawing astonished looks from East Berliners, they won't be spending much of their money there. Many, however, can be seen holding bags of fruit – bananas, oranges and kiwis – hitherto unavailable to them.

There are two special events today worth making a detour for. For the political junkies, West Germany's leading politicians will be speaking at RATHAUS SCHÖNEBERG at about 2.30pm. Originally merely the town hall of the Schöneberg district, the building has been the seat of the Berlin Senate and the mayor's office since 1950 – Berlin's traditional seat of government, the Rotes Rathaus lies in ruins still in Mitte on the other side of the wall. The cast includes West German Chancellor HELMUT KOHL, only recently arrived in the city after breaking his official visit to Poland, and his foreign minister HANS-DIETRICH GENSCHER; WILLY BRANDT, a native of the city and Chancellor of West Germany in the 1960s and early 1970s; and WALTER MOMPER, the current Mayor of West Berlin. It will be an old-fashioned media scrum as the photographers, cameramen and boom operators jostle at the front. Kohl's key moments come when he says, 'Long Live a free German fatherland! Long live a free Europe,' and 'I want to call to all in the GDR we're on your side, we remain one nation. We belong together.' Willy Brandt, visibly moved, will offer a moment's caution: 'This is a beautiful day after a long voyage, but we are only at a waystation. We are not at the end of our way.'

To get to the Rathaus Schöneberg, take a train on Line 2 heading west from the centre and change at Nollendorfplatz for line 4; you'll be looking for a train heading south to Innsbruckerplatz.

Music lovers should head for the section of wall just to the West of CHECKPOINT CHARLIE. There you will find the great Russian cellist MSTISLAV ROSTROPOVICH playing. Rostropovich defected from the Soviet Union in 1971 and has just flown in from Paris to offer this impromptu concert in honour of those who died trying to cross the Wall. He will be opening with a sensational rendition of Bach's Second Suite for cello, the Sarabande.

SATURDAY NOVEMBER 11:
A GAME OF FOOTBALL

Saturday continues very much in the vein of Friday, with ever larger numbers of East Germans flooding across the now routinely open border crossings, still being met by ecstatic West Berliners. New crossings will be opening today at the GLIENICKE BRIDGE and on EBERSWALDERSTRASSE, where an East German army bulldozer will actually smash down a segment of the Wall to relieve pressure on the other checkpoints.

Mid-morning will see a more DIY effort to do the same in Potsdamerplatz, where a group of ALT-WEST BERLINERS will be showing up in an old jeep. Parking up close to the Wall they will attempt to fix a huge chain to the concrete slabs and then to the jeep. Around them the crowd will take up the cry 'The Wall must go!' as well the now ubiquitous 'One land, one people.' The bohemian feel of the moment is enhanced by a group of pan-pipe players nearby. These efforts will be thwarted, however, by East German border guards turning a water cannon on the jeep crew. They will be ably supported by the West German police, who will park a phalanx of vans up against the Wall to prevent a reoccurrence of the event. The crowd will respond to the East German guards, now on the Wall itself, with cries of 'Come down! Do you want to starve over there?'

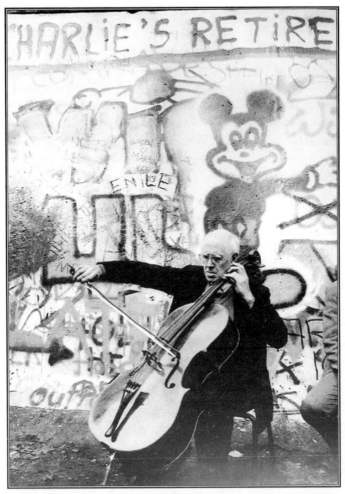

ROSTROPOVICH PLAYS BACH IN FRONT OF THE WALL: NOTE THE GRAFFITI
'CHARLIE'S RETIRED'. THEY DON'T WAIT AROUND WITH THE SPRAYPAINT.

Alternatively, head for the FOOTBALL MATCH between HERTHA
BERLIN and WATTENSCHEID kicking off at 3.00pm at the Olimpiastadion, the centrepiece of the 1936 Berlin Olympics, in the
west of the city. Prior to the opening of the Wall, it was billed
merely as a top-of-the-table clash in the German Bundesliga 2,

but since the morning of 10 November it has become a remark-able opportunity for all of Berlin to celebrate the historic moment.

Until 1971 Hertha Berlin were located in the Wedding district of the city, at their old stadium, the Gesundbrunnen. In 1961 the Wall was erected just a few hundred yards east of the stadium, closing it off to the large body of support in East Berlin. For many years, East Berliners would gather near the Wall to hear the sounds of the crowd as Hertha played on the other side. Today they have the chance to go and see them in their new home, the OLIMPIASTADION, with 10,000 free tickets available to anyone who can produce an East German ID card. Don't worry if you can't, though; there will be plenty of opportunity to just show up and buy a ticket.

Prior to the kick-off, the stadium announcer will call out the names of all the districts of Berlin – both East and West – and the crowd will respond heartily. Wattenscheid will take the lead after sixteen minutes of the first half, but in the sixty-fourth minute nineteen-year-old Sven Kretschmer will grab a scrappy equaliser for Hertha. The team will go on to win promotion to the Bundesliga's first division at the end of the season.

To get to the game, you'll need to head south of the Brandenburg Gate to one of the stations on the U1 metro line – either Möckernbrücke or Gleisdreieck – and head west on the trains bound for Ruhleben. Olimpiastadion is the penultimate stop.

PART THREE

Cultural & Sporting Spectaculars

The 235th Olympiad

AUGUST AD 161 ✳ OLYMPIA, GREECE

IN THE FIFTH CENTURY BC THE POET Pindar called the Olympics the 'pinnacle of contests' – and the ancient games held at Olympia, almost a millennium old when you arrive, still fit the bill. Our trip offers the chance to spend a week in this beautiful complex of temples, shrines, stadiums and bathhouses on the rolling plains and meadows of Elis in the northwest Peloponnese. With its Olympic site recently and extensively refurbished by the Roman Empire, the 235TH OLYMPIAD offers all the ritual and the spectacle of the Classical Hellenic era, and a level of comfort and quality of accommodation that is unmatched in the ancient world. With unrivalled access to the whole sanctuary, you will enjoy a week of processions and sacrifices, pentathlon and pankration, chariot racing and wrestling; and the unique opportunity to see a real wonder of the ancient world. Note that events at the games can only be witnessed by MEN, so all travellers will be dressed and made up accordingly.

BRIEFING: THE ANCIENT OLYMPIC GAMES

The SANCTUARY OF OLYMPIA, set in the foothills of Mount Kronos in the eastern Peloponnese has been a place of spiritual pilgrimage and worship for over a thousand years before your arrival in AD 161. As early as the eighth century, permanent shrines were built here to worship the ancient Hellenic mother gods. At some point, conventionally dated as 776 BC, RITUAL GAMES began to be played at Olympia, though they were just local affairs. In the sixth century BC these games began to attract a wider audience and take on a Panhellenic quality, while Olympia itself acquired the magnificent TEMPLE OF ZEUS, whose giant sculpture of the god was considered one of the seven wonders of the Ancient World. Reflecting the fanatical body culture of the gymnasiums and the barracks of Greece's growing city-states, the Games took on ever greater significance and popularity. In the early fifth century BC the programme of events at the Games was fixed as a five-day festival of athletics, and it remained substantially unchanged until the Romans conquered Greece in the second century and added an extra day to the party.

As with so much else about Greece, the ROMANS left things pretty much intact but improved the infrastructure. At these Olympics, visitors have truly never had it so good. Back in the day, visitors spending a week at Olympia would

SPOT THE DIFFFERENCE! AN ARTIST'S IMPRESSION OF THE WALLED ALTIS AT ANCIENT OLYMPIA, SHOWING THE TEMPLE OF ZEUS IN THE FOREGROUND. YOU WILL STRUGGLE TO FIND THE LARGE AMPHITHEATRE ON THE LEFT, WHICH IS ENTIRELY FANCIFUL.

find there were no public toilets and no supplies of running fresh water; they would stay in tent villages that emerged in the fields around the sanctuary, beset by the intense heat and dust of a Greek August.

Epictetus the Stoic, true to form, thought even that worth enduring: 'Are you not scorched with heat? Are you not cramped for room? Is not washing difficult? Are you not wet through when it is wet? Do you not get your fill of noise and clamour and other annoyances? Yet I fancy that when you set against all these hardships the magnificence of the spectacle you bear them and put up with them.' Aelian, by contrast, decreed it a fate worse than forced labour: 'A man from Chios got angry with his house-slave and said, "I shan't put you on the treadmill, but I will take you to Olympia." For the master thought it a much harsher punishment that he should watch at Olympia, and be baked under the sun, than that he should be sent to grind corn on the treadmill.' Either way, the informal Olympic village remained riotous enough to need its own dedicated police force known as the whipbearers.

THE TRIP

We plan to offer future trips, for keen Hellenists, to the more ascetic pre-Roman Olympics. However, visitors on this trip will witness the games – the 235TH OLYMPIAD – in Roman style, and in comparative luxury. The Romans have already added luxurious accommodation and proper bathhouses and toilets, and this year there will be running drinking water for the first time. The site as a whole is looking fresh, too. Over the last ten years HERODES ATTICUS, the richest man in Athens, has been building the NYMPHAEUM – a great memorial water feature dedicated to his late wife – and a plumbing system to supply it. At this Olympiad it will be in working order for the first time, making your stay infinitely more pleasant and the environment infinitely more healthy. You will ARRIVE BY BOAT on the afternoon before the game, landing on the north bank of the KLADEOS RIVER, where you will be taken to your room in the nearby ROMAN HOTEL COMPLEX. You will be DEPARTING from here on the evening of the sixth and final day of the festival.

THE FESTIVAL SITE

At the centre of Olympia is the sacred walled compound, THE ALTIS, that contains the site's temples and shrines. The Romans have built up and repaired the ALTIS WALL, added porticos and monumental arches and laid out paths and gardens. Normally, this would be a very tranquil place, but over the next week it is going to make the Roman Forum look quiet. Thousands of visitors from all across the Roman Empire will mingle with athletes, trainers, priests, dignitaries, poets, judges and umpires. There will also be plenty of servants, cooks and factotums from amongst the entourages of the elites, as well as itinerant soothsayers, conmen and hawkers spilling over from the TENT CITIES in the surrounding meadows.

You will enter the Altis through the PROPYLON, a monumental arch set into the wall, at the northwest corner of the compound. To your immediate right will be the PRYTANEION, the nerve centre of Olympia and its games; nearby is a small circular monument, the PHILIPPEION. Built in the sixth century BC, the Prytaneion houses the high priests of Olympia and an eternal sacred fire still burns here. During the Games, officials will use the building and entertain Olympic champions in its dining chambers. The Philippeion is a small circular memorial, its carved marble roof held up by a colonnade of Ionic columns. It was commissioned by Philip of Macedon to commemorate his victory at the Battle of Chaeronea in 338 BC and serves as a reminder of his victory in the horse racing at Olympia in 356 BC. Inside you will find a family scene in ivory and gold: Philip, his father; his son Alexander the Great; and his fourth wife and Alexander's mother, Olympias.

THE TEMPLE OF HERA

Standing with your back to the Philippeion you will be able to see the TEMPLE OF HERA to your left and the PELOPION to your right. Beyond the Temple look for the tiny shrine known as the

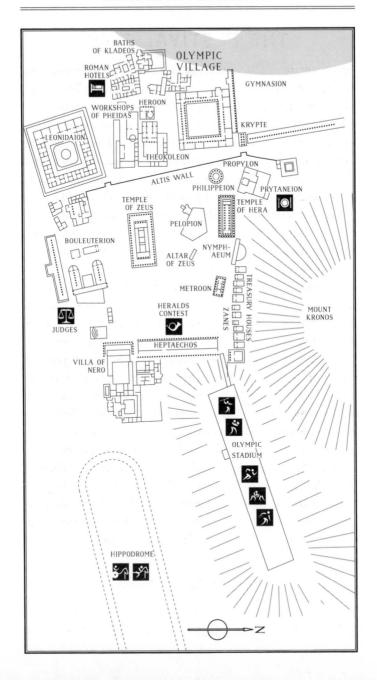

BATHS
OF KLADEOS

OLYMPIC
VILLAGE

ROMAN
HOTELS

GYMNASION

WORKSHOPS
OF PHEIDAS

HEROON

KRYPTE

LEONIDAION

THEOKOLEON

PROPYLON

ALTIS WALL

PHILIPPEION

PRYTANEION

TEMPLE
OF ZEUS

TEMPLE
OF HERA

PELOPION

BOULEUTERION

NYMPH-
AEUM

ALTAR
OF ZEUS

METROON

TREASURY HOUSES

HERALDS
CONTEST

JUDGES

ZANES

MOUNT
KRONOS

HEPTAECHOS

VILLA OF
NERO

OLYMPIC
STADIUM

HIPPODROME

N

METROON and behind it, on a raised terrace, a string of small TREASURY HOUSES. The Pelopion is already an ancient grave-yard built atop ancient burial sites, now enclosed by a irregular pentagonal wall with a Doric portico for an entrance. Inside you can enjoy the tranquillity of its poplars, olive trees and statues and its mounds of funereal and sacrificial ash. During your stay you may well see both formal and informal rites in here, especially the roasting of meat. Do be aware of the consequences of partaking. The writer PAUSANIAS, on a contemporary visit to the games, noted that 'the magistrates sacrificed a black ram to honour Pelops and whoever ate from the sacrificed animal was not allowed to enter the temple of Zeus'. If you have a taste for the black ram, perhaps it would be best to try and see the Temple of Zeus first.

Built in the early sixth century, the Doric TEMPLE OF HERA will appear strangely remodelled, as Roman stone and sculpture have recently replaced the old Hellenic work, including its wooden columns. During the Games this temple's main function will be to display the olive wreaths for Olympic victors on a long wooden table. Note, just to the right of the temple as you look north, a large conical mound of compressed ashes; this is the AL-TAR OF ZEUS where many centuries of sacrificial remains have accumulated to form a small hill over twenty feet high.

Immediately beyond the Temple of Hera, and most likely with an appreciative crowd around it, is the newly opened NYM-PHAEUM. Built by Herodes Atticus in about 160, in memory of his late wife Regilla, a priestess of Demeter here at Olympia, it is in effect a vast monumental spring and water feature. You will see a huge oblong pool backed by a two-storey marble apse, festooned with carved figurines and topped by half-cupolas. The niches within the apse hold Atticus's ancestors and the obligatory sculptures of Zeus, while the centrepiece of the building is a huge marble bull set in the pool. However, the real genius of the Nymphaeum is hidden, for it is just the decorative frontage of a huge piece of Roman civil engineering that has, for the first time, brought fresh water from a spring a few miles east along a

stone viaduct to Olympia. An equally remarkable system of storage tanks and pipes makes the water available across the sanctuary
for drinking and bathing.

The nearby METROON is a small Doric temple, built in the
early fourth century BC and dedicated originally to RHEA, daughter of the original Greek earth mother, Gaia. At the back, there is
still a small altar to her, but over the last century or so the Metroon
has moved into Roman Emperor-worship; inside the colonnade
are statues of the Emperors Augustus, Claudius, Titus and Ves-
pasian, Nero's mother Agrippina and Domitian's wife Dominitia.

The path that leads from the Metroon to the KRYPTE, the
large monumental arch in the north east corner of the Altis, and
thence to the Olympic stadium, is lined with an eclectic collection of bronze sculptures of Zeus. These are the ZANES, paid for
by fines levied on cheats and transgressors of Olympian law and
inscribed with warnings and admonitions for athletes on their way
to the Games. The first dates from the 98th Olympiad, held in
388 BC, when the boxer Eupolos of Thessaly was fined for bribing three of his opponents. Half a century later, six were erected
by the Athenian Kallipos. He had been bribing other athletes in
the Pankration. By the second century AD the TREASURY HOUSES
which sit on the terrace behind the Zanes are a real curiosity. Built
over half a millennium ago by the small city-states of the Hellenic
Mediterranean diaspora, they once housed the votive offerings of
their athletes and champions.

EAST SIDE: HOUSE OF NERO

A COLONNADE occupies almost the whole of the east side of Altis.
Built in the fourth century by Philip of Macedonia to celebrate
his victories in the Olympic chariot races, its unusual acoustics
will give rise to its contemporary Greek name of HEPTAECHOS
(seven echoes). This is the place to come and hear the competitions amongst the trumpeters and heralds that are an integral part
of the Olympic Games. Both were, and continue to be, part of

the sporting ceremonies, announcing the beginning of a competition with a fanfare on their enormous elongated instruments, or declaiming the name, the father and the home town of Olympic victors. In addition to these duties they will be sparring among themselves in contests throughout the Games.

At the southeastern corner of the Altis, just beyond the colonnade, sits the VILLA OF NERO. The volatile emperor came to Olympia as part of a long tour of his Hellenic realm, a schedule that required, for the first time in centuries, that the Games be delayed for two years to accommodate him. You will no doubt hear plenty of Nero stories while you are here, notably how back in AD 67 he crashed his ten-horse chariot, and how to everyone's amazement he won all of the musical and literary competitions in which he participated. He also had an ancient Greek shrine to Hestia ripped down and put up his own brash Imperial condo. It has been enlarged since then and equipped with its own baths to accommodate the very pinnacle of the Roman elite visitors.

THE TEMPLE OF ZEUS

The largest building in the Altis and the spiritual centre of the Games is the TEMPLE OF ZEUS. The temple, started in the early fifth century BC, is considered an exemplar of Doric temple architecture. However, the building was eclipsed around 430 BC, when it received the great seated STATUE OF ZEUS carved by PHEIDAS and designated one of the Seven Wonders of the Ancient World. Before you head inside, do take a moment look at the sculptures on the triangular pediments at the east and west end of the building: the former depicts the mythical CHARIOT RACE BETWEEN PELOPS AND OINOMAOS, presided over by Zeus; the latter, the BATTLE OF THE LAPITHS AND CENTAURS, arranged around the god Apollo. Note too the lion-head water spouts on the marble roof, the gold cauldrons that sit at each corner, and the twelve panels, or *metopes*, that illustrate the twelve labours of Hercules.

THE STATUE OF ZEUS LOOKS ON APPROVINGLY AS WRESTLERS FROLIC.

Once inside you will cross a small rectangular space paved with hexagonal marble slabs: this is where the Olympic champions will receive their olive wreaths. ZEUS, of course, is at the very heart of the temple. Over forty feet high, made of gold and ivory, he won't be hard to find, but just in case: he is the guy on the throne, crowned by a wreath of olive leaves, holding a sceptre topped by an eagle in his left hand and a winged NIKE, goddess of victory, in his right. The Nike figure alone is six feet high. Enjoy it while you can it, as it will be taken off to Constantinople in the fifth century and destroyed in a fire.

South of the Temple of Zeus you will find the SACRED OLIVE GROVES that provide wreaths for Olympic champions and the BOULEUTERION or Council House which combines a central open-air hall and two wings of offices and storage rooms. There will be plenty of action here during the Games as the building serves as the seat of the ELEAN SENATE who are the organising committee of the Games, and the HELLANODIKAI, who are the umpires and referees. This is where athletes will be registered for competition and, when necessary, lots will be drawn to determine either their opponents or starting positions in races. The central hall will be used during your visit for hearing any accusations of bribery, corruption, cheating or other breaches of Olympic convention. The place is dominated by a mean-faced STATUE OF ZEUS clutching some equally mean thunderbolts. Do take a look at the inscription of the pedestal which curses perjurers and cheats.

THE OLYMPIC VILLAGE

The large collection of buildings that lie on the western side of Altis, on the plain that runs down to the river, is the OLYMPIC VILLAGE. At the northern end sits a cluster of sporting and training facilities: the GYMNASION, the XYSTOS and the PALAESTRA. Next comes a block of older buildings and shrines that currently houses Olympia's priestly caste and its workforce. Finally, at the southern end, are the new ROMAN HOTELS and the fabulous BATHS OF KLADEOS for well-heeled visitors and the connected, and their ancient predecessor, the LEONIDAION.

The GYMNASION, entered through a vast portico, is a very large quadrangle building whose central court is 200 yards long. A roofed colonnade – the XYSTOS – divides this into two, with one space for DISCUS AND JAVELIN PRACTICE, the other for RUNNING. Look for the small green door at the southern, colonnaded end of the courts; it will open out on to the PALAESTRA, a large square building set around a courtyard covered with sand. You will find it thickly populated with BOXERS, WRESTLERS, COACHES and MEDICINE MEN. On the south side of the courtyard, the internal colonnade leads to the APODYTERION or undressing room, while on the north side you will find the EPHEBION, or clubroom, for post-training relaxation and socialising. A wander round should also reveal the ELAIOTHESION or oil store, the KONISTERION or dusting room, and a few SPHAIRISTERIA, which are rooms for ball play. Note the strip of concrete pavement in front of the club room and its alternate pattern of ribbed and smooth tiles – this is used as a form of BOWLING ALLEY.

The central cluster of buildings in this section of Olympia is dominated by the THEOKOLEON. The *theokoloi* are the full time priests of Olympia, attending to all its spiritual business between Olympiads – as well as presiding over many of the week's celebrations. They share their office space with a small interpreting service, full-time soothsayers, and the quarters of the sanctuary's musicians, sacrificial animal experts and the woodsman charged with keeping the many temple fires and votive flames stocked with kindling. Despite all the powerful mystic knowledge gathered here, no one really quite knows what the neighbouring HEROON is for any more. Once a small baths, then a Greek temple, it is now a cultic Roman shrine, with an altar to Pan. Finally there are the buildings referred to as PHEIDAS'S WORKSHOP and still a centre for masonry and stonework in Olympia. Pheidas was the fifth-century Greek sculptor responsible for some of the most important statuary of classical Hellenism – above all the bronze goddess Athena at the Acropolis in Athens and the seated Zeus that you will have seen in the Temple of Zeus here in Olympia.

The Greeks did build a few small dormitories and hostels in the third and fourth centuries and even some rudimentary baths, but all of this has been swept away by the Romans. At the same time as remodelling the Altis and generally sprucing the place up, the Romans replaced the primitive Greek hostels with a series of grand HOTELS, installed fine mosaic floors and built the BATHS OF KLADEOS on the banks of the river. This building, less than eighty years old by the time of your arrival, is in excellent shape, featuring grand vaulted ceilings, multicoloured marble cladding, a sweat room, bathtubs and public lavatories, not to mention Olympic-size hot and cold pools.

By contrast, the LEONIDAION, although extensively renovated by the Romans, will be showing its age – almost half a millennium by the time of your stay. It was commissioned and designed by Leonidas of Naxos in 332 BC and his statue can be seen at the northeast corner of the building. Again it is a quadrangular structure with a central courtyard and has previously served as an athletes' hostel but it has been commandeered by Roman officials and given a nouveau riche twist with a huge ornamental pool in the old court.

THE SPORTS FIELDS

Follow the path that runs down from the triumphal arch and you will see the OLYMPIC STADIUM in front of you. First laid out in the sixth century, this late Roman version is about fifty yards south of the original, nestled at the foot of Mount Kronos. The arena is an oblong of sand over 200 yards long, 40 yards wide and surrounded on all sides by grass-covered embankments large enough to accommodate 45,000 spectators. When the Games are on, most of them will be standing, though the Romans, keen as ever on home improvements, have added banks of wooden benches on part of the long sides and improved the drainage by installing a new stone water channel around the track.

In the centre of the south embankment there is a stone platform reserved for the Hellanodikai. On the north bank, note the marble ALTAR OF DEMETER whose priestess will be the only woman permitted to watch the Games. Behind the west end of the stadium you will be able to see the APODYTERION – the undressing room – where athletes will prepare during the Games. This is a secure area.

Immediately to the south of the stadium, and three times its size, is the HIPPODROME with a gravel track over 800 yards long and 80 yards wide, surrounded by low artificial banks. The track itself is divided down the middle by a stone barrier, the EMBOLON, while a column at each end marks the starting and turning point of each circuit. You will see a sculpture of the Hippodamia (wife of the cheating charioteer Pelops) and a circular altar dedicated to Taraxippos, the generic ghost and horse-worrier that haunts hippodromes in the ancient world. Recent reports from Pausanias suggest that this might be an interesting place to locate yourself during the races: 'There stands, at the passage through the bank, Taraxippos, the terror of the horses. It is in the shape of a round altar and there the horses are seized by a strong and sudden fear for no apparent reason, and from the fear comes a disturbance. The chariots generally crash and the charioteers are injured. Therefore the drivers offer sacrifices and pray to Taraxippos to be propitious to them.'

THE GAMES

The programme of the ancient Olympics was first fixed in 486 BC as a five-day event. The arrival of the Romans has seen it extended to SIX DAYS. Please note that all of the ATHLETES will be competing NAKED, a tradition supposedly established in 720 BC by Orsippus of Megara, who won his race after his loincloth fell off and attributed his speed to this. A Spartan sprinter called Acanthus went on to win the second race naked too, sealing the worth of the innovation. Many athletes will tie tight leather thongs strings around their foreskins and thighs to prevent unwanted motion and erection.

VICTORY CEREMONIES will occur relatively soon after each event. First a trumpeter will bow a fanfare, then a herald will announce the champion as 'the best in all Greece' and be awarded a ribbon. Informal parties, feasts and the award of palm leaves will then break out. In the stadium, victors will also take a *periageirmos* – a victory lap. The more formal ceremonies and the presentation of the olive wreath will come later in the week.

DAY ONE: OATH TAKING

The main event on the opening day will be the gathering of the HELLANODIKAI – literally the 'judges of the Greeks' – notable for their purple cloaks. As well as being in overall charge of the

Games, they are also responsible for overseeing the taking of the Olympic oath at the TEMPLE OF ZEUS. Pausanias reports that 'competitors, their relatives and their trainers swear that they would be guilty of no foul play in the Games, and judges swore that they would be fair and would not accept bribes'. Note: when both athletes and judges take these oaths they will be standing on wild boars' genitals.

Later in the afternoon, wander down to the ECHO COLONNADE, where the KERYX – the competition for heralds – and the SALPINKTES – the competition for trumpeters – will be going on. Today is also good opportunity to watch the ATHLETES TRAIN at the PALAESTRA and GYMNASION, explore the more informal OLYMPIC VILLAGE in the meadows south of the Altis, and to see whether you an crash any of the more upmarket PARTIES in one of the grand villas.

DAY TWO: HORSE RACING

DAY TWO begins with a procession. The priests of Zeus and the Hellanodikai will gather at the PRYTANEION, light up torches from the eternal flame and visit dozens of the many small altars to the god that are scattered around the Altis. There will be BLOOD SACRIFICES conducted at many of these, so do expect a lot of flies. Once this process is completed, it will be time to get to the HIPPODROME.

Horse racing is a rich man's game. It is no mean financial and logistical feet to get your rides to this obscure corner of the Peloponnese from across the Roman Empire. The oldest and most prestigious of the three types of racing is the FOUR-HORSE CHARIOT RACE. There will also be TWO-HORSE CHARIOT RACES, originally contested with lowly mules, and simple HORSE AND RIDER RACES.

The chariot races are contested by teams of adult horses, who do twelve circuits of the Hippodrome, and by foals, who do eight. There may up to forty teams in any one race, making the hairpin turns exciting and perilous. The horse and rider event is notable for that absence of saddles and stirrups and thus the ever-present danger of jockeys being dismounted. Whoever wins, it won't be the rider who get the laurels and the glory; this goes to the owners of the teams.

Do take note of the HIPPAPHESIS – the igneous starting mechanism that has been devised for these races. This will release the horses on the outside of the track before those on the inside of the track, which gives a running start advantage to the outside lanes, compensated for by the shorter distance faced by the inside lanes. The ropes that secure the horses in their starting gates are held by a bronze eagle in a small altar in the centre of the track and bronze dolphins at the other ends.

DAY THREE: THE PENTATHLON

Today is given over to the PENTATHLON – the fivefold challenge – beginning with RUNNING, followed by DISCUS, JAVELIN and JUMPING, and concluded with bouts of WRESTLING. The running race will be a sprint, one length of the stadium.

The DISCUS, which began life at the Olympics as a stone and then a bronze disc, will now be made of iron, and subject to the peculiar rule that the contestant who brings the heaviest disc will have it used by everyone. Don't expect the kind of balletic spin and heave that you will have seen at modern Olympics. Here, the discus is thrown from a fixed position, the athlete standing on a small podium or BALBIS. Distances will be marked out by the judges using wooden pegs. Do bear in mind there are no safety nets at Olympia and the average weight of the discuss coming your way is five pounds.

The JAVELIN, also thrown for distance, is a light wood shaft, tipped with metal. Most contestants will also have a long, leather string wrapped around the javelin which uncoils and imparts spin and control when thrown. This is the event most closely associated with music and may well be accompanied by DOUBLE-PIPERS.

The JUMPING COMPETITIONS are more opaque. Contestants take a series of jumps from standing starts on a wooden board, but swinging variety of weight and dumbbells to aid their take-off.

WRESTLING takes two forms at the olympics: sand wrestling or KATO PALE, a grasping, rolling in the sandpit struggle; and the more formal standing wrestling or ORTHOS PALE, in which the fighters stay on their feet, embrace in a clinch and look for opportunities to trip or throw their opponent. The Romans, always more extreme in their violence, have introduced knuckledusters to some bouts. The referees will be keeping control with the use of a wooden rod, though there are few constraints. The breaking of fingers, however, is expressly prohibited, as is gouging.

Note that if an athlete has already won three of the first four events in the Pentathlon, they will be declared the winner without the need for a final wrestling decider.

FOUL! THIS VASE SCENE OF A PANKRATION COMBAT SHOWS A FIGHTER TRYING TO GOUGE HIS OPPONENT'S EYE, AND THE UMPIRE ABOUT TO DISQUALIFY HIM.

DAY FOUR: THE FESTIVAL OF PELOPS

Today is the FESTIVAL OF PELOPS, an intriguing and complex cult figure at Olympia. As a boy he was cut up and cooked by his father Tantalos and served to the gods – who were not fooled. The boy was reconstructed from the meal by the divines and he went on to win the hand of Hippodamia, daughter of Oinomaos, King of Pisa, in a race against her father's chariots – themselves gifts from the gods. Pelops only won the race because he bribed the opposing rider – a course that saw tragedy descend on him and his descendants. Nonetheless, by the late sixth century BC he had become a deity in Olympia, where he was buried.

The entire Hellanodikai as well as the many hundreds of ambassadors attending from distant cities and Roman provinces, will all join the procession to the ALTAR OF ZEUS, where they will sacrifice and roast a hundred oxen. It's a cue for feasting. Once you've filled up on beef, take a stroll back to the Stadium, where BOYS' DAY will be under way, with Olympic competitions reserved for the youth.

DAY FIVE: RACING AND COMBAT

The day begins with the FOOT RACES, which will be contested over three distances: the DOLICHOS, literally the long-one, a twenty-four-circuit race nearly three miles long; then the STADE, a single dash of 210 yards; and finally the DIAULOS, twice the length, up and down the stadium with a single hairpin turn. There may be up to twenty-two competitors in each race and, depending on the numbers attending the Games, there may well be heats as well as final races. As the runners arrive, you should be able to see them position their feet in specially designed stone grooves built into the track that work as starting blocks.

The races will be followed by COMBAT SPORTS. First WRESTLING, conducted along the same lines as the Pentathlon, and then BOXING. Recognisable to contemporary eyes, the fighting is much fiercer and rougher than now. Don't be surprised to see bare fists wrapped in leather thongs and occasionally embellished with studs. Next up is the PANKRATION, the 'all-power thing'. There really are no rules here, apart from no biting and no gouging, so expect ugly scrapping till somebody gives in or passes out.

The day will end with the HOPLITODROMOS, a race in armour where the otherwise naked contestants don helmets and carry a small round shield. In the Hellenic era athletes also wore greaves, but these have been abandoned, much to the chagrin of some.

DAY SIX: FESTIVITIES AND CHAMPIONS

On the final day, there will be a PROCESSION OF ALL THE OLYM-PIC CHAMPIONS to the TEMPLE OF ZEUS, where they will receive their crown of olive leaves. Along the route the crowd will gather to shower them with fruit, twigs and flowers. If you can't get into the temple – it will be crowded – do hang around outside to hear a rendition of the OLYMPIC HYMN sung to the champions.

A special banquet will then be held by the Hellanodikai for champions in the Prytaneion back in the Altis. There is no point trying to get yourself an invite to this occasion. In any case, you will note that the crowd is beginning to thin as people head for river, boats and carriages. Lucian, a visitor to the next Olympiad in 165, found himself caught out by the crowds: 'The end of the Olympic Games soon came – the best Olympics which I have seen, of the four which I have attended. It was not easy to get a carriage since so many were leaving at the same time, and therefore I stayed on for another day against my will.'

Best not to tarry, and to make your way to the DEPARTURE POINT at the hotel complex by the river.

Opening Night at Shakespeare's Globe

THE RECONSTRUCTED GLOBE THEATRE on London's South Bank gives contemporary audiences a flavour of what it might have been like to see the work of the world's greatest playwright in its original setting. But why not see what it was *actually* like? On this trip our travellers will attend the very first play ever staged there – the PREMIERE OF JULIUS CAESAR. Amidst the electric atmosphere of an Elizabethan theatre, you will enjoy the excitement, thrills and spectacle of this historic moment, and hear some of the most quoted lines ever written uttered for the very first time.

While theatre today is an eminently respectable art form, back in Shakespeare's day it was the target of much hostility and criticism. Accommodating the poor alongside the well-to-do, thereby erasing the social distinctions and hierarchies that defined and ordered the Elizabethan world, theatres were an egalitarian force, a shared ritual that offered not only entertainment but a running commentary on the state of the nation. As a consequence they were constantly under attack from religious figures, and London's governing bodies were always looking for an excuse to close them down, and periodically did so. However, nothing could stem the public's appetite for drama, and it was the genius of Shakespeare – and his brilliant contemporaries, Christopher Marlowe and Ben Jonson – that helped elevate its status. For the first time playwrights were named and credited for their work, and plays began to appear in print alongside poetry and prose. Though, for many, the theatre would never be respectable, it was institutions like the Globe that secured the legacy of Shakespeare and his fellow scribes, ensuring their words would survive to inspire future generations.

This thirty-six-hour trip will also include a day's sightseeing in London, allowing you to experience this great metropolis – the largest in Europe at the time – as it inspired and nurtured Shakespeare, the country boy with stars in his eyes. The Bard clearly fed off its cosmopolitan energy and the rapid social change affecting the city – and England – as the medieval world faded away and a more dynamic one came into being.

BRIEFING: THE BIRTH OF THE GLOBE

Around dawn on 28 December 1598, a dozen armed men trudged through the snow towards the site of The Theatre Playhouse (or simply The Theatre) in Shoreditch. Built in 1576, this was one of the oldest and most renowned theatres in London and was home to the Chamberlain's Men, a company of actors formed in 1594 under the patronage of Lord Hunsdon, the Lord Chamberlain, which included William Shakespeare, Richard Burbage, Will Kempe, John Heminges, Augustine Phillips and Thomas Pope.

Having performed over 100 plays at The Theatre, the Chamberlain's Men had a problem: they had failed to renegotiate the lease with the landlord, Giles Allen, while a plan to open a new venue in Blackfriars had fallen foul of its well-heeled residents. An alternative site had been found south of the river in Southwark – beyond City limits and the long arm of the Privy Council – near the ROSE THEATRE, used by their main rivals the ADMIRAL'S MEN. This was secured on a thirty-one-year lease to run from Christmas Day 1598. However, the company still needed to construct an actual theatre. Starting from scratch would be ruinously expensive. So they came up with an audacious scheme. Though Allen owned the land The Theatre stood on, the Chamberlain's Men owned the building. Why not dismantle the whole thing and transport it lock, stock and barrel to the new site?

With Allen on holiday in Essex and a royal performance pencilled in for New Year's Eve, time was of the essence. Having faced down some of Allen's friends, the men went to work, supervised by the Master Builder Peter Street. By dusk they had removed the whole frame of The Theatre, with its huge, heavy square posts, and stored it in a warehouse by the river. Four days later, the job was done, and the materials were ready to shift by boat and cart once the foundations of the Globe were dug. (Allen later sued the Chamberlain's Men but lost the two-year court case).

This part of the process was near completion by early spring 1599, but then a cold snap slowed construction work and was followed by heavy rain and flooding at the end of May. However, once the weather cleared, the foundations were finished and the carpenters and sawyers moved in to fit the reassembled frame together. The outer walls were hoisted into place, and cross-frames and curved braces added for stability. Then 'setting up' could start: with fresh timber arriving every day, new joists, rafters, partitions, seating and staircases were built. Glaziers appeared, as did plumbers, smiths, thatchers (for the roof), plasterers (who used lathe, lime and hair to cover the wood frame to give it the appearance of stone), and painters and specialists to marble the wooden columns on stage.

As summer approached, the new theatre – named the Globe – was nearing completion. Saturday 12 June was chosen for the grand opening. The date (on the Tudors' Julian Calendar) coincided with the SUMMER SOLSTICE, a full Moon, and the appearance of Venus and Jupiter in the night sky, all signs that augured well for the theatre's future. For a society obsessed with astrology, such auspicious portents could not be ignored.

All the Chamberlain's Men needed was a new play to open with. Shakespeare, who had recently moved home to Southwark, close to the old Clink Prison, had already written *Henry V* that year, and now turned his attention to the classical world. He quickly knocked out *Julius Caesar* – 2,500 lines total, almost all verse – had it approved for performance by the chief censor, the Master of the Revels, and rehearsals began. At these, each actor learned his part from individual scrolls, with only his bits of the text written on it – the whole company working flat out to be ready for the premiere.

THE TRIP

You will arrive at 9.30 am on Friday 11 June 1559 in the fields that straddle the fringes of urban SOUTHWARK. Bear due east for about a quarter of a mile and you will hit the main route to LONDON BRIDGE, the entry point for every kind of visitor from the continent and from the grand estates, farms and villages of south-east England.

DRESS, ROOMS AND VICTUALS

DRESS CODE in the Elizabethan era is used to distinguish social rank or profession. You will be wearing items that place you amongst the middling sort; not gentry or nobility, but still affluent and successful, borne aloft by self-made money, much like Shakespeare. Current trends are for colourful, eclectic, European styles: Spanish sleeves, French gowns, Dutch cloaks.

As the weather will be pleasantly warm, you won't be needing too many layers of clothing, but WOMEN TRAVELLERS will require a number of different garments under their dresses (bared arms and legs are out, but generous displays of cleavage are OK if you're unmarried). To cover your delicate parts you will have a length of washable linen, over which will be a chemise, then a linen smock with foreparts laid over it, and around that a fabric-covered framework (*farthingale*) to support your petticoat. Finally, you can put your gown on, with its ruffs and ruffles to add a touch of class, a neckerchief (*partlet*) and optional *mantles* to decorate the shoulders. You will have silk stockings and, considering the amount of walking you are likely to do, soft leather slippers with buckles. Extra adornments will include jewellery and a wig. To combat the sheer stench of the city, you will be wearing strong perfume – *amberg*, made from whale sperm, or *civet* from the cat of the same name – and carry a linen pouch stuffed with lavender.

MEN will have less clothing to negotiate: a linen shirt with a doublet and waistcoat, a cloak for theatrical effect, hose, breeches and high leather boots. A felt hat with a coloured hat band and dyed feather, an earring, and dagger worn at the waist, complete the ensemble. You may fancy one of the latest hairstyles imported from the continent, while a neatly trimmed beard is the fashionable choice.

ROOMS

The standard of ACCOMMODATION in London's taverns is quite high. Your room will be spacious and comfortable, its walls decorated with painted cloths. There will be a large four-poster, curtained bed with a feather mattress on top and feather pillows and pillowcases to rest your head on. There will be clean linen sheets, blankets, coverlets and quilts. Men will don a NIGHTSHIRT and CAP, while women will pull on a smock-like NIGHT RAIL. Additional items include a candle, candle holder, and a cham-berpot by the bed, or, if you're lucky, a CLOSE STOOL: a square box with a hole in the top and a padded seat to plant your behind on. You are best off using the facilities in your room, as the public latrines (*jakes*) are pretty foul. If you are caught short when you're out and about, there are three communal privies on Tower Street, while the largest is on London Bridge and empties directly into the Thames.

VICTUALS

Those hoping to gorge on a Tudor roast will be disappointed. To encourage people to consume more fish, it is against the law to eat meat on Fridays and Saturdays. Expect your FISH to be poached or boiled in heavily spiced sauces, with added fruits and natural sugars, served with vegetables and

PIPE AND A PINT AT AN ELIZABETHAN TAVERN.

a salad (*sallat*) option, followed by cheese and dessert.

Most of your food will be sourced from one of London's many MAR-KETS, which you will encounter everywhere you go. Open six days a week, from 6am to 11am and 1pm to 5pm, they are all under the control of the Lord Mayor and his councillors, who fix prices and levy fines for offences like forestalling (intercepting goods before they reach the market). Your fish will come from Stocks Market, Billings-gate, and the fishmongers of Fish Street, your FRUIT AND VEGETABLES from Greenchurch Street Market or Queenshithe by the river (or any of the City's 377 grocers), while CHEESE will come from one of these markets or the cheese shops of Bread Street. Though you won't be able to eat any meat, you'll see plenty of it, whether alive and kicking at Smithfield or straight out of the slaughterhouses at Cheapside, where there are carcasses and joints hanging from hooks and skewered on spits.

Nobody drinks water. Instead, it's BOTTLED BEER, made from malt barley, water and hops; ALE, which has no hops and a three-day shelf life; or WINE, of which there are 30 named brands available.

FRIDAY 11 JUNE: THE CITY

Jammed with traffic, human and animal, and lined with impressive buildings on either side, LONDON BRIDGE offers visitors a spectacular introduction to the CITY OF LONDON. Immediately you step foot on it you will see two corn-grinding mills, then a drawbridge (no longer functioning) with a tower that sports the skulls of sixteen executed traitors and, midway across, a disused chapel.

Interspersed between these landmarks are large four-storey dwellings belonging to wealthy merchants, some with shops on the ground floor. The most grandiose of these is NONSUCH HOUSE, a Renaissance extravaganza, pre-fabricated in Holland and erected on site, with turrets, gilded columns and carved galleries projecting out over the river. As you approach the northern end you will be confronted with an arch containing a massive water wheel. Passing this you will now be close to ALDGATE, the City's front door.

Criss-crossed by broad thoroughfares and linked by narrow streets and twisting alleyways, the CITY is a hotchpotch of dwellings, from the slums of the dirt-poor to the mansions of the filthy rich, all rammed together alongside official buildings, trading houses, retail outlets and churches – many of them disused, There are many gardens and, always within walking distance, open green spaces, though many of these are occupied by laundresses drying their washing.

Wandering the streets, some paved or cobbled, others covered with gravel and beaten earth, you will notice how young everybody looks; half the population is under twenty. You will hear people being referred to as *Goodman This* or *Goodwife That*, and if somebody calls you *snout fair*, it means they think you are good looking. If, by contrast, they consider you *as much worth as a piss in the Thames*, take that as the insult it is clearly intended to be. Be wary of COURTESY MEN who prey on visitors, befriending then robbing them, while male travellers should be on their guard against A DEMANDER OF GLIMMER, an attractive women who promises you her body, takes your money and runs. You may also find yourself being accosted by TOURIST GUIDES, ready to lead you a merry dance around town and relieve you of your cash. Don't be suckered into accepting their help.

You will meet SELLERS *crying their wares*, flogging *timely* (fresh) fruit and pies from baskets, BUSKERS, STREET PERFORMERS and BALLAD SELLERS; at some point you will probably be handed a playbill advertising the grand opening of the Globe. BEGGARS will be hard to avoid – they are all licensed by church authorities to operate in a particular area for a specific period of time. You may also come across people being paraded around on CARTS (*carting*); these are minor offenders being publicly humiliated for their misdemeanours. Some may be tied to horses, but facing backwards. You will see individuals with either one ear or both ears missing: these are ex-cons who have been subject to a brutal punishment called *pillioring*.

LUNCH IN BISHOPSGATE

The main meal of the day is at midday. We recommend you dine at either THE BULL or THE GREEN DRAGON in Bishopsgate. You will be expected to wash your hands before eating and will be given a towel to dry them with. The menu will not be as elaborate or extravagant as some of the more extreme examples of Elizabethan cuisine. Nevertheless, you will be able to choose dishes like ELUS BAKYN, eels baked in red wine sauce; PYKES IN BRASEY, grilled fish in wine; or SALMON poached in beer, vinegar and herbs. CHEESES on offer will include green (new) cheese, hard cheese (Cheddar) or soft cheese with herbs. DESSERT will come in the form of a fruit tart, perhaps filled with strawberries in red wine with sugar, cinnamon and ginger, or cherries with mustard, cinnamon and ginger. Or you might feel like a TRIFLE made with a pint of thick cream, seasoned with sugar and ginger and rosewater.

The best BEER to drink is *March Beer*. If you have an aversion to sweet varieties of WINE, then avoid the ever-popular *Sack*, a dry, amber wine from Spain that has added sugar; *Malmsey*, from Crete; *Muscatel*, from France; and *Rumney*, from the Balkans. For lovers of a full-bodied red, there is *Bastard* from Burgundy or, for a lighter bouquet, *Claret* from Gascony. The premium white wines are from La Rochelle or the Rhineland. After the meal, you may want to order a shot of Flemish BRANDY (*brandewijn*).

AFTERNOON SPORTS AND THE TOWER

Eating done, you can plunge back into the hurly-burly of the city, or you might prefer something a bit more recreational. If you fancy a spot of SWORD PLAY, we can book you a fencing lesson at Ely Place in Holborn. Beginners (*scholars*) will get instruction in the rapier, quarterstaff and broadsword. Your teacher will be a member of the Company of Masters of the Art of Self-Defence. If PISTOL SHOOTING is more your thing, then head to ARTILLERY YARD, just to the east of Bishopsgate, an enclosed space with brick walls and targets at each end. Or, if ARCHERY appeals, make your way north out of the City to FINSBURY FIELDS, where there are 200 *butts* (targets) available for experts and novices alike.

Fans of the GRUESOME AND GROTESQUE might take a guided tour of the TOWER OF LONDON. However, do bear in mind that its dungeons and torture chambers are not just for show: they are very much in demand. Once inside, you will see THE PIT, a twenty-foot-deep hole where prisoners rot in total darkness; the infamous RACK, where limbs are stretched and bones broken; and THE LITTLE EASE, a cave too small to stand upright in. You will also be introduced to a particularly fiendish contraption known as the *Scavenger's Daughter*, a multifaceted instrument that comprises an iron band to compress the victim's feet and head into a circle, iron gauntlets to crush their hands, and *jetters* (irons) to encase their arms and ankles.

EVENING PURSUITS

You will be staying the night at THE BELL INN by St Paul's Cathedral – the original Norman version of 1087. A LIGHT SUPPER will be served at 6pm with a musical accompaniment provided by fiddlers, bagpipers and ballad singers. The atmosphere will be very smoky; you can add to the tobacco haze by purchasing a small-bowled PIPE. Those with a competitive streak may fancy a game of CHESS or a crack at the BOWLING ALEE. There will also be GAMBLING going on around you, whether on card games – *gleek, primero, one and thirty, new cut* and *trumps* – or dice, which are almost always loaded. Don't get involved unless you are very skilled with a blade; disputes over money and honour can escalate rapidly into duels to the death.

Whatever you do, you must be off the streets by the 9PM CURFEW, which is signalled by the ringing of church bells. Watches, with powers of arrest, patrol the city to ensure that the taverns are shut, the shops shuttered and all good citizens are safely behind closed doors.

SATURDAY 12 JUNE: SOUTHWARK

The City Gates reopen at dawn. BREAKFAST will follow shortly after: a bottle of beer and buttered white or brown bread, each loaf sealed so the baker can be identified, the price and weight set by the Lord Mayor. After breakfast you will have a couple of hours to kill before having to be at Blackfriars to catch a WHERRY (water taxi) over to Southwark. You may want to take a look inside ST PAUL'S. Though famed for its beauty, the cathedral is now in a pretty sorry state, having suffered the depredations of the Reformation – its icons, tapestries, sculptures and gold ornaments have all been ripped out. Nevertheless, it retains the awesome architectural scale and majesty we associate with Gothic churches. If you are feeling energetic, why not climb its three hundred steps to the roof, from where you will get uninterrupted views of London.

You may also want to browse the BOOKSHOPS congregated round St Paul's Churchyard, selling editions in ancient Greek, Latin, Italian, French and English; top of the bestseller list is *Foxes Book of Martyrs* (1563). Also popular are almanacs, saucy Italian verse and home-grown plays, including some of Shakespeare's. (We regret that you may not make any purchases). It is also worth a walk to nearby St Paul's Cross, where you will be harangued by fiery EVANGELICAL PREACHERS, radical Protestants with a mission to remind you of your Sins and the dreadful ordeals awaiting you in the afterlife.

Once you are at BLACKFRIARS you will have no trouble finding a WHERRY. There are hundreds working the river, each one with two upholstered seats at the back, a canopy to shield you from the elements, and an oarsman up front who has done a two-year apprenticeship and been certified as competent by the Eight Rulers (overseers). The journey will cost you a penny.

As you cross the Thames you will be struck by the sheer number of vessels afloat. Asides from the wherries, there will be larger passenger barges with ten oarsmen, long tilt boats with a separate steerage boat attached, and dozens of large ships queuing up to unload their cargoes at the custom houses by London Bridge. Masses of fish inhabit the river's murky grey waters, while swans glide over its surface.

AROUND THE GLOBE

Southwark stretches south for a mile from the riverbank, and is heavily built up. Its squalid tenements are crammed together along packed streets and are home to watermen, craftsmen and foreigners, who rub shoulders with an underworld of criminals and prostitutes. Many of Southwark's three hundred inns double as BROTHELS, the most well-known being the CARDINAL'S HAT. Mixed in with all the usual frightful odours is the unpleasant smell of the *stink* trades of brewing and tanning.

Your best bet for LUNCH is the ELEPHANT TAVERN on Horseshoe Alley, right next to the Globe and only a short walk from where your wherry docks. Don't expect fine dining: this is Southwark, and you're here for the theatre. To guarantee your place for the 3pm performance be there at least an hour early. As the GLOBE – a hundred feet in diameter, with a flag flying from the roof and the motto *Totus mundus agit histrionem* (The whole world plays the actor) inscribed above the entrance – has a 3,300 capacity, the crowds gathering outside will swell considerably as you wait to go in. You will see a few noblemen on horseback, some on foot, well-dressed members of the gentry and gaggles of Law students from the Temple Bar and Inns of Court mingling with tradesmen, apprentices and labourers.

There will be CONJURORS AND JUGGLERS dazzling you with their skills, sellers offering refreshments: oranges, apples, nuts, gingerbread and bottled beer, as well as pipes and pouches of tobacco at threepence a pop. Be on the alert for PICKPOCKETS and PROSTITUTES on the prowl. The queuing arrangements will be more disorderly than orderly until you reach the GATHERERS who will take your money at the door.

Once inside the AUDITORIUM you will be impressed by the gilded decor, rich with classical motifs expressed in paintings, sculptures, tapestries and hangings. Here you will turn either left or right to enter one of the three galleries lined with wooden benches that surround the fifty-foot wide stage (2d admission). Be prepared to fight for a good seat, as there are roughly 1,000 other playgoers who want one too. If you want to rough it, you could pay just a penny to enter the seatless PIT, an open yard that slopes towards the stage, covered with ash, slag and hazelnut shells, crammed with over 2,000 people from the lower sort – the *understanders* – jostling for a good view of the action.

While you will be exposed to the full glare of the June sunshine, the five-foot-high stage will remain totally in the shade. You will immediately notice how bare and functional the performance space is. There are two exits/entrances on either side; between them is curtained area used for DISCOVERY SCENES, which might feature a character asleep in bed or in their death throes, while a canopy is supported by two wooden pillars.

Otherwise, asides from a few props – tables, chairs, etc, that are kept under the stage (*Hell*) – the boards are bare. There is a trap-door but it won't be needed this afternoon. Just above the stage is a balcony that houses half a dozen MUSICIANS armed with trumpets, drums, other horns, recorders and lutes. Torches and candles provide whatever on-stage lighting is required, and rudimentary sound effects, such as horses' hooves, birdsong and bells, are supplied by the BACKSTAGE TEAM comprising a bookkeeper, assistant stage keeper, a carpenter and two further stagehands.

Throughout, the audience will be fully engaged with the action. Cries of *mew* indicate displeasure. Expect the galleries to rise to their feet during the most intense scenes, while from the Pit there will be boos, hisses, shouts of encouragement and cheering and applause for memorable speeches. Though rowdy, the punters are generally attentive and appreciative; some even bring table-books with them to note down significant passages from the play.

THE PLAY'S THE THING

Julius Caesar will last just over two hours, with no act breaks; the scenes, seventeen in all, will simply flow together to give the impression of continuous movement. Of the sixteen actors in the company – six of them boys who will take on the female roles – the leading man is RICHARD BURBAGE, the best of his day, and a pioneer of a more naturalistic approach to his craft.

Generally, the style of acting will be what we would call *hammy*. This is partly to compensate for the fact that much of the audience will struggle to see the performers' faces, while any dialogue spoken quietly will simply be lost in all the crowd noise. As a result, voices are big and declamatory, the verse projected with a booming rhetorical flourish. Gestures will be equally theatrical; the actors have a repertoire of fifty-nine hand gestures

THE FIRST FOLIO OF JULIUS CAESAR – NOT YET PUBLISHED.

to communicate different emotions and states of mind. Though all the cast are adept at *thribbling* (improvisation), today they will stick to the script. The actor's costume is called his *shape*, while his place on stage is his *habitation*. Over the course of *Julius Caesar*, they will be wearing togas, tunics, cloaks, robes and armour (for the battle scenes), all the responsibility of the wardrobe keeper.

Once *Julius Caesar* begins, there will be many HIGHLIGHTS to look out for. After a group of plebs set the play in motion with their disparaging comments about Caesar's ambitions to rule single-handedly, SCENE 2 will begin with blaring music from the balcony, heralding the entrance of the main characters and a throng of citizens. Night falls during SCENE 3, and the plot thickens as the would-be assassins make last-minute preparations for murder most foul, accompanied by a wild and unholy thunderstorm, courtesy of the sound effect guys: a sheet of metal will be used to make the thunder, fireworks for the lightning, a canvas tied to a wheel to produce the wind, and dried pies rattled on tin to create the rain.

The intense noise of the storm continues into the next scene, where Caesar ponders his potential fate, and then onto the killing itself in SCENE 8. When each conspirator plunges his dagger into Caesar's stricken body, bladders of sheep's blood, strategically placed on the actor's body, will erupt, spilling their contents onto the stage. As Brutus delivers the final thrust, Caesar, dismayed by the treachery of his closest companion, will speak those three words of Latin that will echo down the ages: 'Et tu, Brute?'

This coup de grâce is followed by the famous funeral orations of Brutus and Mark Antony; both actors will ascend to the musicians' balcony to deliver their speeches. Mark Antony's stirring tribute to Caesar, featuring the immortal opening lines, 'Friends, Romans, countrymen, lend me your ears. I come to bury Caesar not to praise him,' will turn the people of Rome against the assassins and an angry mob will scour the city for them, happening upon the hapless poet Cinna in SCENE 10: thinking he is someone else, they will pummel him to death (more sheep's blood).

The play is now entering its final third: Brutus and his fellow conspirator Cassius are with their army near the town of Philippi, preparing for battle with Mark Antony and Octavius. There will be a lot of drumming, trumpet blasts and off-stage shouting to help create a military mood. During SCENE 12, the night before the decisive battle, the ghost of Caesar will visit Brutus in his tent and issue the chilling warning, 'Thou shalt see me at Philippi.' To give their meeting a spooky, supernatural quality, stagehands will place lights behind coloured bottles; the shapes and shades shed by them will bathe the actors in unearthly hues.

The last four short, fast-paced scenes, encompass the battle and its grisly aftermath (lots more sheep's blood). Fearing all is lost, first Cassius, then Brutus, will fall on their swords, leaving the victors, Mark Antony and Octavius, to bring proceedings to a close.

Before you file out, however, the next play will be announced, the actors will kneel together and offer a prayer to the Queen, and then the whole ensemble will perform a boisterous and ribald JIG to send you merrily on your way.

POST-PLAY

It is customary after the performance to promenade through PARIS GARDENS, a mere stone's throw from the Globe. Here you will be able to buy alcohol and watch games of bowls and cards. You will also be close to its BEAR-BAITING ARENA. This hugely popular form of entertainment features star bears with names like George Stone, Harry Hunks and Harry Tame. Costing a penny to stand in the stalls, or tuppence for a gallery seat, punters will be treated to the sight of the bear being led in on a chained leash and then tied to a stake before being viciously assaulted by hunting dogs, usually Great English mastiffs. These ferocious contests can last several hours, before the combatants are too exhausted or wounded to continue.

DEPARTURE

With dusk fast approaching, and the streets becoming more dangerous for outsiders, you should make your way south-west out of Southwark, past farmsteads, woods and marshy ground. You will soon be at the fields where your journey began and from where you will depart.

The Birth of Bebop

15–16 FEBRUARY 1942 ✳ HARLEM, NEW YORK

DURING THE SECOND WORLD WAR, JAZZ music underwent a profound evolution and a new style was born – bebop. Drenched in the blues, this fast, rebellious music, with its insider cool and outside status, had an incalculable influence not only on jazz, African-American culture and popular music, but also on literature (the Beats, especially Kerouac), art (the abstract expressionists), comedy (modern stand-up pioneers such as Lenny Bruce and Mort Sahl), European cinema (the French New Wave) and fashion (from movie stars to Mods).

On this forty-eight-hour trip, you will get a ringside seat at legendary venues, experience the humming buzz of New York nightlife, dance till you drop at the Savoy, the world's premier ballroom and attend the ultimate jazz laboratory – the Jam Session – where Young Turks and giants of the swing era share the same stage together, interrogating and reinterpreting jazz standards.

Out of this dialogue between the generations bebop is born. The trip is designed so you see and hear this collaborative process in action; you will enjoy both the glorious power of the Big Bands and the jagged dynamism of the New Thing.

··

BRIEFING: THE BEBOP REVOLUTION

··

This trip is all the more remarkable because the genesis of bop was lost to posterity. A strike over royalty payments called by the American Federation of Musicians, which lasted from 31st July 1942 to November 1944, banned all union members (and if you wanted to work you had to be in the union!) from doing *any* sessions – whether in the studio, on radio, or live – for *any* recording company. As a result, when artists like Charlie Parker and Dizzy Gillespie unveiled their music at the end of the war, it would seem like it had come from nowhere, fully formed, a perception that caused a damaging rift within the jazz community between Modernists and Traditionalists and obscured bebop's true roots. Thus you have the unique opportunity to visit a moment in time when they all played on the same side of the street.

You'll be spending time at three key venues in New York, all of which are based in the city's jazz heartland of Harlem.

THE SAVOY BALLROOM

Opened in 1926, and taking up an entire block on 140th Street and 596 Lenox Avenue, the Savoy – *The Home of Happy Feet* – is the leading jazz dance venue not only in New York, but the whole world. Dance crazes first invented here soon spread across the USA and onto Europe. Owned by the entrepreneur Moe Gale and run by Harlem businessman Charles Buchanan, it costs half a million dollars a year to run, while taking twice that at the door. It is also home to BATTLES OF THE BANDS or CUTTING CONTESTS, during which the house band takes on out-of-towners.

For much of the 1930s the CHICK WEBB ORCHESTRA ruled the roost at the Savoy. The diminutive drummer and bandleader (severe spinal deformities led to his death in 1939 aged just 30) was a genius behind the kit and the first to record that perennial favourite "Stompin' at the Savoy". His all-conquering outfit, featuring the young Ella Fitzgerald, outplayed Benny Goodman in 1937 and Count Basie a year later.

For your visit, the Savoy's house band will be the LUCKY MILLENDER ORCHESTRA, a hard-swinging outfit with a penchant for R&B-inflected monster grooves.

MINTON'S PLAYHOUSE

Minton's is the focal point of the New York jamming scene and is located in the first-floor dining room of the Hotel Cecil, an elegant five-storey building on West 118th Street, near 7th Avenue. It's owned by HENRY MINTON, a former tenor-sax man, and the first ever black union delegate, who had previously managed the Rhythm Club – which hosted big names like Louis Armstrong and Fats Waller. With the musical tides flowing in fresh directions, Henry closed and then reopened Minton's in 1940 and hired the ex-bandleader TEDDY HILL to run it.

Hill immediately installed a new house band brimming with young talent. Most notably, he recruited as his Musical Director the explosive drummer KENNY 'KLOOK-MOP' CLARKE, whose off-beat blows on the snare and bass drums had already raised eyebrows in the bands he'd played with. His redefinition of the drummer's role – less tied to holding the beat and inter-acting more with the soloists – was one of the foundations of bebop. Clarke then brought in THELONIOUS MONK, a mercurial genius with a highly individualistic approach to the piano who was already on the verge of composing masterpieces like "Round Midnight" and "Ruby My Dear".

But what drew swing-era giants like Benny Goodman, Count Basie, Coleman Hawkins and Lester 'Prez' Young to Minton's was the presence of CHARLIE CHRISTIAN on guitar: the most precocious axeman of his generation, he'd cut his teeth in the brilliant small groups of Basie and Goodman, and pioneered a new approach to his instrument which anticipated rock'n'roll – though, sadly, this hard-partying cat was hospitalized with TB in 1941 and passed away not long after.

MONROE'S UPTOWN HOUSE

Known as THE PIRATE'S DEN, Monroe's is the go-to place for an after-hours jam, and is located at 198 West 134th Street in a dingy cellar-like basement – appropri-ately enough given its underground reputation. It is run by CLARK MONROE, a dedicated jazz head who inherited the club from the gangster Barron Wilkins after he was gunned down by a pimp called Charleston.

THE TRIP

You will arrive at 3.45pm on Sunday 15 February 1942 on the CORNER OF 125TH STREET AND 7TH AVENUE amidst the crowds of Harlemites gathered for their Sunday promenade, strutting their stuff and dressed to impress. For the duration, you will be based on 7th Avenue, the broadest boulevard in HARLEM, cov-ering 23 blocks and referred to as *Black Broadway* or *The Great Black Way*. Most of the places you visit will be along here or within walking distance on Lenox Avenue, which runs parallel to 7th and almost matches it for length (21 blocks) and reputation: Lang-ston Hughes, that fine Harlem Renaissance writer, dubbed it *The Heartbeat of Harlem*, and it inspired his poem 'Midnight On The Legendary Street'.

To overcome the COLOUR BAR that runs through American so-ciety, and to ensure that you can enjoy your trip (whatever your ethnicity) without encountering any hassles, you will assume the identity of a French aristocrat. As a fugitive from Nazi Europe you have been travelling the continent before reaching the Big Apple. Your English is passable but not fluent. You love jazz.

Ever since that amazing performer Josephine Baker (*The Black Pearl*) hypnotised Paris in 1925, jazzmen have been big stars in France; revered as great artists and, most importantly, treated like human beings. For decades to come, the city will offer them a place of refuge. As a result, the tight-knit jazz community will welcome you with open arms. At the same time, being a member of the European aristocracy will ease your entrée into New York's highlife (the VIP PACKAGE).

SUNDAY 15 FEBRUARY

Right in front of your arrival point is the HOTEL THERESA, the most upscale, exclusive hotel in Harlem – a very tall white building with Gothic features that takes up a whole block. Owned by Walter Scott, it is a magnet for the big names in entertainment – you might meet Duke Ellington in the elevator – plus business tycoons and politicians. Permanent residents, paying $8 a week to rent a room, include NAT KING COLE, the bandleader JIMMIE LUNCEFORD and pop sensations THE INK SPOTS.

As you approach the marquee entrance, you will notice taxis and limos disgorging guests, many from Chicago and Detroit, carrying sets of golf clubs – the ultimate status symbol – and wearing riding gear – the latest fashion for those keen to flaunt their wealth. You will go through the double doors into the wide foyer and lighted lobby with its green and beige floral wallpaper, and stroll past glistening mirrors towards the Registration Desk, manned by the slender, golden-brown Eloise Scott. Seated just behind her is Miss Mattye Jean, the college-educated switchboard operator. Adjacent to them are the elevators and three public phone booths.

Your $2-a-night room is on the first floor. Wandering the corridors, decorated by white square tiles with black stripes, you may smell the unmistakably pungent aroma of MARIJUANA, which is referred to as *Reefer*, *Muggles*, *Mary Jane*, or simply *Tea*. It is a staple of the jazz life and there exists a whole subgenre (*Viper Music*) of songs celebrating the mighty herb: "Gimme a Reefer", "Reefer Man", "Reefer Hound Blues", "The Stuff is Here and It's Mellow". If you don't come across any at the Theresa, you definitely will at Minton's and Monroe's. Rather than trying to score any dope yourself, which could prove hazardous, you are advised to loiter outside the clubs or out back by the kitchen exits, where much crafty toking will be taking place. Play your cards right and you will be able to drag deep on the odd joint.

By the deluxe double bed in your comfortable room, you will find a copy of *Cab Calloway's Cat-o-logue: A Hepster's Dictionary*. The veteran bandleader (his biggest hit is "Minnie the Moocher"), has put together a collection containing 200 *jive* (SLANG) terms, the preferred argot of the jazz world. Take a few minutes to absorb some key phrases that might come handy during your stay: *hip* = wise and sophisticated; *blow their wigs* = show great excitement; *dime note* = $10 bill; *early black* = evening; *fine dinner* = good-looking woman; *slide your jib* = talk freely.

In the wardrobe you will find three different OUTFITS. For tonight, men will wear a tuxedo with necktie, while women will slip into a sequinned evening gown and white gloves. For daytime tomorrow, both genders will be dressed more conservatively: men in a dark blue suit, women in a plain dress. For your jamming evening, men will sport zoot suits – broad shoulders, wide lapels, pinstripes and turned-up baggy trousers – and women a brightly patterned top and a pencil skirt. It's February in New York, so men will be provided with a trench coat, women with a floor-length mink (fake).

At 4.30pm exactly, switch on the RADIO in your room; it will be pre-tuned to a local station that broadcasts a fifteen-minute performance by the new arrivals at the Savoy Ballroom. This Sunday afternoon it's the JAY McSHANN BAND, a hard-swinging outfit from Kansas City who have on alto sax the twenty-one- year-old

THE BIRD TAKES FLIGHT. CHARLIE PARKER (FAR RIGHT), PLAYING IN
THE JAY MCSHANN BAND.

CHARLIE PARKER (*Yardbird* or simply *Bird*). This is only Bird's
second visit to the Big Apple. His first saw him gain a few admir-
ers but no paid work; he had to stay with a friend and wash dishes
in a club for small change. Pretty much an unknown quantity up
to this moment, the broadcast you are about to hear will turn the
spotlight on him.

The Jay McShann Band will do five numbers; Bird will be the
featured soloist on "Cherokee", a fiendish tune with sixty-four
bars and tricky harmonies. Bird's improvisation – juggling the
chord progressions, dancing both behind and in front of the beat,
waiting patiently for exactly the right moment to unfurl blister-
ing runs of notes – stuns everyone who hears it. Ears prick up all
across New York, the Five Boroughs and beyond. His debut radio
performance will draw packs of hungry jazzheads to the Savoy
tonight to sample Bird in the flesh – and you will be there too.

STOMPIN' AT THE SAVOY

When you are ready, leave the Theresa and walk the few blocks to the SAVOY, where queues to get in will already be forming; the cost of admission before 8pm is 60 cents, after that, 85 cents. Stepping into its spacious lobby you will be struck by its ostentatious glamour; more like a palace than a dance hall. Hanging above you is a massive cut-glass chandelier; ahead of you, a curved marble staircase. There is a roomy check-in for your coats, and carpeted and mirrored lounges to *take five* (try not to say 'chill out'). Climb the staircase and enter the huge ballroom – 10,000 square feet with 4,000 capacity. This giant space is divided into two: one zone has tables and settees where you can sit, watch the action, rest weary feet and drink cheap beer; the other is for dancing.

The dense, heaving crowd includes all types of people of all ages. Such is the Savoy's fame, you might glimpse a film star or two; Clark Gable and Greta Garbo have both been spotted here. You will notice a dozen well-built, heavy-set men in tuxedos prowling the room. They are the bouncers – ex-boxers and basketball players on $100 a night – under the command of JACK LA RUE. Troublemakers will be discreetly, but forcibly, removed. Also working the floor are the Savoy Hostesses, *café au lait* girls, mostly from Sugar Hill, a prosperous black neighbourhood. Their main job is to make sure everybody is having a good time. Male travellers should avoid getting too friendly, as the Hostesses can be fired for consorting with the patrons. However, if you buy a 25 cent ticket, one of them will be your dance partner for the evening.

The especially sprung DANCE FLOOR, all polished maple wood and lined with coloured lights, is a thing of beauty. The main section is known as THE TRACK; 250 feet long and 50 feet wide, it can hold thousands doing much loved and imitated dances that originated on this very strip: the *Jitterbug*, *Suzie-Q*, *Hucklebuck*, *Camel Walk*, *Snake Hips* and the *Flying Charleston*, to name a few. The Track will be dominated by young African–Americans out to dazzle with their moves, demonstrate their prowess and look good with it: a local marijuana dealer, MALCOLM LITTLE (street name *Detroit Red*), a regular at the Savoy who would later change his name to Malcolm X, never forgot 'the black girls in way-out silk and satin dresses, their hair done in all kinds of styles, the men sharp in their zoot suits and crazy conks'. For those who prefer a gentler pace, there is a space reserved for the *Tango*, *Fox Trot* and other classics; the top dancer here is known as *The Sheik*.

The most ambitious hoofers hoping to prevail in the Savoy's hypercompetitive DANCEOFFS will congregate in the CAT'S CORNER, a 10-foot-square area to the right of the two bandstands, as will a throng of spectators, some taking side-bets on the outcome. The winners will be invited to join the 400 CLUB, allowing them to rehearse in daylight hours alongside the bands. Longevity and stylistic innovation are what counts and will separate the genuine contenders from the no-hopers. Don't even think about stepping into the arena unless you are really hot to trot.

Also featured in the Cat's Corner are the SAVOY LINDY-HOPPERS (from the dance the *Lindy-Hop*, conceived in 1927 to honour Charles Lindbergh's maiden flight across the Atlantic), professional dancers under the control of their mentor and erstwhile agent, HERBERT 'MAC' WHITE, an ex-boxer who came through the bouncer's ranks and has been in charge of the Lindy-Hoppers since 1938, recruiting fresh talent and helping to get his dancers work on movies like *Hellzapoppin'* (1941). With a distinctive white streak running through his black hair, he will be hard to miss. Look out of for his star performers: FRANKIE 'MUSCLEHEAD' MANNING, who has a highly original technique, positioning his body at an acute angle to the floor, like a runner waiting in the blocks for the starting gun, bent low so he can execute his flying aerial leaps; the youngster AL MINNS, known as *Crazy Legs* because of his dazzling speed; and the indefatigable multi-contest-winner NORMA MILLER.

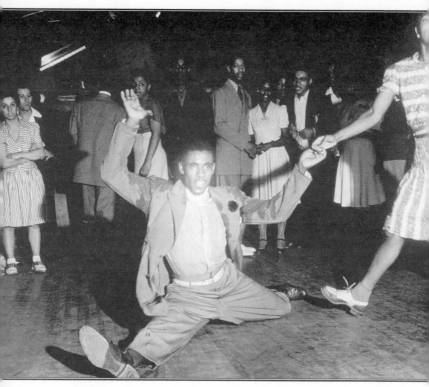

LINDYHOPPERS SWING-DANCING IN THE CAT'S CORNER OF THE SAVOY.

The pumping heart of it all, which keeps everything moving, is the turbo-charged music coming from the bandstands. First up is the JAY MCSHANN BAND. You will see Dizzy Gillespie – with his distinctive horn-rimmed glasses, beret and goatee, trumpet case in hand – and the inscrutable Monk amongst the coterie of musicians assembled close to the stage, all eager to catch Bird in flight. During Jay's set, BIRD, a slight figure in a shabby, crumpled suit and sunglasses, will solo on "Clap Hands Here Comes Charlie" and "Cherokee", his rapid fingers unleashing sizzling pyrotechnics, driving the band to ever-heavier heights.

Having left the bandstand steaming, it's the turn of the resident outfit, the LUCKY MILLINDER ORCHESTRA, with the wonderful

CLYDE HART on piano (in a few weeks Dizzy will join them, having been fired by Cab Calloway because of his onstage antics). Though they are no slouches, Lucky Millinder's crew are out-gunned by McShann and co; once the BATTLE OF THE BANDS commences, Jay's mob will blow them away.

AFTER-HOURS

For POST-SAVOY EATS AND DRINKS, you could do worse than BRAD-DOCK'S BAR AND GRILL, right next to the famous Apollo Theatre, situated on 7th Avenue and 125th Street; its two-for-one policy is popular with musicians and the steaks are pretty good. CLUB BARON is a very sophisticated and luxurious venue on 132nd and 437 Lenox; here you will be entertained by the MC Larry Steele, some up-and-coming comedians, and the talented singer ETHEL WATERS. If you fancy something a little less swish, head over to the DAN WALLI CHILI HOUSE on 7th Avenue between 139th and 140th, often host to impromptu jam sessions.

Otherwise, you can return to the Theresa, which is still very much alive and kickin'. You can get a decent meal in the restaurant and then head to the bar which is open until 2am. The manager, John Thomas, has a team of seven bartenders working under him, all male and wearing white tunics, and you can get a shot of whiskey for 75 cents. Asides from other late-night drinkers, high-rollers and city gents, you will notice a number of stunningly beautiful women loitering here, some prostitutes, others local girls hoping to land a rich husband, and a smattering of fellow European aristos. If you are not yet ready for bed after the bar closes, then head down to the lobby, where there will still be fun to be had; you may run into members of the Lucky Millinder Orchestra who are staying at the hotel.

For a more rough-and-ready, but no less jazzy scene, check out the Woodside Hotel, just round the corner from the Savoy on 7th Avenue and 141st Lenox. Many of the clientele reflect the criminal demi-monde inhabited by its owner, Love B. Woods, a slum landlord with flop houses and shabby apartments all over Harlem; you will encounter pimps, gamblers, hustlers and sassy dames. However, mixed in are the jazz fraternity: the hotel is Count Basie's base in New York (he penned "Jumpin' at The Woodside" in 1939) and Jay McShann's boys are in the house. Head for the basement restaurant, where you will catch the musicians working on their *chops* (technique).

VIP PACKAGE: THE STORK CLUB

For a small additional fee, you will have the chance to check out New York's most exclusive late-night venue, THE STORK CLUB on 3 East 53rd Street. Opened in 1929, the Stork Club is owned by former bootlegger SHERMAN BILLINGSLEY and attracts A-listers like CHARLIE CHAPLIN, BING CROSBY and FRANK SINATRA; literary heavyweights like ERNEST HEMINGWAY; real heavyweights like JOE LOUIS (world champion from 1937 to 1949); and major players in business and finance. Throw in presidents and the occasional royalty, and you have the full array of the East Coast elite mingling here.

A limo will pick you up outside the Savoy and whisk you across town to the club, which opens at 11am and shuts at 4am. From the street, the entrance appears fairly nondescript; an ordinary door with a narrow marquee leading to the sidewalk. The only hint of what lies inside is the fourteen-carat solid gold chain barring your way. But don't worry; the top-hatted doorman is expecting you. Once inside, be on your best behaviour. Sherman will not hesitate to eject you if you get out of hand. Even big celebs are not immune: HUMPHREY BOGART is one high-profile victim of Sherman's no-nonsense approach.

The Stork Club provides a variety of spaces to meet your entertainment needs; there is the tropically themed ISLAND BAR; a COCKTAIL LOUNGE; the glassed-in main DINING ROOM with a band and dancing; the CUB ROOM, a small, intimate venue; while upstairs you will find a LONER'S ROOM for singletons and the BLESSED EVENT ROOM for catered parties. By now you will have built up quite an appetite, so make your way to the dining room, where the menu offers haute cuisine with an American twist: dishes like *Tournedos Baltimore* (tenderloin steak with mushrooms, onions, sliced veal kidney and stewed tomatoes), *Pheasant*

Casserole Derby, *Royal Squab Knickerbocker* and *Aiguillette of Duckling Florida*, followed by Gallic cheeses and rich desserts.

Though you may prefer wine with your meal, you'd be a fool not to try the club COCKTAILS, which are without doubt the best in New York. The barman, JULIUS CORSANI, will mix you up his own creation, the *Julius Special*, made with Cointreau, Jamaican rum and a twist of lime, or the house speciality, the *Stork Club Cooler* – gin, sugar, the juice of half an orange, shaken, strained and served with shaved ice. Other unique concoctions include the *Champagne Cocktail Gloria Swanson* – a pint of very dry champagne, Cognac and lemon peel; the *Alexander the Great* – vodka, crème de cacao, coffee liqueur and fresh cream, shaken together until ice cold; the *Snow White* – Southern Comfort, vodka and orange juice; or the *Millionaire Cocktail* – sloe gin, apricot brandy, Jamaican rum and a dash of grenadine.

At MIDNIGHT, female travellers should gather in the main dining room to participate in a Sunday night ritual. As the clock strikes twelve, masses of balloons will be released from the ceiling, New Year's Eve style, each one containing a RAFFLE TICKET. Only women guests are allowed to take part in this light-hearted scramble to grab a balloon and be part of the prize draw; you could win anything from a charm bracelet to a motor car (at least three of the balloons have a $100 bill inside).

At closing time, your limo will be waiting to drive you back to the Theresa for a well-earned rest.

MONDAY 16 FEBRUARY

Given the late hour you hit the sack, you may opt for a lie-in on Monday morning. However, if you are determined to cram in some sights, the familiar Manhattan landmarks await you: TIMES SQUARE, FIFTH AVENUE, CENTRAL PARK, etc. For lunch, we recommend the RAINBOW GRILL on the 65th floor of the ROCKEFELLER CENTER, with its stunning views of Midtown and the ice-skating rink down below. Opened in 1934, the Rainbow

Grill's menu contains mostly French dishes, prepared to a high standard, while more regulation American fare is available from the Cold Buffet and Hot Grill selections.

If you can't summon the energy to venture out of Harlem, then a great spot for lunch is WELL'S CHICKEN SHACK, serving moreish waffles and fried chicken. Plus it's a favourite hangout for musicians; you may be treated to a spontaneous solo set from the exquisite pianist TEDDY WILSON – Billie Holiday rose to prominence in his band – who likes *woodsheddin'* (practising) here in the afternoon.

Having eaten, take the time to explore 7th Avenue. You will see RADICAL SPEAKERS on street corners preaching revolution, real preachers preaching the Word of God, and all manner of folks going about their daily business. Of particular interest are the BLYDEN BOOKSTORE, run by Dr Willis Huggins, and the NATIONAL BOOKSTORE, owned by Lewis H. Michaux; both stock unrivalled selections of African-American literature, history and political thought.

CELEBRITY NIGHT AT MINTON'S

Having returned to the Theresa and changed into your jazzy evening wear, head over to the Cecil Hotel, with its dark-blue awning extending over the sidewalk. Go up to the first floor, where you will find MINTON'S itself. Walking in you will see a long bar to your left, its stools occupied by big-wig politicos, penniless dancers, wannabe gangsters, and anxious aspiring jazzers hoping to sit in during the jam and leave with their reputations intact. The barman, Herman Pritchard, dispenses beer at 25 cents a glass and fine sippin' whisky at 35 cents a pop. To your right is an extremely attractive coat-check girl, who will look after your coat and *lid* (hat). Passing through swing doors, you will enter the music room; on the left-hand side is the tiny bandstand about twelve inches off the ground, and an equally titchy dance floor in front of it. Behind another set of doors is the kitchen. Take a pew at one of the dozen tables, each one draped in a white tablecloth and displaying flowers in a little glass vase, and tuck into Minton's excellent home cookin': fried chicken, ham hocks, barbecued ribs, grits, black-eyed peas and hot biscuits.

Tonight is CELEBRITY NIGHT, sponsored by Bobby Schiffman, manager of the Apollo Theatre, which is closed Mondays. Minton's offers an open invitation to the bands booked in there, plus free drinks and munchies. This, and Minton's reputation as a happening place, guarantees their presence. By 10pm the room will be packed for the beginning of THE JAM. On stage already are KENNY CLARKE, the prodigal nineteen-year-old pianist BUD POWELL, who is *depping* for Monk (though Thelonious will probably sit in on a few numbers), and ebullient tenor man DON BYAS. Soon they will be joined by the likes of BIRD, DIZZY, BILLIE HOLIDAY,

THELONIOUS MONK, HOWARD MCGHEE, ROY ELDRIDGE AND TEDDY HILL OUTSIDE MINTON'S PLAYHOUSE.

COLEMAN HAWKINS, HOT LIPS PAGE, BEN WEBSTER, LESTER YOUNG, and many more. At some points there will be as many as fifteen musicians on the bandstand. Not that it's a place for the faint hearted. Any jammer who hasn't got their shit together won't survive long. The others will carve them up with high-velocity tempos, unusual chord patterns and esoteric key signatures.

Nevertheless, aside from the odd wounded apprentice, the atmosphere is collegiate, though when the temperature rises you'll see two titans of the tenor, LESTER YOUNG and BEN WEBSTER, locked in combat: barman Herman Pritchard compares their duels to dogs fighting in the road. But it's a communal, collective vibe that prevails as the musicians astound and dazzle the audience and each other with their takes on standards like *Body and Soul*, *I Got Rhythm*, *How High The Moon*, *April in Paris* and *Get Happy*. It's Dizzy who best sums up the mood: 'on Monday nights we had a ball'.

JAMMING AT MONROE'S

You may want to stay at Minton's until it closes at 4am, but a number of the younger players – Bird, Diz, et al. – will leave at around 2am to get to MONROE'S for when its jam begins. Be prepared for considerably less salubrious surroundings. The club is essentially a basement dive with a rudimentary bar, small kitchen and barely adequate stage. Yet it exudes an edgy, dark cool befitting its owner, CLARKE MONROE, a hustler who knows all the pushers and dopers, and fences stolen goods in his spare time – silverware, jewellery, furs and watches. He is here every night from midnight, digging the sounds and making deals. Handsome, charming, six-feet-tall, with light-brown skin, straightened hair, flashy suits, glossy shoes and women hanging offa him, Clarke will stand out.

What transforms his venue from a seedy fleapit into a place of magic is the music. Zinging with ideas after their workout at Minton's, BIRD and co will join the house band – AL TINNEY piano; RUSS 'POPEYE' GILLON trumpet; VICTOR COULSON tenor sax; EBENEZER PAUL bass; and the teenage MAX ROACH, who will go on to raise jazz drumming to a new level – for hours of experimentation. You will hear them stretch time, rhythm and harmony to the limit, take snatches of melody and fragments of riffs and run with them, speaking a language that will translate later into bonafide bebop tunes; every note hinting towards the future, every bar leading Jazz into the unknown.

Monroe's shuts its doors at 7am. Stumble out into the light of day, head singing, and go grab breakfast at SIMON JOUB'S RESTAURANT on 161st and Lenox, the epicentre of the growing Latino presence in Harlem. Not only can you get strong black coffee and yummy sweet and savoury Cuban *pastelitos* (pastries) – made from puff pastry and filled with either cream cheese, guava, pineapple and coconut, or ground beef in a tomato sauce with raisins and green olives – you will also be nodding your head and tapping your feet to some seriously infectious beats; the set of conga drums in the corner are always in use.

DEPARTURE

Once you've had your fill at Simon Joub's, make your way back to your room at the THERESA, from where you will DEPART.

The Beatles in Hamburg

EACH YEAR HALF A MILLION VISITORS from across the world – many not even born when the Fab Four were making records – make the pilgrimage to a nondescript zebra crossing next to Abbey Road studios in northwest London to recreate the band's celebrated 1969 album cover. But how much more fun to hang out with The Beatles themselves – and before they were famous. This trip offers the chance to follow the original Fab Five as they transform themselves from a teenage beat group into a successful working band during a series of engagements in Hamburg. This will lead them to the cusp of Beatlemania and enduring fame and fortune. To chart their progress, you will take THREE SEPARATE TRIPS, each in a different year – 1960, 1961 and 1962 – to see three different gigs at three different venues on three separate weekends.

The map shows the St Pauli District of Hamburg, with the following labels:

- LENNON DOORWAY
- PAUL - ROOSEN - STRASSE
- BAMBI KINO
- N
- FREIHEIT
- ST PAULI DISTRICT - HAMBURG
- INDRA CABARET
- SIMON - VON - UTRECHT - STRASSE
- GROSSE
- STAR CLUB
- SCHMUCKSTRASSE
- TOP TEN CLUB
- KAISER KELLER
- REEPERBAHN
- GRETEL & ALFONS HAROLD'S CAFE MOLLER'S

BRIEFING: ST PAULI

Each visit is designed to reflect the Beatles' own experience of Hamburg; the money in your pocket, the clothes on your back, the hours you keep, the places you hang out, will all be dictated by the Beatles' own habits and life-style at the time. This way, you will be able to chart the changes they went through en route to stardom.

You will spend the majority of your time in St Pauli, a tough working-class neighbourhood close to the docks and home to the notorious red-light district. Nowadays, the area is something of a tourist attraction. At the time of your visit, it is a quarter avoided by most Hamburg residents, due to its reputation for violence and crime. St Pauli's transient population of prostitutes, pimps and assorted low-life, its sex shops, strip clubs, bars and brothels, make it the favoured haunt of the Hamburg underworld, and attract tough guys of all shapes and sizes. Adding to this volatile mix is a constant stream of sailors and seamen looking for a good time while on shore leave. As a result, fights are constantly breaking out and murders are not uncommon. It is in this heated environment that The Beatles become The Beatles.

TRIP ONE

On Monday 8 August 1960, Bruno Koschmider, a squat, hard-nosed ex-circus performer and owner of the Kaiserkeller club in Hamburg, is in London trying to find a five-piece band to open his new club, the INDRA CABARET, in a week's time. Allan Williams, the Beatles' booking agent, convinces Bruno to hire them and they are contracted to play nightly from 17 August to 16 October, with Mondays off.

After a scramble to sort out their passports – none of them had ever left the country before – JOHN, PAUL, GEORGE, STUART SUTCLIFFE (Stu) and PETE BEST (who was reluctantly added at the last minute, making him the group's fourth drummer in 13 weeks), make the thirty-six-hour journey, Williams driving them in his Austin J4 minibus to save money. They travel down from Liverpool, through London (the boys' first glimpse of the capital), then on to Harwich for the night boat to the Hook of Holland, followed by a long haul across Germany, arriving in Hamburg just after midnight on Wednesday 17 August. That evening, they step out on the Indra stage for the first time.

FRIDAY 26 AUGUST 1960

You will arrive nine days later, at 5pm, in the darkened stalls of the BAMBIKINO, a pornographic movie theatre. It is around an hour into the afternoon feature. A few feet away from you, the Beatles will be just stirring from their slumbers in their tiny digs in the back room of the cinema, located beyond the screen with its own side entrance.

While you may be tempted to remain in your seats to catch the climax of the film, we suggest you slip out early and explore the area while it's still light, and less dangerous. However, before leaving the BambiKino, check out the toilets, as this may be your first chance to cast your eyes on the band. This is where they wash,

THE FAB FIVE IN THEIR LEATHERS, PHOTOGRAPHED BY ASTRID KIRCHHERR:
FROM LEFT, PETE BEST, GEORGE, JOHN, PAUL AND STU SUTCLIFFE.

shave and clean up before their night's work begins. Stepping out onto the street, you will find yourself directly opposite the INDRA club at Grosse Freiheit 64, with its crimson red frontage, Indian elephant signage and gated entrance adorned by a guitar and saxophone.

Male travellers will be DRESSED as the band: Teddy boy style, with quiffs, shades, lilac jackets, black shirts, black drainpipes, and crocodile shoes; women travellers will be wearing cream or polka-dot dresses with the skirt above the knee, bobby socks and flat shoes. You will each have 30 Deutschmarks SPENDING MONEY, the same amount as the band gets paid per night. This is a comparatively meagre sum, less than the wages of a manual labourer. Therefore, you will have to be economical, which may prove tricky, as there will be no shortage of people trying to con you out of your last *pfennig*. As the Beatles have no fixed abode, neither do you, but you don't need one, as you (like the band) will be pulling an all-nighter.

The Beatles spend most of their time on GROSSE FREIHEIT, and so will you. Note the contrast between the tall older buildings, some still bomb-damaged from the war, and the squat, almost shack-like ones hosting an array of bars, sex clubs and fast-food joints, patrolled by hulking employees 'barking' for your custom, and watched over by a hoarding of a giant bikini-clad lady, a fake Eiffel Tower on the horizon – the whole thing is reminiscent of a Wild West or Gold Rush town. As you walk the narrow cobbled street, you will see a substantial venue next to a strip joint, Studio X; this is the KAISERKELLER, where the band will have an ill-fated residency later in their stay.

Reaching the end of Grosse Freiheit, turn left onto the main drag, the REEPERBAHN (Ropemaker's Way). Somewhat glitzier, busier and a shade more cosmopolitan, this offers the same range of facilities but on a slighter grander and more expensive scale. Don't be fooled, though, it's still very rough and ready. Here neon rules the night, turning the whole strip into a flashing and blinking carnival of sex and debauchery.

Those keen to see more of St Pauli's seamy underbelly should turn off Reeperbahn into DAVIDSTRASSE, which leads to the docks, and take the third right into HERBERTSTRASSE, a dingy alleyway where prostitutes stand in windows offering their wares.

THE GIG

Aim to be back at the Indra by 8pm. The venue is tiny, with the small stage at the back of the room, a heavy, faded red curtain behind it, and tables gathered in front. The clientele are a mix of strippers, hookers, transvestites – drag acts are popular here and at many of the St Pauli clubs – some sailors and a scattering of 'rock kids', young local music fans who have summoned the courage to venture into Grosse Freiheit at night. You are best off taking a seat as close to them as possible. Chances of a brawl breaking out are fairly high, especially as the waiters, often ex-Nazi thugs with a grudge, are looking for any excuse to start one. According to George Harrison, 'all the waiters had tear gas guns, truncheons, knuckle-dusters'. As far as drinks go, bottled beer is the cheapest option; avoid the over-priced schnaps and ersatz champagne.

The Beatles will be doing four one-hour sets: 8.30–9.30pm, 10–11pm, 11.30pm–12.30am and 1–2am. Filling this amount of time will stretch the band's catalogue of covers to the limits; you will be treated to versions of the whole of their favourite albums by artists like Carl Perkins, Elvis and Gene Vincent, some Jazz Age standards like "Summertime", "Somewhere Over the Rainbow" and "Moonglow", classic hits by Chuck Berry and Fats Domino, current chart-toppers such as The Shadow's "Apache", and a fifteen-minute version of Ray Charles's R&B stonker "What'd I Say".

Their renditions will be often clumsy and incoherent, not helped by the constant flow of free drinks sent to them by appreciative punters, and the fact that Paul is on rhythm guitar, an instrument he is uncomfortable with, Stu is almost a beginner on bass, and Pete is a barely adequate drummer, unable to keep time properly. To try and help him hold onto a beat, the rest of the band will stomp their feet hard on the stage; Pete will respond by giving his bass drum a hefty kick – thomp, thomp – raising the noise level to such an extent that the old woman who lives above the Indra is forced to complain to the manager, Wilhelm 'Willi' Limpensal. Despite these flaws, it's hard not to be impressed by the boys' sheer energy and charisma, enough to send a shiver up your spine. Most startling will be their attitude, not dissimilar to early punk bands; you will see them spit, belch, curse and hurl abuse at the crowd. John is particularly fond of taunting them about Hitler.

At 9.45pm, you will hear an announcement come over the PA, and fifteen minutes later you will notice members of staff going round to check the IDs of anyone young-looking – it is against the law for anybody under the age of eighteen to be in a club after 10pm – and chucking out all the offending punters. Luckily, nobody seems to mind that George is only seventeen!

POST-GIG

After the Indra closes at 3am, you may well be in the mood to hit the Reeperbahn and check out other clubs like the BEER SHOP, MAMBO, WAGABOND and CHUGS. Don't: they all operate a system known as the *nep* – 'additional charges' added to your bill so that when it arrives it will be considerably larger than you expect and considerably more than you can afford. Failure to pay will result in a severe beating.

Instead, head over to HAROLD'S CAFÉ at 15 Grosse Freiheit, one of the Beatles' favoured post-show hangouts. There you can get cheap eats – burgers, fries, hot dogs – and bottled beer.

JOHN LENNON IN HAMBURG, 1960, ON HIS ROCK'N'ROLL ALBUM.
YOU'LL BE DEPARTING FROM THIS VERY DOORWAY.

Occupy one of the booths with plain wood tables and hopefully you will see the band come in and order their regular breakfast of cornflakes and milk, a choice that reflects their lack of cash and sophistication.

DEPARTURE

By 8am, the Beatles will be ready to stagger off to their make-shift beds at the BambiKino. This is your cue to leave. Walk along Grosse Freiheit to the corner of Paul-Roosen-Strasse. Turn into it and proceed to Wohiwillstrasse – second on the left. Carry on a few yards until you reach an alley way that leads into an OPEN COURTYARD flanked by tenement buildings. You will depart from here, the spot where a few weeks later John will have his photo taken standing nonchalantly in a doorway, an image that will later grace the cover of his 1975 *Rock'n'Roll* album, which features many of the tunes bashed out night after night in Hamburg.

TRIP TWO

The Beatles' stint at the Indra ends prematurely on 4 October 1960, due to the din they are making. Bruno Koschmider shifts them over to his Kaiserkeller, but there things go from bad to worse. Their already fraught relationship with Bruno descends into open conflict. Matters come to a head after George is deported when the authorities find out his true age, while Bruno has the rest of the band arrested for damaging the stage. By 10th December 1960, John, Paul and Pete have all been sent packing.

One bright spot during this period is their burgeoning friendship with two young Hamburgers: Klaus Voormann, an art-school graduate, and Astrid Kirchherr, a graduate in fashion and photography. At twenty-two, they are a touch older than the band and will open their eyes to different aspects of the city beyond St Pauli. Stu and Astrid quickly fall head over heels in love, getting engaged on 28th November and Stu remains in Hamburg, where he plans to continue his art studies.

Despite the debacle at the Kaiserkeller, the band had made an impression and are invited back to Hamburg to do a seven-night residency at the TOP TEN CLUB. On Tuesday 28 March 1961, John and George, travelling by train this time, set off from Liverpool Lime Street, arriving via the Harwich–Hook of Holland route at Hamburg's main station, Hauptbahnhof, at 3.16am on Thursday 30th, where they are met by Stu and Astrid. Two days later, Paul and (for want of a better alternative) Pete join them, and the band open at the Top Ten on Saturday 1 April. George will describe this residency as 'fantastic'.

SATURDAY 15 APRIL 1961

At 5pm on Saturday 15 April, you will arrive at the courtyard in Wohlwillstrasse with 35 Deutschmarks in your pocket, slightly more than last time. Men will be dressed to match the Beatles' latest HAMBURG LOOK – black leather jackets, black velvet shirts, black leather trousers, cowboy boots. Women will be wearing black leather jackets, black polo necks, black leather skirts, black tights and boots. All these items have been sourced for you from the uptown HAMBURGER LEDERMODEN, where the band saw the gear that inspired their new style (the store proved too expensive for them, so they engaged the services of a St Pauli tailor to reproduce its clothes at a fraction of the price).

Again you have no accommodation; you will spend another night on the tiles. This time it will be a good idea to fill your belly before the gig; it's never wise to take amphetamines on an empty stomach. Make your way to SCHMUCKSTRASSE, just off Grosse Freiheit, where transvestite hookers linger in doorways, and at number 9 you will find CHUG-RU, a cheap and cheerful Chinese restaurant where the Beatles often go to eat – they are very fond of the pancakes. Once you are done, head to the Top Ten Club at 136 Reeperbahn.

THE GIG

You will enter the TOP TEN CLUB, housed in an old, narrow-gabled building, with an extended lip over the entrance bearing large blue signage, at 7.30pm. Consisting of one large room, the raised stage is set alongside one wall, the sizable dance floor (*Tanzfläche*) directly in front of it, the bar to its right.

You may well encounter the owner, HORST FASCHER, a thirty-six-year-old former champion amateur boxer who did nine months in jail for killing a man in a St Pauli street fight, and you will certainly see his younger brothers, UWE and MANFRED, also boxers, whose job it is to shield the band from any unwarranted attention. On the whole, however, the Top Ten's clientele is a bit less seedy than at the Indra and there is a larger proportion of rock fans. Horst wants Top Ten to be all about the music and has had his manager, Peter Eckhorn, instal a state-of-the-art sound system and Binso echo microphones – which The Beatles love using.

The Beatles will be playing from 8pm until 4am, with fifteen minutes' break every hour. With Paul on piano, having gladly ditched his rhythm guitar, the band dynamics are better, though some stomping will still be required to keep Pete in line. You also might get to hear Paul on bass, as Stu, now enrolled at Hamburg Art School, is often absent. Belting out a similar setlist to the one they mined at the Indra, you will appreciate how much more together they are, their vocal harmonies smooth and sophisticated.

These improvements are partly due to the fact that they will be joined on stage by TONY SHERIDAN on electro-acoustic Martin guitar. Sheridan is a gifted musician whose promising career as a rock 'n' roller has stalled in the UK because of his chronic unreliability. A Hamburg veteran, he has worked most of the clubs with visiting artists and pick-up bands. The Beatles really dig him – they will go on to record with Sheridan while in Hamburg, their first ever studio sessions – and are forced to raise their level to match his.

THE BEATLES RAISE THEIR GAME, INSPIRED BY TONY SHERIDAN (FRONT
RIGHT), AT THE TOP TEN CLUB.

Another factor effecting the band's performance is SPEED – the
drug not the tempo, which they are all taking on a nightly basis,
along with pretty much everybody else in the club. Preludin (*prellies*) is the stimulant of choice. Licensed in Germany in 1954, it is
an appetite suppressant that is available on prescription from any
chemist. Aside from giving them the stamina to keep doing these
marathon sets night after night, it also adrenalises them onstage;
cranked up, buzzing hard, there is an unhinged wildness to the
show, a thrilling edge and danger to every note played.

We suggest you take some Preludin yourself. As a one-off experiment it should do you no harm and will put you in sync with the band and all the other night owls that inhabit the area. To get your hands on the pills, simply go downstairs to the Gents, where you will encounter Rosie Hoffmann, the sixty-two-year-old *toiletten frau* who sits at her small table with a bowl for tips and a big glass jar full of what look like mints but are actually *prellies*. Rosie, who is well-liked by the band, charges 50 pfennigs a pill. One or two will be quite sufficient for your requirements and will match the band's consumption – except for John, who will be necking a handful over the course of the evening.

At around 1pm you will see a group of well-dressed gangsters swagger into the club, take tables right near the stage and start lavishing drinks on the band. These are some of The Beatles' most dedicated fans: VIP criminals led by WILFRIED SCHULZ, king of the Hamburg underworld, dubbed 'Der Pati von St Pauli' (Godfather of St Pauli) by the press, and including hardened muscle like WALTHER SPRENGER, the proud owner of fifteen convictions for grievous bodily harm. Whatever you do, don't spill your drink on him! The hoods are so into the music that you will see them make requests and even get up onstage and sing along with some of the numbers.

POST-GIG

Around 4am you will be turfed out on the Reeperbahn. Ignoring the usual temptations, head over to GRETEL & ALFON'S BAR at 29 Grosse Freiheit. Its low ceilings, nautical themed decor and cosy fireplace make it feel like an Olde English pub, an impression enhanced by its white exterior, small windows, hanging baskets and modest signage. The Beatles feel especially at home here; the owner, Horst Janowiak, is letting them all crash in his apartment at 66 Grosse Freiheit. So get the drinks in and enjoy the convivial, intimate atmosphere as you enter the wee small hours.

DEPARTURE

Around nine on Sunday morning, the Beatles are in the habit of strolling over to the BRITISH MARINERS' MISSION at 20 Johannisbollwerk, just a few minutes walk away via St Pauli Hafenstrasse and adjoining the Gustav Adolf Church. This venerable establishment is open to UK sailors and seamen looking for somewhere to lay their heads – for 4 Deutschmarks per night, men only – and offers free fry-ups every morning. The familiar nosh, plus the British newspapers and authentically strong tea, is what attracts the band. Find yourself a table and tuck into a full English breakfast – liver, bacon, sausage, eggs, grilled tomatoes, mushrooms and toast/fried bread. After your heavy night, it will really hit the spot and take the edge off your comedown from the Preludin.

Meal finished, leave the Mission. Right next to is a railway bridge. Go stand in the tunnel underneath it, and you will depart from there.

TRIP THREE

The Beatles' career takes a huge step forward on Wednesday 24 January 1962, when BRIAN EPSTEIN signs on as their manager. Soon after, they make their first appearance on BBC Radio and start gigging at the Cavern Club in Liverpool. Meanwhile, they are head-hunted by MANFRED WEISSLEDER, who has made a fortune from his chain of St Pauli sex clubs and is planning to open a brand new rock venue in a converted cinema. Having outbid Peter Eckhorn, who wants the band back at the Top Ten, Weissleder secures The Beatles for a two week residency, starting 13 April.

This time the money is better and the band get to fly to Hamburg, but the whole trip is overshadowed by the sudden death of Stu from a brain aneurysm on 10 April, the very day the band land at Hamburg airport. This tragedy hits them all hard and turns their time at Weissleder's STAR CLUB into something of an emotional endurance test. John is most deeply affected and his anger and grief leads to onstage craziness. One night he comes on dressed as a cleaning lady, another stripped to the waist with a toilet seat around his neck.

Having survived this nightmare, the band's return to the UK sees them back on an upward curve. On 16 August, having finally fired Pete (Brian Epstein did the honours), Ringo takes on the drum duties. Ringo first met his future bandmates in Hamburg during their ill-fated stint at the Kaiserkeller in 1960 while he was playing with Rory Storm and the Hurricanes and their paths crisscrossed from then on, both in Liverpool and Hamburg. On 4 September they complete their first session for EMI, guided by George Martin's cultured ears. On the 22nd they appear on TV for the first time; on 5 October "Love Me Do" is released; by the end of the month it sits at number 27 in the *NME* charts. However, there is unfinished business in Germany. Epstein has booked them in at the Star Club again from the 1st to the 15th of November, even though the band, as John observed, had 'outlived the Hamburg stage and wanted to pack it in'.

SUNDAY 11 NOVEMBER 1962

You will arrive this time in the lobby of the HOTEL GERMANIA, an old building in decent condition with three floors and an attic on Detlev-Bremer-Strasse, about five minutes' walk from Grosse Freiheit. Your room is booked and paid for in advance. You will find it perfectly adequate with all the basic amenities. The Beatles are also staying here courtesy of Weissleder's cheque book.

Reflecting the band's new-found celebrity, you will have 73 Deutschmarks to burn, over double what you had on the first trip. And there's a new DRESS CODE. Men will be sporting dark blue mohair suits, white shirts and slim ties, sartorial choices dictated by Epstein's desire to make the band more appealing to a mainstream pop audience. Women will be wearing black sleeveless dresses with high necklines and ankle boots. As it is winter and below freezing at night, you will provided with coats; for the men, knee-length navy blue duffel coats; for women, dark grey trench coats.

Looking sharp, you will step out of the hotel and walk south towards Simon-Von-Utrecht-Strasse, which takes you onto Grosse Freiheit. The Star Club is at number 39, next door to an erotic film theatre, and instantly recognisable by the large hoarding covered with the names of the big acts who've played there, positioned over the darkened entrance, with the club logo in neon above.

THE GIG

Once inside the Star Club you will be struck by its size compared to the other venues you have visited: it has a 2,000 capacity and a huge dance floor – a site of exuberant, frenzied non-stop motion. The stage is standard, with a cityscape backdrop behind the bands. The crowd will be predominantly rock fans, interspersed with the usual suspects. The place will be packed and you may struggle to find a seat until 10pm, when the under-18s are all ejected.

Armed with your extra cash you will be able to afford to drink your fill without fear of retribution. Look out for one of the barmaids in particular – BETTINA DERLIEN. Known as Big Betty, she is a beautiful, buxom, curvaceous and outspoken character who is infatuated with John – an interest he is happy to repay.

The Beatles will be doing two hour-long sets, one before 10pm, and one late, and sharing the bill with other acts: TONY SHERIDAN; ROY YOUNG, a London born artist in the mould of Jerry Lee Lewis; DAVY JONES, a Manchester-born singer who will go on to star in America with The Monkees, the first ever manufactured boy band; and another Liverpool group, KING SIZE TAYLOR (the six-foot-five lead singer and guitarist) AND HIS DOMINOES.

When The Beatles hit the stage, you will immediately notice the difference that Ringo makes to the overall sound of the band

IT'S RINGO – AT LAST. THE FAB FOUR SHAKE IT ALL UP AT
THE STAR CLUB IN 1962.

by maintaining a rocksteady beat. Gone is the ragged quality of earlier performances. The band will be tight, slick and in command as they knock out the usual combination of rock'n'roll stonkers – "Twist and Shout", "Be-Bop-A-Lula", "Roll Over Beethoven" – selections from the Great American Songbook – "Red Sails Over the Sunset", "Falling in Love Again"; and novelty covers like Fats Waller's "Your Feet's Too Big".

The undoubted highlight of the night will be the headline act, none other than the already legendary LITTLE RICHARD and his backing band, SOUNDS INCORPORATED. Born in 1932, this flamboyant, hugely gifted pianist with deep roots in gospel, blues and R&B, author of such hits as "Tutti Frutti", "Long Tall Sally", "Lucille" and "Good Golly Miss Molly" – all staples of The Beatles' repertoire – is currently at a crossroads in his career as he contemplates abandoning secular music all together in favour of the church. However, this dilemma will not affect his performance and you will experience Little Richard at his outrageous best. Starting the show in a tuxedo, white shirt and bowtie, he will slowly strip off his clothes until he is down to just his trousers, which he will remove while standing on the piano to reveal a pair of bulging bathing trunks.

Every night, The Beatles will watch awestruck, learning at the feet of the master, while offstage Little Richard will offer them spiritual guidance. Another bonus for the band will be their friendship with the teenage prodigy BILLY PRESTON, keyboardist with Sounds Inc. Preston will go on to appear with The Beatles on tracks like "Get Back" during their last ever performance, filmed on the rooftops of Apple HQ on 30th January 1969.

DEPARTURE

After the gig, make your way to the junction of Grosse Freiheit and Reeperbahn, where you will find CAFÉ MOLLER. This one-storey, lemon-sherbet building, with a flat roof and a hoarding featuring a large chef in a white hat next to a waitress bearing multicoloured ice-cream cones, resembles an American diner. There are tables outside if you want to sit and watch the action on Reeperbahn or, if you'd rather not expose yourself to the cold, take a pew inside and order the Beatles' current breakfast of choice – ham and eggs. Moller's home-made cakes are also highly recommended.

By 8.30am, you should be back at the HOTEL GERMANIA. Given this is the first time you will have access to a bed, you will now have two hours to enjoy this luxury before DEPARTURE from your room.

The Rumble in the Jungle

29–30 OCT 1974 ✳ KINSHASA, ZAIRE

SPORT LENDS ITSELF TO HYPERBOLE, but this fight really was extraordinary. First, the setting: the Rumble in the Jungle took place in the heart of Africa, in a stadium built over a prison of medieval ghastliness in which 50 criminals had just been executed at random to discourage their associates from misbehaving while the eyes of the world were on their country. Then the timing: in an era of elevated black consciousness, the African setting was inspired, while the new technology of satellite television allowed Kinshasa to become the authentic centre of planetary attention, at least for an hour. Next, the cast of characters: the bout was promoted by a vertical-haired ex-numbers racketeer, financed by a dictator who knew no bounds, and featured boxers – Muhammad Ali and George Foreman – who were respectively arguably the most charismatic man alive and the Platonic embodiment of brooding menace.

Finally, there was the fight itself: it was David vs Goliath, Age vs Youth and Beauty vs Beast rolled into one, a bullfight in which the tables were turned on the matador. There was only one way

MOBUTU INTRODUCES FOREMAN AND ALI TO ZAIRE, ON THEIR
ARRIVAL IN KINSHASA.

to beat Foreman, and Ali found it. This was his apotheosis. Even
Foreman would ultimately be transformed by the magic of the
occasion. You don't often get to see a myth unfolding in real life,
but you will tonight.

BRIEFING: STAGING THE FIGHT

The organising genius behind the fight is Don King, a character whose manipulations Machiavelli might have found distasteful. A former illegal gambling magnate from Cleveland, Ohio, King saw the light, or at least the dollar signs, while serving a four-year stretch for beating a man to death (he owed King $600). He had a dream. It wasn't as nice as Martin Luther King's, but boy it was compelling. He would take over the world of boxing.

On leaving prison in 1971, King managed to entice Muhammad Ali to take part in an exhibition bout in

Cleveland to raise funds for a local hospital. Within three years, he was hatching plans for the most ambitious bout in the history of boxing. Using his sorcerer's tongue, he persuaded both Ali and Foreman to sign contracts to fight one another for the unprecedented sum of $5 million. Now all he needed was someone to put up the cash.

He found what he was looking for in the person of Joseph-Désiré Mobutu, or Mobutu Sese Seko Kuku Ngbendu Wa Za Banga, as the President of the vast central African Republic of Zaire restyled himself in 1972. The name translates as 'all-powerful warrior who, because of his endurance and inflexible will to win, goes from conquest to conquest leaving fire in his wake'. This has certainly been the experience of his political opponents. Ali probably wishes he had thought of the nickname first.

By systematically creaming off the wealth derived from Zaire's extraordinary natural resources, Mobutu has already become either the third- or the seventh-richest man in the world, depending on who you speak to. (His subjects are among the poorest, with an average annual income of around $70.) He can thus foot the bill for the fight with ease. And, as King has correctly calculated, staging it deeply appeals to his vanity. Mobutu is no mug, however, and is not about to let himself be outshone by Ali's charisma. Accordingly, he will watch the fight from the considerable comfort of his palace on closed-circuit television.

In future years, King will miraculously appear by the side of almost every new world champion, his grinning visage becoming as much a part of the post-fight ritual as the handing over of the title belt.

PLEASE NOTE: The fight was originally scheduled for 25 September but has had to be pushed back five weeks due to Foreman sustaining a cut to his eye in training. This scuppered plans for the bout to coincide with the ZAIRE 74 MUSIC FESTIVAL, which took place from September 22–24 at the Stade du 20 Mai. It featured James Brown, BB King, Bill Withers and The Spinners, as well as African artists including Miriam Makeba, Tabu Ley Rochereau and Franco's TPOK Jazz, and will soon be available as an additional journey for our travellers.

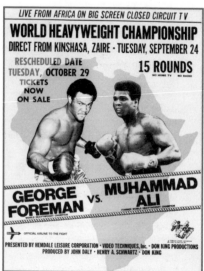

LIVE FROM AFRICA ON BIG SCREEN CLOSED CIRCUIT TV

WORLD HEAVYWEIGHT CHAMPIONSHIP

DIRECT FROM KINSHASA, ZAIRE · TUESDAY, SEPTEMBER 24

RESCHEDULED DATE
TUESDAY, **OCTOBER 29**

15 ROUNDS
NO HOME TV NO RADIO

TICKETS NOW ON SALE

GEORGE FOREMAN VS. **MUHAMMAD ALI**

OFFICIAL AIRLINE TO THE FIGHT

PRESENTED BY HEMDALE LEISURE CORPORATION · VIDEO TECHNIQUES, INC. · DON KING PRODUCTIONS
PRODUCED BY JOHN DALY · HENRY A. SCHWARTZ · DON KING

THE TRIP

On the morning of 29 October 1974 you will arrive at the GARE CENTRAL on Kinshasa's PLACE DE L'INDÉPENDENCE. It is less than fifteen years since the Belgian colonists packed their bags: Leopoldville has turned into Kinshasa, and in a short period of relative stability it has grown into a thriving and lushly green capital city, its colonial squares flanked by new hotels, highrises and the trappings of modern urbanism. You should have no difficulty getting a taxi here.

WEATHER, ROOMS AND FOOD

The WEATHER will be hot and humid, in the mid-90s F during the day and dropping no lower than 80°F in the middle of the night. The night of the fight itself will be beautiful, clear and lit by a full moon, but bear in mind that just half an hour after the contest finishes there will be a prodigious rainstorm.

Local CURRENCY is the ZAIRE, and the official exchange rate is currently half a zaire to the dollar. You will be able do better on the black market. This would be unwise for regular travellers, who on leaving the country have to prove exactly where they have changed money, but as you will be departing in a time machine this shouldn't be a problem. Regular tickets for the fight are going at 5 zaires ($10) a shot, though many locals will find a way to get in for less.

You'll be lucky if you manage to get to bed as early as 7am on the night of the fight (which *begins* at 4am local time), but you'll certainly be looking forward to some sleep thereafter. We can offer rooms at the INTERCONTINENTAL on Ave Batetela where Foreman and his entourage are staying, as well as the American novelist Norman Mailer. Alternatively, the HOTEL MEMLING, 5 Avenue Rep du Tchad, is a grand old pile recently refurbished by Belgian airline Sabena. And, close to the airport, the airline has a SABENA GUEST HOUSE, which provides rooms and

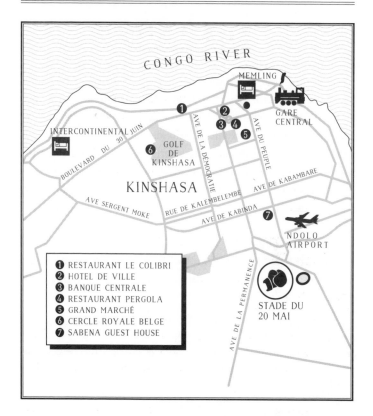

delightful cottages in its immaculately kept grounds.

For top-end EATING, try the PERGOLA restaurant opposite the BCC (Banque Centrale du Congo) building. Similarly priced is the CERCLE ROYALE BELGE, situated by Kinshasa's golf course (entrance on Avenue du Cercle). Another good choice is LE COLIBRI, a French-stye bistro at 61 Avenue Lusaka, founded in the 1950s, whose speciality is *Le Toast Cannibale* – a take on steak tartare.

OH KINSHASA!

Boxing aside, KINSHASA offers travellers plenty of other diversions. Most SHOPPING needs can be met at the fabulous Art Deco SEDEC BUILDING (Boulevard de 30 Juin), previously a motor showroom and now the city's first self-service grocery store. For African crafts, head for the MARCHÉ DES VOLEURS, where you will find plenty of malachite and ivory trinkets and Kasai carpets; but do remember our clients are not allowed to bring souvenirs home.

A vibrant post-independence THEATRE scene is developing on the Kasa-Vubu Road, but Kinshasa's strong suit is MUSIC, DANCE AND NIGHTLIFE. In fact, you have arrived in the midst of a golden era and are likely to find superb sounds in almost neighbourhood bar. Among the leading bands of the time playing Kinshasa, look out for ZAÏKO LANGA LANGA, FRÈRES SOKI & L'ORCHESTRE BELLA BELLA, EMPIRE BAKUBA and, above all, FRANCO & L'ORCHESTRE TPOK JAZZ . You are likely to hear one of these at the SCOTCH CLUB, LE BODEGA (though do bear in mind this is also a house of ill repute) or the landmark LA PERRUCHE BLEU. The HOTEL OKAPI on a hilltop in the Binza Ozone district (west of the old city) has a great dance floor but tends to be very expat heavy.

For a taste of Kinshasa high society, be sure to take in LA DEVINIÈRE in Binza, opposite the presidential Palais de Marbles. Behind its outer walls you will find a delightful garden, fine French cuisine and leading figures in the government and the Lebanese business community.

THE FIGHT

THE FIGHT will take place at 4am local time in the STADE DU 20 MAI in the Quartier Matonge, about half a mile from Ndolo Airport. Despite the weird hour (to fit with US TV schedules), around 60,000 locals – and a rather poor showing of VIPs – will be attending. The ring sits in the centre of football pitch, a canopy of corrugated erected over it and the VIP area. An enormous poster of Mobutu in trademark leopard-skin hat sits behind one the goals. Most of the locals will be pitching up several hours before the fight between 10 and 11 pm. If you choose to join them, you will be treated to several displays of TRIBAL DANCING.

Take a look at the people in the RINGSIDE SEATS. Alongside many members of Mobutu's entourage, there will be a smattering of American celebrities. Ex-heavyweight champion JOE FRAZIER can be seen in a very groovy green and yellow Hawaiian shirt under a maroon sports jacket. Also present are American literary luminaries NORMAN MAILER, GEORGE PLIMPTON and HUNTER S. THOMPSON. Seats have been reserved for our clients at the back of the VIP zone on the side opposite Mobutu's portrait.

GEORGE FOREMAN

The 1974 version of GEORGE FOREMAN is light years from the cuddly bald electric grill tycoon of the future. The twenty-five-year-old World Heavyweight Champion is a snarling fighter with a distinct aura of menace. He has got off to a bad start with the people of Zaire by pitching up with his pet German Shepherd, a breed indelibly associated with the police force of their Belgian former overlords. He will go into the fight with almost the entire nation rooting for his opponent. But he doesn't seem particularly troubled by this.

As economical with words as Ali is profligate with them, Foreman conserves his energy to maximise his menace. Raised in Houston, Texas, he was by his own admission a teenage hoodlum of the kind you would most definitely not want to meet on a dark night, before finding salvation of a kind in boxing. He stormed his way to Olympic Gold in 1968. Since then he has won all forty of his professional fights, thirty-seven of them by way of a knockout. Two of his recent victims have been JOE FRAZIER and KEN NORTON, both of whom have beaten Ali since his comeback (though Ali has subsequently levelled the scores). Foreman demolished both of them within two rounds, knocking Frazier to the canvas six times.

Foreman is considered one of the hardest punchers in history, as a glance at the heavy bag he uses in training graphically confirms. After each session, it has an indentation several inches deep. If Ali allows Foreman to corner him, his body

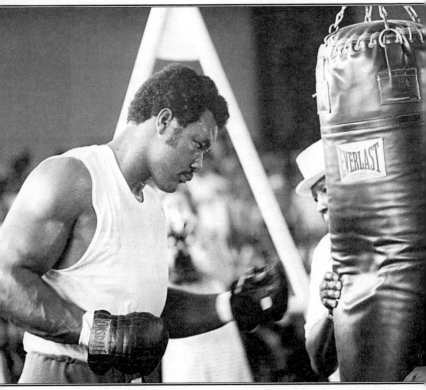

FOREMAN IN TRAINING. HE PLANS TO DO SOMETHING SIMILAR TO ALI
WITH ONE OF HIS 'HAYMAKER' PUNCHES.

will become that bag. At as least as frightening as the power
of the Champion's blows is the relish with which he delivers
them. Archie Moore, the wily ex-Light Heavyweight Champion
who is co-training Foreman for the fight, is seriously worried he
might kill Ali if the latter doesn't do the sensible thing and let
himself get knocked out quickly.

During the unforeseen delay, Foreman has holed up in the
Inter-Continental Hotel in downtown Kinshasa. His daily workout takes him and his crew on a six-mile run along the banks of
the Congo river, just north of the hotel.

MUHAMMAD ALI

Where do you begin with MUHAMMAD ALI? Born Cassius Marcellus Clay in Kentucky in 1942, the 'Louisville Lip' was one of the most controversial figures of the 1960s and remains a profoundly divisive character going into this fight. He 'shook up the world', in his words, by winning the World Heavyweight boxing crown at the age of twenty-two with a stunning display against the terrifying Sonny Liston. He hasn't stopped shaking it since.

Shortly after capturing the crown, Ali became a Muslim, changed his name and joined Malcom X in the Nation of Islam, further alienating the wide section of white America that was already none too fond of this boastful nonconformist. After three years and nine dazzling title defences, the establishment got its opportunity for revenge when Ali refused to be inducted into the US Army to fight in Vietnam ('No Vietcong ever called me nigger'). His boxing licence was revoked and he was not allowed near a ring for the three and a half years that would, under normal circumstances, have coincided with the peak of his boxing prowess. There are those who will never forgive Ali for refusing to fight for his country, but the wheel of history has turned and his anti-Vietnam stance is now much more in tune with the times.

Ali fights like no other heavyweight boxer. He has the speed of a lightweight schooled in the Shaolin monastery, and can throw a bewildering six jabs per second. He defies convention by holding his hands low, aiming his punches almost exclusively at his opponents' heads, and leaning out of the way of shots aimed at his own, rather than attempting to block them with his arms. As a child, he used to ask his brother to throw rocks at him to sharpen his reflexes, and it shows.

Ali doesn't act like other fighters, either. A promoter's dream, he is an inspired self-publicist who composes poems ridiculing his opponents, predicts the round he will knock them out and does anything in his considerable power to upset their composure both before and during his fights. Humility is not his middle name – he has been describing himself as 'THE GREATEST' for a decade – and his breathtaking self-confidence tends to be self-fulfilling, as well as highly entertaining. But there are many who are itching to see him get his comeuppance.

Ali's performances since his comeback in 1970 have been a mixed bag. Though retaining unfeasible hand speed – he still STINGS LIKE A BEE – the lay-off and his advancing years seem to have compromised his ability to FLOAT LIKE A BUTTERFLY, dancing round the ring and evading his opponents at will. Ali can still undeniably talk the talk, but can he walk the walk? We are about to find out. Ali has based himself in a villa in NSELE, near one of Mobutu's palaces on the eastern side of the city. The gym where both fighters have been training is also located here.

THE TALE OF THE TAPE

The size difference between the two fighters is distorted by their auras and reputations. They are the same HEIGHT (6'3") and, while Ali has a slightly longer REACH, at the weigh-in Foreman is the heavier in WEIGHT (though by a mere 3.5 lbs). You are prohibited from betting because you know the result, but the most widely quoted ODDS on an Ali victory are 3–1 against.

	MUHAMMAD ALI	GEORGE FOREMAN
AGE	32	25
WINS	44	40
KNOCKOUTS	31	37
LOSSES	2	0
HEIGHT	6'3"	6'3"
WEIGHT	216.5 lb (98.2kg)	220 lb (99.8kg)
REACH	80"	78.5"

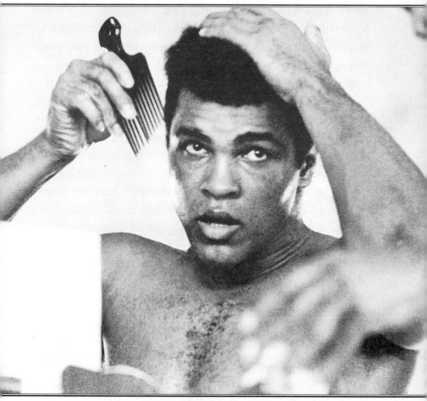

'I AM THE PRETTIEST OF ALL TIME.' ALI PREPARES FOR THE FIGHT.

THE BUILD-UP

ALI is the first to emerge from the dressing room, preceded by an American flag and wearing a white dressing gown with stripy African trim. The huge moustachioed man towards the front of his entourage is his younger brother RAHMAN. The other key figures are his trainer ANGELO DUNDEE, his doctor/cornerman FERDIE PACHECO and his best friend and cheerleader DREW 'BUNDINI' BROWN, who sports a natty silk jacket with Ali's name emblazoned on the back. FOREMAN will keep Ali waiting so long – about seven minutes - that his eventual appearance in a crimson red gown is greeted with sporadic boos. Ali won't appear unsettled by the delay. He takes the opportunity to conduct the crowd's chanting of the phrase 'Ali boma ye!' ('Ali, kill him!'). Foreman will be attended by his manager DICK SADLER and his trainer ARCHIE MOORE.

A rather jerky, tuneless rendition of the STAR-SPANGLED BANNER with a touch of New Orleans jazz funeral about it begins the ceremonies. Then the crowd will sing along to ZAIREAN NATIONAL ANTHEM. A lengthy pause follows during which gloves are put on the fighters in the ring (their hands were strapped under supervision back in their dressing rooms). Finally referee ZACK CLAYTON will call the boxers to the centre of the ring. In the pre-fight huddle, Ali counters Foreman's death-stare with constant chatter. You won't be able to hear the words but his flashing white gumshield leaves no doubt that they are tumbling out.

As the fighters go to their corners, Ali dances, breaking off briefly to pray to Allah. Foreman will perform some highly intimidating shoulder stretches, grasping the top rope on either side of his padded corner post and sending the whole structure quivering. The message is clear: 'I own this ring.'

ROUND 1

Ali will come out on the offensive, dancing like he did in the mid-1960s. Significantly, he will land the first punch. Indeed, he will land most of the punches – stinging, cat-like jabs invariably aimed at his opponent's head.

It will quickly become apparent that Ali is adopting the first of two high-risk strategies he will employ during the fight. This is LEADING WITH HIS RIGHT HAND, despite his conventional, left-foot-forward stance. His punches thus have further to travel, giving Foreman fractionally more time to respond. Other things being equal, this would seem a suicidal tactic. But other things are not equal. Ali has the hand speed of a karate master and George is hard-wired to expect him to lead with his left.

One minute in you will see Ali pull Foreman's head downward and whisper in his ear. He will do this throughout the fight. But Foreman will advance relentlessly, attempting to corner Ali and cut him off from the relative safety of the open ring. Every time he manages this, he will unleash fearsome hooks to the body. You will be unable to help but fear for Ali's safety. But even while Foreman is pummelling his torso, Ali will be landing sharp blows on the Texan's head.

ROUND 2

The pace will drop somewhat after the frenetic opening round. Ali will now reach for the second counterintuitive tool in his locker: retreating to the ropes and inviting Foreman to hit his body at will. The unspoken deal is that he is not allowed to hit his head. Ali will enforce this with intense watchfulness, holding his gloves in front of his face in an almost airtight guard, and using the elasticity of the ropes to lean out of the way of any head punches that do get through. Ali's tactic of LYING ON THE ROPES and encouraging Foreman to hit him goads the champion into huge, curving body punches, leaving a channel in the middle, which Ali will use to pick him off with head shots almost at will. Ten seconds before the end of the round, Ali will shake his head, pantomime style, to indicate that Foreman's punches are not hurting him.

Do look out for the vigorous disagreement conducted at ringside between JOE FRAZIER, who reckons Ali will get slaughtered if he retreats to the ropes, and the American football star JIM BROWN, who will argue that he is the one landing the best shots despite being on the ropes.

ROUND 3

One minute in, Ali will show incredible hand-speed, landing a sequence of COMBINATION PUNCHES. Then Foreman will launch a scary flurry of BODY SHOTS. Two minutes in, Foreman will lands his best punch yet on the left side of Ali's jaw. But by the end of the round, Foreman will be feeling in front of himself with his fists with the tentativeness of a person stumbling in the dark. After the bell rings, watch Ali glare at Foreman as the two fighters separate. 'I will not be cowed by you,' his wide-eyed stare will say.

ROUND 4

The genius of Ali's 'ROPE-A-DOPE' tactics will become ever more apparent. You will see him make no effort to avoid what has been the focus of Foreman's training – cutting him off from the ring. Instead he will yield to his opponent's intention. This will allow him to focus all his energy on throwing his own punches and absorbing Foreman's, rather than evasion. This is pure judo. When a shot does get through, much of its energy is transmitted to the ropes. Ali is tearing up the rule book, making what should be his enemy into his best friend. Throughout the round, listen out for Ali taunting Foreman: 'Is that all you got?'

ROUND 5

This will be an EPIC ROUND, the best of the fight. From 30 to 120 seconds in, Ali will stay in more or less the same position on the ropes while Foreman gives him everything he's got. But, in Norman Mailer's memorable metaphor, Ali will lurch out of the way and back in with counter punches 'with all the calm of a man swinging in the rigging'. Foreman won't be hurting him, just exhausting himself. Between the 5th and 6th rounds, attempts will be made to tighten the ropes, to prevent Ali from leaning back. You will notice his trainer, Angelo Dundee, screaming at the ring technicians to desist.

ROUND 6

A SLOWER ROUND, in which Ali will appear to be assessing Foreman's remaining strength, like a chef testing a sauce. He will deliver a series of unanswered left jabs towards the end of the second minute.

ROUND 7

 This will be the QUIETEST ROUND of the fight. There is something zombie-like about Foreman's constant, unthinking forward motion. He looks like he is sleepwalking. Ali is just biding his time.

ROUND 8

 Ali will start the round SCORING AT WILL. Then, after 25 seconds, Foreman will throw a huge, missing haymaker – the

ALI THROWS THE BIG ONE. CUE GLOBAL PANDEMONIUM.

momentum of which almost carries him out of the ring. Halfway through the round, Ali will make his way to the opposite corner of the ring and stay there, dodging or absorbing Foreman's now perfunctory punches. With fifteen seconds to go, Foreman will throw, miss and lean over the ropes. Ali's eyes will suddenly light up. He will launch a devastating MULTI-PUNCH COMBINATION, culminating in a straight right to the face, which will send Foreman wheeling to the canvas like a broken helicopter. Absolute pandemonium breaks out in the ring. DAVID FROST, commentating at the ringside, will squeak: 'This is the most joyous scene ever in the history of boxing.'

THE AFTERMATH – AND DEPARTURE

After his victory, Ali will collapse briefly, but you probably won't see this, as he will be surrounded by leaping and rejoicing members of his corner, as well as fans and hangers on. You may also notice DON KING floating towards Ali seemingly without moving his feet. Eventually several white-helmeted Zairean policemen will pile into the ring as well, not least to avoid missing out on the moment.

Kinshasa will be partying and celebrating long into the night and the next day. Feel free to join in, but do bear in mind that your DEPARTURE is scheduled for midnight today back at La Gare Central.

PART FOUR

EPIC JOURNEYS & VOYAGES

In Xanadu with Marco Polo

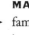 **MARCO POLO IS PROBABLY THE MOST** famous traveller who ever lived. His name is a global brand, fronting everything from cruise ships to clothing. But to what exactly does he owe his fame? His journey was not that arduous or hair-raising, by true explorer standards, and nor was he even the first European to make the trip to the Far East. In fact, what earned him his place in posterity is the seventeen years he spent in Mongol-ruled China and at the court of Kublai Khan – the legendary Xanadu.

This trip concentrates on Polo's first six months in the great Khan's orbit, during which time you will initially stay in Xanadu (*Shangu*), the wondrous city built by Kublai as his summer residence. Polo's descriptions of this oasis of tranquillity echoed down the ages and was the inspiration for Coleridge's celebrated opium-induced dreamscape. Today, nothing at all remains of Xanadu, but you will see the city at its shimmering best.

From Xanadu, you will accompany Polo and Kublai's court on its imperial progression south to the Khan's new capital, Beijing (*Dadu*), which he has completely rebuilt, making good on the destruction wrought by his grandfather Genghis Khan. Having settled on a name for the city after consulting the *I-Ching*, he has redesigned it and constructed a stunning array of palaces and parks.

Here, at the centre of the largest land empire in history – encompassing Russia, Persia, Central Asia and China – you will be immersed in the polyglot mass of humanity drawn to Beijing. You will witness the elaborate rituals of the court, revel in a wide variety of entertainments and participate in the two most extravagant ceremonies in the Imperial calendar: KUBLAI'S BIRTHDAY and MONGOLIAN NEW YEAR, a massive and magnificent banquet of great symbolic and cultural significance.

BRIEFING: KHAN AND THE POLOS

Having outmanoeuvred his rivals, Kublai was proclaimed the Great Khan of the Mongol Empire in 1260. Though his realm technically included the western swathes of Mongol territory, his focus would be on China and its immediate neighbours. He added Tibet, Korea and Yunnan to his portfolio, then turned his attention to the unfinished business of conquering the whole of China; Genghis had brought the northern half, ruled by the Jin dynasty, under his control, but the heavily populated and prosperous southern regions, home of the Song dynasty, remained independent. A long campaign, involving hundreds of ships, thousands of men and some of the most sophisticated siege weaponry ever built, eventually ended the Song's resistance.

Word of Kublai's deeds filtered its way along the Silk Road trade routes back to Europe. Keen to discover more, Marco Polo's father, Niccolo, and uncle, Maffeo, who had been wandering the Caucasus in search of business opportunities, made their way slowly to China.

As luck would have it, Kublai was looking to develop a Christian presence in China – his mother was a Nestorian – alongside the Taoists, Buddhists and Muslims that competed for his attention. Kublai understood that if he favoured one faith above the others he was inviting trouble: the followers of those given secondary status might plot against him, while the devotees of the primary religion might prove strong enough to act as an alternative source of power. Consequently, keen to add another church into the mix, he welcomed the Venetian travellers with open arms.

Having enjoyed Kublai's hospitality, Polo's father and uncle were dispatched homewards with a mission: to return as soon as possible with 100 high-ranking emissaries of the Pope and to bring valued Christian relics. When they finally got back to Venice after their extended round trip, Polo was only fifteen years old, but ready and eager to join them. Two years later, in September 1271, the group set off with a letter from the Pope and some holy oil from the sepulchre of Christ, purloined by the Venetians during a stopover in Jerusalem.

The journey to China took the party around three years. Their start had been delayed by papal politics, and their journey involved lengthy diversions across brutal deserts and snow-covered mountains to avoid

MARCO POLO IN TARTAR COSTUME.

hostile locals. But in 1275 they reached the borders of Kublai's territory, and from then on it was plain sailing. Kublai had the party accompanied by a large Mongol contingent and furnished them with a gold *piazi* – a travel pass that ensured they completed the journey unmolested, arriving at the Emperor's court in the summer of 1275.

THE TRIP

YOU WILL MEET UP WITH THE POLOS at one of the many relay stations (*yamb*) that appear at regular intervals across the Khan's territory and act as both crucial nodes in his communications infrastructure and as refuelling stations. Your *yamb* is at XUANHA, a few days travel from Xanadu, located on a level basin between mountains, and with well-appointed, comfortable lodgings. Here you will take on supplies and around 300 fresh horses, mostly for the military escort that will now accompany you on this first leg of your journey.

It is at Xuanha that you will become part of the Polo entourage, and you will go on to play a range of supporting roles over the course of the trip. Expect some light menial duties and a certain amount of bowing and scraping. Nevertheless, you will share the exclusive access of the Polos to Kublai's court; this privilege will surely outweigh any unpleasantness you may encounter as a domestic helper.

A the same time, both in Xanadu and Beijing, you will be able to merge seamlessly into the small army of staff and attendants needed to keeps the wheels of Empire turning – cooks, artisans working in gold, silver, porcelain and textiles, servants, managers, entertainment specialists, historians, translators, interpreters, astronomers, doctors, librarians, shrine-keepers, musicians, architects – and lose yourself amongst them, giving you the freedom to wander and explore as you choose.

During the summer months you will wear pyjama-like CLOTHING; for the winter, you will be supplied with coats made of sheepskin, furs and animal pelts, thick boots and the ubiquitous Mongol furry hats. You will also be provided with enough cash to cover your expenses for the duration of the trip. Kublai is very keen on PAPER MONEY, which has been in circulation in China for several hundred years, and has introduced three new notes – two backed by silver, one by silk. These currencies are made from paper that comes from the beaten inner bark of mulberry trees, and is printed using carved wooden blocks. With a wad of these notes, you will have plenty in the way of spending money.

XANADU (SHANGU)

You will approach the city of XANADU through open grasslands, passing a series of hills marked with shrines of sacred stones (*obo*). Notice the steady build-up of traffic – mostly carts pulled by bullocks or yaks – on the many tracks converging towards it. Up to 500 vehicles a day travel this route in order to supply Xanadu's 120,000 citizens.

You will be sticking to the main thoroughfare, the ROYAL ROAD, from which you will marvel at the thousands of pure white horses, the most prized animals that Kublai possesses, ranging over the plain, and a similar number of musk deer, much coveted for their distinctive perfume. Your route then takes you into the OUTER CITY, with its dense conglomeration of simple mud-brick houses, traders and thousands of cooking stalls wafting tantalising aromas.

Passing on, you reach Xanadu proper. The site for the city was chosen by Kublai's foremost town planner, Liu Bingzhong, and members of his Golden Lotus Advisory Group. As the area was previously known as the Dragon's Ridge (*Lung Gang*), spells were cast to evict said dragon and a magical iron pennant was raised to prevent its return.

Xanadu divides into three sections, all squares, with a twenty-five-foot-high outer wall, marked by bastions, towers and large gates, that stretches for more than a mile on each side. Above the walls, you will glimpse a mass of roofs with blue, green and red tiles glinting in the sun. Once inside your senses will be assaulted by another mass of street traders peddling their wares amongst densely packed dwellings. Be careful where you tread. The very poorest live in pits dug in the ground with planks and dry grass for roofs. Step too heavy and you might find yourself in somebody's living room!

Making your way across the city, check out the WEST GATE MARKET, which does a brisk trade in horses, sheep, cows and even slaves. Another attraction worth visiting is the NORTH YARD, a kind of zoo featuring pumas, lions, eagles and other rare animals.

Your focus, however, will be on the inner square walled section of Xanadu that contains the IMPERIAL CITY. You will reach it via the South Gate, or GATE OF SPLENDOUR. After crossing a moat, you will walk along a road lined with houses for about half a mile to a second wall and a second gate that opens into an area of the Imperial City, laid out in grids that includes sub-palaces for Kublai's family and staff, temples, government buildings and the houses of officials.

Finally, once you are over another moat, you will be inside the last and most important square: the PALACE CITY, with its series of splendid tented pavilions, their names testament to their imposing stature and beguiling aura – CRYSTAL, AUSPICIOUSNESS, WISDOM, CHARITY, FRAGRANCE and CONTROLLING HEAVEN. Then take a deep breath as rising before you is the ROYAL PALACE, a two-storey building on a 350-foot-high brick-faced platform, much of it made from white marble especially imported by Kublai.

As befits the ruler of most of the known world, Kublai tends to keep his visitors waiting, and you and the Polos will have to linger a while for your first audience and your first glimpse inside his Imperial Palace. Having changed into the special footwear, beautiful slippers of white leather that all visitors are required to wear, you'll be escorted into a labyrinth of over 120 rooms – two wings, a central courtyard and its grand Pavilion of Great Peace – which the poet Zhou Boqi describes as 'rafter upon rafter, the storied pavilion reaches the azure sky, a picture painted in gold floating atop seven precious pillars'.

You will then follow the Polos into Kublai's chamber and lay your eyes on the Great Khan – who is short, stocky and shows signs of the gout that will plague his later years. He will be dressed in glorious robes of gold laced with intricate patterns, his black-eyed gaze scrutinising your every move.

You and the Polos should prostrate yourselves before his majesty, worried that the failure to bring along a bevy of Papal officials will anger him. Fear not. Kublai is delighted to see the Polo family and welcomes them and, by association, you, into the bosom of his court.

LIFE IN XANADU

You will be staying in a GER (or yurt), the traditional Mongolian habitat, on a camp site for VIPs and merchants near the East Gate. Your *ger* has a wooden circular frame, covered in felt made from sheep's wool, with a frame of expanding lattice wall sections. The interior will also be lined with felt and decorated with patterns that represent savage beasts, the five elements (fire, earth, water, metal and wood), plus geometric patterns such as the continuous hammer (*alkhan kee*).

Considering the nomadic lifestyle of the Mongols, it'll come as no surprise that their toilet arrangements are pretty rudimentary: expect to find yourself squatting above a stinking hole in the ground.

But, on the bright side, toilet paper is available – the Chinese have been using it for six hundred years. Note that these open latrines are thought to harbour ghosts. To combat the presence of malicious spirits, the Ruler of Heaven (China's main deity) blessed these latrines with their very own god, the Purple Maiden. Legend has it that a first wife, jealous of her husband's second wife, murdered her rival by shoving her into a communal shit pit. The Ruler of Heaven then took pity on her poor befouled soul and made her divine.

Toilet issues aside, the time spent in your *ger* will allow you to appreciate the alfresco simplicity and back-to-nature vitality of the

Mongol way of life. With warm weather and long hours of daylight, it will be a refreshing pleasure to stay under canvas, dining out every night under the panoramic, star-speckled sky.

EATING AND DRINKING

Though most of the city's population is Chinese, Kublai is determined that Mongolian culture will predominate at Xanadu. The life-blood of their diet is the mildly alcoholic drink *airag*, derived from MARE'S MILK which has been poured into a huge sack and churned with a club before turning sour and fermenting, and then churned continually until butter can be extracted from it. You better get a taste for it quickly, as it will be offered to you constantly. The mare's milk is also boiled to get clotted cream (*orom*), with the remains processed into cheese (*byaslag*). This emphasis on dairy produce may present a challenge for those with a lactose intolerance.

As for other foods, the Mongol's most popular delicacies include steamed or boiled minced meat DUMPLINGS (*buuz*) and MUTTON cooked over hot stones. Broths are also common fare, su ch as BORBI SOUP, concocted by reducing thirty or so sheep bones in a bucket of water.

There will be more sophisticated dishes on offer that combine ingredients and culinary techniques from other parts of Kublai's realm such as RUSSIAN OLIVE SOUP, consisting of one leg of mutton, five cardamom seeds, and shelled chick peas, which are boiled and strained before Russian olives, sliced sheep thorax, Chinese cabbage or nettle leaf are added to the mix.

Another option is butter skin YUGBA that uses a fine cut of mutton, sheep's fat, sheep's tail, mandarin orange peel, sprouting ginger, salt, sauce and spices, while the skins are from a blend of vegetable oil, rice flour and wheat flour. You will also come across NOODLE DISHES with mutton, egg, ginger, sheep intestines and mushrooms in a broth seasoned with pepper, salt and vinegar.

VEGETARIANS may find Mongol fare a struggle. Your best bet is to stick to noodle dishes, with the meat extracted, or rice dishes that use curds or raisins for flavour. Vegans may prefer to stay at home.

HUNTING

One of the highlights of your time in Xanadu will be the opportunity to enjoy Kublai's private GRASSLAND PARK, just to the north-west of the city. While its fountains, brooks, immaculate lawns and hidden groves summon up visions of paradise, the real purpose of the park is HUNTING, the defining activity of Mongolian

KUBLAI KHAN HUNTING WITH A GYRO-FALCON – A MINIATURE FROM THE
FIFTEENTH-CENTURY LIVRE DES MERVEILLES DU MONDE.

culture. Kublai's park is well stocked with deer, hares, rabbits and
birds. Much of the hunting is done on horseback using bows and
arrows; this is a tricky art and will be impossible to master without
some equestrian experience.

Kublai also employs a range of hunting dogs – mastiffs,
greyhounds and retrievers. But most spectacular of all is the
massive GYRO-FALCON. Bred mainly in Korea and Manchuria,
this sub-Arctic bird is either white with black flecks or pure white,
and has a massive wingspan. You will watch open-mouthed as
this immensely powerful falcon brings down a deer by battering
it round the head and eyes with its wings. Equally awe-inspiring,
indeed a bit terrifying, will be the sight of Kublai letting his PET

CHEETAHS loose. Marvel at the speed and agility of one of nature's most sublime predators as it pursues its prey.

Another not to be missed park attraction is Kublai's BAMBOO PALACE, also known as the PLEASURE DOME. This regal *ger*, where the Khan conducts much of his official business in lavish luxury – with animal skins for a carpet – is on a scale unimaginable to his forefathers and required a considerable feat of engineering to make it large enough for his purposes while still being portable. The *ger* is secured in place by two hundred silken cords, and rests on top of pillars, each with a great golden dragon. The whole thing, despite its size, seems to float in the air, defying the laws of physics, rendering it somewhat fantastical to the eye, like something wrought out of legend.

WORSHIP

Xanadu is host to a multitude of BUDDHIST AND TAOIST TEMPLES, the biggest of them attended by several hundred monks. They are in the pagoda style that is still with us today, with multiple roof sections, bright colours and dragon motifs, while inside the ornate interiors are golden statues of the gods and incense burning continually. Feel free to enter and take part in ceremonies that have remained practically unaltered for thousands of years.

Though Kublai is careful not to over-privilege either religion, he has chosen to adopt MAHAKALA, the Buddhist god of war, as his patron saint; its black face, fierce, blazing eyes, fixed snarl, wild yellow hair and headdress of skulls are an appropriate image for a serial conqueror. However, this does not mean Kublai has deserted his own spiritual roots. At Xanadu, MONGOLIAN SPIRITUAL PRACTICES will be the most frequently seen.

Based on a circular concept of time, this is a pantheistic faith, particular animals acting as totems or symbolic ancestors, the most famous being the BLUE WOLF and RED DEER, the mythical progenitors of the Mongols. Ruling over their universe are the SKY GODS (*tengri*), the foremost being ETERNAL BLUE HEAVEN, with the sun (fire) and moon (water) for eyes. Beneath him are 99 other male divinities, 55 of them benevolent (white) and 44 terrifying (black). As an equal-opportunity religion, there are 77 female divinities (*natigai*), governed by the ALMIGHTY EARTH MOTHER.

This celestial pantheon will be available to you through the ritual machinations of the SHAMANS. Gifted with psychic powers (*hii*) and the ability to travel between the worlds of the living and dead, human and divine, man and animal, they can also access three categories of ancestral spirits: Lord Spirits, Protector Spirits and Guardian Spirits. During their rituals, you will be transported by mysterious chants and the incessant rhythmic beating of a one sided hand-held drum (*tuur*). You will notice that the shaman wears an amulet (*dalbuur*) and a metallic circular mirror (*toil*), which not only acts as armour to deflect spirit attacks but also absorbs energy from the universe. To intensify the experience you will be offered alcohol and tobacco, and be expected to inhale the fumes from burning juniper, producing a mildly hallucinogenic high. Suspend your disbelief, open your mind, go with the flow, and you will find yourself travelling through time and space.

DEPARTURE AND IMPERIAL PROGRESS

Your stay in Xanadu will finish on 28 AUGUST, the traditional end of summer, when Kublai will depart south for Beijing. This auspicious day is marked by a LEAVING CEREMONY. You will witness Kublai sprinkling milk taken from his white mares onto the ground by hand to honour the gods, followed by the mystic men, who will drink the sacred milk that is poured out especially for them before they offer their blessings to Eternal Blue Heaven.

This ceremony complete, you will begin the journey to Beijing along with a vast train of carriages and carts filled with hundreds of Kublai's staff. Covering 20km a day, it'll take you roughly three weeks to reach your destination. En route, you will be stopping at a string of towns, whose only function is to welcome Kublai once a year. The first port of call is HANGZHOU, followed by LIANG

TAI and CHAGAN NOR – known as the White Lake and famous for its swans, partridges, pheasants and cranes. Then onto ZHONG DU, ZHANGBEI, ZHANGJIAKU, XUANHU, TUMU and KHARA-BALGASAN (Black City), finally dropping down through a gorge between mountains to the plains.

From here there are thirty miles of open ground between the mountains and the city of DADU (modern Beijing). You will approach it on a road that has been especially cleared and smoothed over by labourers.

DADU (KHANBALIQ)

The Imperial Progress will take you through the suburbs of DADU, or KHANBALIQ as it has been renamed by Kublai. This is the city that will become Beijing, and already it is a massive conurbation with a sea of houses and little plots of land for vegetables and other crops, alongside larger houses and inns reserved for foreigners and merchants. You will immediately be struck by the thick haze of smoke. This is the product of constantly burning FUNERAL PYRES; Kublai has outlawed the burial of bodies within the main city. You will also be struck by the multitudes of prostitutes hustling for business; Kublai banned them as well from his new capital.

THE SUBURBS

The suburbs form a thrillingly cosmopolitan and multicultural township, where you will rub shoulders with Chinese, Mongols, Turks, Arabs and Indians, haggle with merchants offering silks, spices, jewels and pearls, be entertained by buskers and tempted by the STREET FOOD being prepared on every corner. This is largely of Chinese origin and based on the northern school of cooking, Lu, and will not be that different from a takeaway back home, with similar ingredients, spices and seasoning. And, of course, there is more tea than you could ever possibly drink.

This is also the area to come for a night on the town. The numerous INNS offer rice wines and local beers and the opportunity to participate in games such as MAHJONG and indulge in a spot of GAMBLING. Playing cards have been around in China since the early ninth century and you may have an edge at the tables, as one of the most popular card games is very similar to poker. Otherwise, you might want to try Chinese dominoes, using tiles (*kwat pai*) with symbols/characters on them and many-sided dice, or Chinese chess, with pieces that resemble elephants. Backgammon is available, too, but may prove an expensive option, as it tends to attract high-spending high-rollers with cash to burn.

THE CITY

Beijing is organised on the same principles as Xanadu – once again the work of Lui Bingzhong, assisted by an architect from Central Asia, Ikhtiyar al-Din. It takes the form of a palace within an inner city, within an outer city, sporting huge walls all around, then a second wall concealing the Imperial City, then a third one shielding the Palace.

When your procession reaches the thirty-foot-high whitewashed main wall, it will turn south and proceed four miles to the South Gate, or EMPEROR'S GATE, which will usher you into the Imperial City, with streets laid out in grids, raised pavements, good drainage, and whole blocks owned by the wealthiest and most prominent families.

DADU LODGINGS

In the Imperial City, you will notice a tented zone similar to the one in Xanadu, with grand *gers* for VIPs and smaller ones for officials and craftsmen, and for weapons stores. You may pitch up here if you wish; however, given that conditions will turn distinctly chilly and wet over the coming months, you may prefer to abandon the world of the *ger* and opt to take up residence with your masters in the well-appointed and spacious mansions they inhabit while in Beijing. Not for the Polos the lodging houses of the suburbs. Kublai had already taken a shine to them and considers their advice invaluable; he wants them close by at the centre of his realm. Aside from being more comfortable, you will also have access to better toilet facilities: a sheltered wooden structure with a stone seat to perch on and an armrest, set over a pit in the ground that has running water to flush it out, plus highest-quality toilet paper, soft and perfumed.

INNER SANCTUM

Accompanying the Polos, you will make frequent visits to the PALACE itself. You will cross a moat with a three-arched marble bridge, stroll along three passageways to three gates with towers and five doorways, each one gaining you entrance to the IMPERIAL PALACES and Kublai's private gardens with lakes full of fish.

The centrepiece of Kublai's conception is the resurrected JADE ISLAND, which had been left to rot by Genghis Khan. Kublai has rebuilt the bridge that leads to it, landscaped the slopes with rare trees, added winding staircases, temples and pavilions with evocative names – Golden Dew, Jade Rainbow, Inviting Happiness, Everlasting Harmony – and a main temple that sits atop the island, the grand WHITE PAGODA. Here you can spend many blissful hours in quiet contemplation of the island's outstanding beauty.

Then there is the spectacular NEW PALACE, a single-storey structure raised above the ground by marble terraces and staircases, lined with varnished woodwork and sculptures of dragons and other potent animals, and famous warriors. Inside are seven halls, plus dozens of rooms, chambers, treasure troves, offices and apartments for Kublai's four wives and many concubines. Everywhere you go, you will see fearsome-looking heavily armed men. These are the elite warriors that comprise Kublai's personal bodyguard – it's best to stay on their good side.

Within the sprawling building there is a MINI-PALACE where Kublai holds court from a huge bed inlaid with gold and jade. Next to the bed is huge jade urn weighing around four tons, filled with 600 gallons of wine. Perhaps at no point in your stay will you be as impressed with Kublai's majesty and the authority that emanates from his person as he reclines on his bed, completely at ease with the power that he wields so naturally, totally secure at the heart of his vast empire as he watches his servants dispense wine to his grateful guests.

A NIGHT AT THE THEATRE

In accordance with Kublai's wishes, Chinese culture is to the fore in Beijing, and this means, above all else, THEATRE. As a result, you will get to see everything from large-scale productions to smaller shows performed on movable stages. These events will combine music, singing, poetry, pantomime, dance and acrobatics, punctuated by comedic interludes, running gags and audience interaction.

Many of the more formal four-act plays will feature love stories with strong female characters in the leading role (*tan*), often reworking well-known plots and myths. Originality is not at a premium; much of the fun for the audience comes from seeing their favourite bits from other shows, and stock characters such as the clown (*ch'ou*), the comic villain (*chou*) and the malevolent female (*ch'a tan*). Another aspect of these performances that will be familiar to the spectators are the mimes: choreographed and stylised movements from a set repertoire of gestures and expressions: for example, *entering lovesick, having a coughing fit* and *rubbing eyes in disbelief.*

The key element that binds the plays together is music. At first you may struggle to appreciate the atonal and apparently discordant sounds on offer, but be patient, as you will come to enjoy and admire the elegant, complex harmonies and the skill and dexterity of the musicians playing a wide range of string, woodwind and percussion instruments to produce the eight tones (*bayin*). There are various types of zither, harp and lute, which can be plucked, bowed or struck. The woodwind section will consist of bamboo flutes and pipes, as well as conch shells (*hailou*), while there is a whole panoply of percussion – stone chimes, metal bells, cymbals (*bo*), gongs (*lou*) and an array of skin drums. Expertly deployed, they produce sounds of great subtlety and passionate intensity.

BANQUETING

During your stay you will be lucky enough to take part in two of the greatest feasts of the year. First up is the celebration of KUBLAI'S BIRTHDAY on 23 September, which takes place in the 6,000-capacity HALL OF GREAT BRILLIANCE. You will join the other commoners who will be sitting on the floor gawping at Kublai's robes of beaten gold and thousands of nobles and attendants dressed in similar garb.

Take special care when entering the hall to STEP OVER THE THRESHOLD without your feet touching it. This custom relates to life in the *ger*: to touch its threshold with your feet by accident is considered a bad omen; to do it deliberately, a terrible insult. If you happen to trip up as you go into the hall, the massive guards by the doorway will beat you with rods and strip you of your outer garments; oddly, the only mitigating circumstance is if you are too drunk to walk straight.

The other magnificent banquet you will attend is the WHITE FEAST in early February. This celebrates Mongolian New Year and marks the end of your trip. The festivities begin solemnly as you and the assembled guests touch your foreheads to the floor four times, followed by a brief song and a prayer. Then Kublai takes his place at the high table with his head wife, Chabi, known for her wisdom and temperance, next to him, while the princes and their wives sit on a lower platform level with his feet. At the centre of proceedings is a huge decorated buffet table and a vast golden wine bowl from which butlers draw wine into golden jugs. The very first cup is for Kublai; once he takes a sip, everyone else can. The same ritual is repeated with the food, which will be mostly the meat pastries (*buzz*) you will remember from Xanadu. You will notice that those serving Kublai have their mouths and

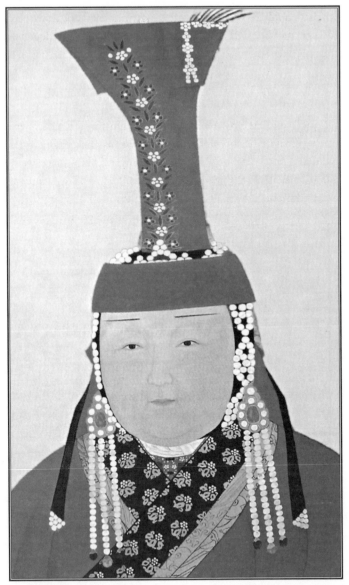

AT THE BANQUET YOU'LL BE AWARE OF EMPRESS CHABI, KUBLAI'S
FAVOURITE WIFE AND SPECIAL ADVISOR. MONGOLIAN-BORN, SHE HAS BEEN
INSTRUMENTAL IN THE RETURN OF THE POLOS TO KUBLAI'S COURT.

noses wrapped in veils of silk and gold, so neither their breath nor smell contaminates his dinner.

Throughout, an orchestra will perform MONGOLIAN MUSIC. Similar to the Chinese tradition, the musicians will play either string, woodwind or percussion. The most common instruments are the horse-head fiddle (*morin khuuur*); a three-stringed strummed lute with a long neck that sounds like a banjo (*shanz*); flutes (*tsuur*); oboes (*everburee*); and a richly ornamented metal trumpet with a brass mouthpiece (*bishguur*). Percussion will include small bells (*damar*) and frame drums (*tuur*). The most evocative and startling element is the THROAT SINGING (*hoomii*) that produces two distinct sounds at the same time: a low guttural drone alongside higher melodic notes. Tune into the ecstatic vibrations of the throat singer's trance-inducing sounds, and it will stir your soul and animate your spirit.

Once the eating is done, there will be a FLOOR SHOW featuring cabaret, acrobats, jugglers and conjurors. Pace yourself. The carousing and merrymaking will go on well into the following day.

DEPARTURE

While your masters are still in bed sleeping or nursing their hangovers, slip quietly away and head for Jade Island. Once there, you will DEPART from the TEMPLE OF EVERLASTING HARMONY.

Captain Cook's First Epic Voyage

CAPTAIN JAMES COOK MADE THREE EPIC voyages to the Pacific – and we are delighted to offer the first and best-known, a three-year odyssey that included the first accurate charting of the New Zealand coastline and the 'discovery' of Australia. As a member of Cook's crew you will experience tremendous highs and devastating lows, and your strength of character and physical stamina will be tested to the limits. But the rewards lie in stunning unspoiled landscapes and untamed shores; you will marvel at wildlife of all kinds, pit yourself against the elements and the raw power of the sea, and stand on deck to watch the sun set over the Pacific.

Setting off from PLYMOUTH, England, your journey will see you cross the Atlantic, with stopoffs in Madeira and Rio de Janeiro; negotiate the perilous passage round Cape Horn into the Pacific; spend several months in Tahiti, the island paradise with its legendarily welcoming inhabitants; then sail on to New Zealand, with its very much less welcoming locals, where you will circumnavigate both the North and South Islands before heading towards Australia. There you will have a close shave with the Great Barrier Reef and make the first European contact with the Aborigines. Having claimed this new continent for the British Empire, you will make a gruelling journey home.

BRIEFING: A SCIENTIFIC EXPEDITION

Cook was not the first European to venture into the Pacific, and at the time of his first voyage there is a generally held view among Europe's geographers that a new continent – *Terra Australis Incognita* – is waiting to be found. This, of course, is of interest not just to Britain, the world's dominant sea power, but to other European contenders for global empire – the French, Dutch, Spanish and Portuguese.

A scientific expedition has been judged to be the best way of furthering British imperial ambitions without raising the suspicions of its rivals. Thus, in February 1768 the ROYAL SOCIETY petitioned George III for cash to fund a voyage to the Pacific to observe the TRANSIT OF VENUS. This rare stellar event that, if measured correctly, can reveal the distance between Venus (and other planets) and the Sun.

CHARLES GREEN, assistant to the Astronomer Royal, has been chosen for the star-mapping, and to boost the expedition's scientific credentials a team of botanists has been enlisted. They are led by JOSEPH BANKS, a very wealthy man who has devoted himself to the system of classifying flora and fauna developed by the Swede Carl Linnaeus. Banks has engaged his pupil DANIEL SOLANDER and a Finnish naturalist, HERMAN SPÖRING, as assistants. By the end of the voyage, his team will have collected 30,000 botanical specimens, including 110 new *genera* and 1300 new species. Two artists, SYDNEY PARKINSON and ALEXANDER BUCHAN, have been invited along to record the trip.

The forty-year-old JAMES COOK is from a humble Yorkshire farming background and has been appointed captain for his skill as a cartographer. He had helped survey and chart the Gulf of St Lawrence in Newfoundland during the Seven Years' War (1756–63). The ship chosen for him by the Royal Society, the ENDEAVOUR, is a one-time coal ship – a sturdy vessel weighing 368 tons. It is 97 ft long and 29 ft wide, with a broad, flat bow, square stern and deep hold. In preparation for the trip, its hull has been sheathed and caulked, and a third internal deck added for extra cabins and storage space. It also houses a longboat and several smaller boats, while ten four-pounder cannons and twelve swivel guns give it some teeth.

The crew comprises fourteen officers, twelve Royal Marines, eight servants (two of them African attached to Banks), and around sixty sailors from all over Britain. Adding to the ship's compliment is a GREYHOUND for hunting, three CATS for killing rats, and a GOAT, which is more a mascot than anything else.

As is customary before departure, anybody suffering doubts is given the chance to quit. Eighteen men vote with their feet. Replacing them at such short notice is the job of the press gangs, part of the IMPRESS SERVICE, and this is how you will be joined up.

THE TRIP

You will ARRIVE on 18 August 1768 in TURNCHAPEL, PLYMOUTH, an area of dark, narrow, cobbled streets right by the harbourmouth. Violent, seedy, full of brothels and bars, it is fertile ground for the Impress Service. Take a pew in the BORINGDON ARMS, a dockside pub, and wait to be approached. Each press gang of twelve men is led by an Impress Officer who is paid by results. He will give you a choice between being taken by force or becoming a VOLUNTEER. The latter is, of course, much the best option. As a 'volunteer', you'll get paid the King's shilling, in advance, and will receive better treatment.

You will spend the majority of the trip with your fellow crew members. It is therefore essential that you adapt quickly to their way of life. If you think you are going to hang out with Cook, or indeed any of the other 'gentlemen' on board, then you will be sorely disappointed. An unbridgeable gap exists between you and them. There will be some interaction concerning the day-to-day doings of the ship, but ultimately your place is with the crew. Together you will be responsible for transporting Cook round the world; without you the ship won't get very far.

Some experience of being at sea – and sailing – would obviously be useful, as would familiarity with the layout of ships and the terms used to govern them. Such knowledge will earn you the title of ABLE-BODIED SEAMAN. However, the Royal Navy doesn't mind if you are a nautical novice; you will simply be referred to as a LANDSMAN. Either way, you will not (unless you are particularly fit and well suited to such duties) be expected to perform the most challenging tasks, such as going aloft to unfurl the sails and untie the topgallants. These dangerous and vertigo-inducing jobs are normally reserved for the youngest and most agile sailors, known as the UPPER YARD'S MEN.

Instead, you will be on DECK DUTIES, hauling sheets, halliards and braces. You will be equipped with a knife for cutting lines that you will carry sheathed on your back. Otherwise, your main duty will be going on WATCH; you will be assigned a specific part of the ship to monitor, and each shift will last eight hours. However, rather than doing three consecutive nights in a row (standard practice at sea), you will only do two, thanks to Cook's largesse.

DEAL
JULY 12
1771

PLYMOUTH
AUGUST 26
1768

MADEIRA
SEPT 1768

PACIFIC
OCEAN

ATLANTIC
OCEAN

BATAVIA
OCT 1770

TAHITI
APRIL-JULY
1769

RIO DE
JANEIRO
NOV 1768

BOTANY
BAY
MAY 1770

CAPE TOWN
MARCH 1771

NEW
ZEALAND
OCT 1769

CAPE HORN
JAN 1769

ON BOARD SHIP: PRACTICALITIES

Your BASIC KIT will consist of a buttoned single-breasted waistcoat (*weskit*), long-sleeved cotton or linen shirts with short cuffs and a single-button, baggy striped *pantaloons* of canvas to cover your knee breeches (*slops*), and heavy trousers and *fearnought jackets* for when it gets cold. Hats are a staple: either variations on the triangular shaped tricorn, turned up so the brim diverts rainwater away from your face, or a brown woollen-knitted *Monmouth cap*. Your shoes will be black leather with a brass buckle, though much of the time bare feet will suffice. You may wish to accessorise with a bandana, often in black to mask the ingrained dirt, and a brightly coloured neckerchief.

FOOD

On a voyage like this, your well-being, both mental and physical, will hinge on the quantity, quality and variety of FOOD on offer: your morale and that of the crew will revolve round your stomachs. The contents of your diet are largely determined by Cook's desire to prevent scurvy, the deadly wasting disease so prevalent amongst sailors.

Drawing on the latest research, especially James Lind's 1753 *Treatise of the Scurvy*, Cook's selection of anti-scurvy food will include 100 pounds of *portable soup* (from dried vegetables), sugar, sago, marmalade of carrots, ground up orchid roots (salop), vinegar, mustard, malt, raw onion, concentrated lemon juice, shore greens and 7,860 pounds of pickled sauerkraut. *Endeavour* will leave Plymouth carrying, in addition, 6,000 pieces of pork and 4,000 of beef, nine tons of bread, five tons of flour, one ton of raisins, cheese, salt, peas, oil, and oatmeal, plus seventeen sheep, four pigs, and twenty-four assorted poultry.

You will have three-quarters of an hour for BREAKFAST and an hour and a half for LUNCH, consuming roughly 4,500 calories per day. Your weekly ration will contain four pounds of salt beef, two pounds of salt pork, three pints of cereal grain, six ounces of butter and twelve ounces of cheese. Mondays, Wednesdays and Fridays are meat-free; you will be served pease pudding and onions instead. SHIP'S BISCUITS, pretty vile and often infested with insects, will accompany every meal.

Over the course of the journey, fresh water will be procured at regular intervals and you will be able to gorge on produce sourced from the many islands you visit; coconuts, yams, bananas, sweet potatoes, yellow apples, sugar cane and plantains. FISH AND SHELLFISH will also make a welcome change. Savour oysters and lobsters fresh from New Zealand's rocky inlets; feast on huge stingrays plucked from the waters off Australia; and tuck into giant turtles, popular not only for their succulent meat but also for the sport to be had diving for them.

Sea birds will also land on your plate, most notably ALBATROSS. Though the crew consider this strange, ungainly bird as the sacred embodiment of the spirits of dead sailors, this doesn't stop the botanist Joseph Banks shooting one. The albatross will then be served up in a savoury sauce, having been skinned, soaked in salt water, parboiled and stewed until tender.

DRINK

After food, ALCOHOL is the main-stay of the crew. On board are 250 barrels of beer, 44 barrels of brandy and 17 barrels of rum. Out of this, you will be given a DAILY RATION of a gallon of beer or a pint of grog – rum diluted with water; sometimes the crew will mix beer with spirits to make a concoction known as *flip*. Not surprisingly, drunkenness is endemic and you will need to be able to handle your liquor without losing control; much of the trouble on the ship will be caused by too much alcohol. One crew member will die after drinking 3½ pints of rum, while four will be flogged for stealing rum.

If you are teetotal, for whatever reason, the best way to explain your abstinence is to claim serious religious convictions – preferably Protestant.

Aside from drinking, recreational activities will include singing SEA SHANTIES and GAMBLING on pretty much anything from arm wrestling contests to cockroach racing. For those so inclined, there will be a RELIGIOUS SERVICE every Sunday morning.

ACCOMMODATION

The quarters where you sleep will be on the lower deck. Your HAMMOCKS are a mere fourteen inches wide with hardly any gap between you and your neighbours, while the ceiling is only four feet high. Anybody over six foot is going to struggle, as is anyone who suffers from even mild claustrophobia.

Going to the toilet will present its own unique challenge. The crew's LATRINE is simply a hole cut in a long plank extending out from the bow of the ship. Privacy and retaining your dignity will be the least of your worries; you will be focused on not falling off the plank. In rough seas, you may prefer just to hold it in.

You will wash yourself regularly using a large bucket full of cold water. Clothes will also be soaked in it and scrubbed with soft soap made from ash lye and animal fat. Your hammock and bedding will be rolled out and subjected to the same treatment. All these items will then be hung out on deck to dry in the sun and the wind.

DISCIPLINE

Once a week you will gather on deck for a reading of the ARTICLES OF WAR. First drawn up in 1652 and last updated in 1757, this has 36 sections governing matters of discipline and punishment on board ship, listing crimes either meriting the death penalty or 'such punishment ... as the nature and degree of the offence shall deserve', which generally means getting FLOGGED by a cat o'nine tails. Known as the 'captain's daughter', this is about 2½-feet-long with nine waxed cords of rope, each with a knot on the end. A maximum of twelve blows will be delivered to your bare back, the whip cutting into your flesh and causing considerable bleeding. Afterwards, salt will be rubbed into the wounds to prevent infection.

who believes in treating his crew humanely. This does not mean Cook is a soft touch. He realises the necessity of maintaining discipline and will act accordingly.

However fed up you are with your diet, don't gripe about the food. ARTICLE TWENTY-ONE forbids complaints about 'the unwholesomeness of the victual', something Cook takes seriously. Two of the crew will get twelve lashes for refusing to eat their ration of fresh beef.

Thankfully many of the Articles will not apply to your voyage. However, a number are worth paying close attention to. Take care not to fall foul of ARTICLE TWO, which covers 'profane oaths, cursing, excretions, drunkenness, uncleanness or other scandalous actions'; ARTICLE TWENTY-THREE, which condemns fighting, quarrelling and winding up your fellow crew members (an easy trap to fall into on such a long and stressful journey); and ARTICLE TWENTY-SEVEN, which warns you not to fall asleep while on watch or slack off from your work, both errors you may unwittingly commit. The clause most open to abuse is ARTICLE THIRTY-SIX, which covers 'all other crimes ... not mentioned in the act', and gives the captain carte blanche to punish any misdemeanours. Luckily for you, Cook uses the lash sparingly. He is a benevolent captain

Even if you avoid such disciplinary measures, you will have to watch the whippings, performed on deck in front of all of you, accompanied by drum rolls, sips of water for the victim and the repetitive crack of the lash.

DEATH

An unavoidable and distressing part of the trip will be the loss of fellow sailors. The first death will occur only two weeks after leaving Plymouth: one of the crew will get dragged overboard by the buoy-rope and anchor. Six months later, either deliberately or by accident, a marine will disappear over the side, while on arrival in Tahiti the artist Alex Buchan will die of a bowel disorder. Overcoming the grief of these unfortunate deaths will help prepare you for when the toll increases dramatically later on in the voyage.

CROSSING THE ATLANTIC

26 AUGUST–13 NOVEMBER 1768

Out of Plymouth, and through much of September 1768, *The Endeavour* will be buffeted by gales and heavy rain; in the worst of the storms, one of the small boats will be washed overboard, along with a lot of poultry. But on the 13th of the month, everyone aboard will get some welcome relief during a four day stopover at the port of FUNCHAL on the island of MADEIRA.

While the ship is being re-caulked and painted here, you will have a chance for a spot of shore leave: Funchal is a busy port, so you can expect the usual conglomeration of bars and brothels. However, there will be little time for sightseeing because by day you will be transporting fresh supplies and loading them onto the *Endeavour*: an extra 20 pounds of onions per seaman, 270 pounds of fresh beef, a live bullock, plus 1,200 gallons of beer, 1,600 of spirits and 3,032 of wine.

On Wednesday 26 October, you will reach the EQUATOR – 'crossing the line' – and have the chance to participate in the Navy's equivalent of bungee jumping: any sailor who has never crossed the line before will be ducked in the ocean three times. Suspended above the yardarm, you will be fastened by rope to three pieces of wood – one between your legs, one between your hands and the other above your head – hoisted as high as possible and plunged rapidly beneath the waves before being pulled up again. You are not obliged to take part in this ceremony, but if you don't you'll forfeit four days of alcohol rations.

By the time RIO DE JANEIRO comes into view on Sunday 13 November, you will be chomping at the bit to sample its many delights. However, the Viceroy of Brazil, Dom Antonio Rolim de Moura, has other ideas. Unimpressed by the *Endeavour*'s scientific credentials, Senhor de Moura is convinced you are up to no good and refuses to allow anybody, even Cook, to set foot in the city, though he will permit you to take on food and water. Annoyed and frustrated, twelve crew members will defy his orders and slip undetected into Rio, where they will be immediately arrested for smuggling and spend a night in a hideous jail cell with other prisoners, who are chained to the walls, only to be released after Cook writes an infuriated letter to the Viceroy.

INTO THE PACIFIC

2 DECEMBER 1768–12 APRIL 1769

As you sail the 300 miles to Cape Horn, the southernmost tip of Latin America, you will notice the temperature drop dramatically and Cook will issue your cold weather clothing. It's a new year, too, and on 11 January 1769, you reach Tiera del Fuego, where you will find locals living in round beehive shaped dwellings with wooden frames covered with sealskins and brushwood. They're a hospitable bunch.

After this brief respite, you will face the toughest phase of your trip so far: getting round CAPE HORN. You will have to negotiate the STRAIT LE MAIRE, a funnel-like passage beset by storms that send tidal surges racing through its bottleneck. Three times *Endeavour*, tossed like a twig on the foaming waves, will fail to get through before finally making it out of this deathtrap.

A few days later, you will drop anchor at the BAY OF GOOD SUCCESS and meet its inhabitants with their distinctive black and red body paint, while the botanists head inland to search for specimens. Leaving here on 21 January, there is nothing but the endless horizon of the Pacific in front of you. Time passes slowly. Weeks stretch into months, the monotony somewhat relieved by warmer weather, the variety of marine life on show, and the knowledge – passed on by some of the crew who had been on HMS *Dolphin* when it visited Tahiti in 1767 – that your next port of call is home to some of the nicest people on earth.

TAHITI

13 APRIL–14 JULY 1769

Finally, you will see land, a tiny speck in the ocean called LAGOON ISLAND. You will then pass a few others like it before MATAVIA BAY appears with its palm trees and pristine beaches, the locals coming to greet you in their sixty-foot canoes, bringing a warm welcome and food to trade for beads and cloth. A decimal system is used for counting; Tahitians have signs for numbers from 1 to 20 – enabling them to count up to 20,000 – and they follow the lunar calendar and use astronomy to interpret the stars.

TAHITIAN LIFE

At the top of the TAHITIAN SOCIAL SYSTEM is the ARI'I (chief), then the TAHU'A (priests), followed by RA'ATIRI (minor nobility), and MANAHUNE (regular folk). These distinctions aren't immediately obvious, as everyone you meet will appear to be on the same level. There are clues, though, across the island in their MARAE – burial sites. These are often just a pile of rocks, but sometimes quite elaborate memorials made of coral stone with steps and an altar with carved wooden posts. The largest is at OPOOREONOO – a pyramid with eleventt huge steps to a platform. According to legend, the MAUWE, the island's gods, giants with seven heads and superhuman powers, inhabited the earth long before man showed up.

All ranks of Tahitians wear little in the way of CLOTHING, which is made from bark. This is peeled from trees in strips, melded together with fine paste and beaten flat with large wooden tools, before other strips of beaten bark are added crosswise. The resulting material is dyed in red, brown and yellow. The Tahitian's are keen on TATAUS (tattoos), created using bone and soot, and you might want to get one of their unique tribal symbols as a memento.

There is an abundance of EXOTIC FRUIT AND VEGETABLES available, pigs run wild, and a Tahitian speciality is ROAST DOG. It's worth conquering any aversion you might have to canine cuisine (Cook will record that he's never eaten sweeter meat). First, the dog has all its hair burned off, then its entrails are removed and washed clean. Meanwhile, a fire is started at the bottom of a hole in the ground about a foot deep. When the flames are strong enough, stones are put on top and, once they are red-hot, the fire is extinguished. Green leaves are placed on

TAHITIAN WOMEN PERFORM THE TIMORODEE. LOOK OUT FOR APPLES.

the stones, the dog and its guts are laid on them with a covering of more leaves, and oven-grilled.

When dining, you will notice that men and women never eat together. This is forbidden (*tapu*). You will also have to bring your own booze if you want any alcohol with your meal; the Tahitians serve nothing but coconut milk and water.

You will be treated to a great deal of MUSIC played on hand drums of hollow wood with a membrane of shark's skin, and four-holed, fifteen-inch-long bamboo flutes, which are inserted in the nostril and blown. The DANCES that these instruments accompany are segregated by gender. The female ones often feature girls on the verge of puberty: during the TIMORODEE DANCE, two groups of near-naked young women split into opposing groups and throw apples at each other. MALE DANCES are more warlike and based around wrestling poses. WRESTLING is popular on the island, so you will get to see the real thing as well.

Property will be the main cause of friction during your stay. The Tahitians have a 'what's mine is yours' attitude; private property is a totally alien concept, and theft, therefore is a meaningless term. Because theirs is a Stone Age culture, the locals are particularly drawn to objects made from glass or metal. One day after arrival, two of the gentlemen will have their pockets picked, one losing his spyglass, the other his snuff box. From then on, things will keep vanishing. On the whole, they will be recovered without bloodshed, but when a musket is snatched from a sailor's hands the 'thief' is promptly shot dead. After an iron rake goes missing on 14 June, Cook, at his wits end, will conficate all the canoes in the bay until it is returned.

There will also be a lot of bartering, done primarily by the Tahitian women, who will exchange sexual favours for coveted objects such as the ship's iron nails. To prevent this, Cook will issue five rules, four of which (the other simply instructs you to be friendly) relate to unauthorised bargaining with the locals; one explicitly forbids trading iron for anything except food. To show how serious he is, Cook will have a seaman flogged for filching nails from the stores.

More often than not, the women will give themselves freely. You will find the Tahitian attitude to sex remarkably liberal. Nor will you witness any resentment, jealousy or possessiveness from the menfolk; both husbands and fathers seem happy to share. In this relaxed environment, it's no surprise that the majority of the crew will have intimate relations with Tahitian women – some casual encounters, others more serious affairs.

TRANSIT OF VENUS

Regardless of the many delights on offer, your reason for being on Tahiti is to observe the TRANSIT OF VENUS. Cook will order a FORT built to safely store the astronomical instruments – a brass quadrant, a newly patented azimuth compass, a high quality sextant, and two telescopes with Gregorian reflectors and parabolic mirrors. Work on the fort will start almost immediately on arrival, and you will help construct a high-spiked palisade with swivel guns at each corner, boxing in a series of big tents. For extra security, the two big on-ship guns will be trained on the woods next to the fort.

The quadrant will be set up on 1 May, only to be stolen the following day. Infuriated, Cook will detain all the large Tahitian canoes until it reappears. Thankfully, that evening it is returned undamaged. On the day itself, Saturday 3 June, the conditions will initially appear perfect, but then clouds will gather and obscure the view – Cook will complain of 'an Atmosphere or dusky-shade round the body of the planet'. As a result, none of the three readings taken match up, making it impossible to get any accurate measurements.

By 9 July, you will be ready to set off again, along with a young Tahitian, Tupia, who has a smattering of English. However, departure will be delayed by the hunt for two seamen, Clement Webb and Sam Gibson, who have not unreasonably decided to desert the ship so they can stay with their Tahitian girlfriends. A search party will be sent ashore and, to ensure the locals' cooperation, their chief is taken hostage. Within twenty-four hours, the two lovesick sailors will be back on the *Endeavour*, and you will begin the next phase of your adventure.

NEW ZEALAND

SEPTEMBER 1769–1 APRIL 1770

En route to New Zealand, the *Endeavour* will call in at the Society Islands, whose inhabitants will sacrifice an eighty-pound hog in your honour. It is an isolated highlight. September will bring violent storms, colder weather and mounting tension; when, if ever, will land appear? Cook knows there is something out there thanks to the Dutch explorer Abel Tasman, who sighted New Zealand in 1642, but Tasman only skirted the North Island; you will trace every nook and cranny of the whole coastline.

Finally, on 8 October, a panorama of white cliffs, sandy bays, wooded hills, river valleys and two majestic purple mountains will come into view. As you get nearer, you will see a string of huts on the beach and Maoris with their warpaint and tattoos paddling towards you in their fifty-foot-long and five-foot-wide

MAORI WAR CANOES – NOT A WELCOMING SIGHT.

war canoes, each capable of holding a hundred men, hurling spears and making aggressive noises. Your musket fire will force them to turn round, with one warrior killed. An attempt to go ashore fares no better; there is a standoff between you and the Maoris, armed with *patoo patoo* – heavy, hand-held weapons with sharp, serrated blades of green stone. Though Tupia will try to chat with the Maoris and offer gifts, there is more musket fire and another dead warrior. A second landing ends just as badly, with four further Maori casualties. It's no wonder Cook dubs the area POVERTY BAY.

Many of your subsequent encounters with the Maoris will be hostile. At the appropriately named KIDNAPPER'S BAY, Tayeto, Tupia's boy helper, is snatched, and force of arms will be required to get him back, while at the BAY OF ISLANDS you will need a volley from the big ship guns to disperse a force of two hundred armed Maoris.

However, there will be friendlier relations, especially at TO-LAGA BAY, where you will stay seven days and get a taste of local life and culture. The Maoris are superb fishermen, using lobster traps made from twigs and huge trawling nets. Their clothes are made from a hemp-like plant (*barkeke*), their homes constructed round a frame of sticks and thatched with long grass. You will be pleased to note that every dwelling has a basic outside toilet. Their music is played on wooden flutes and shell trumpets. During their DANCES, the women wear head dresses with black feathers, while the men's WAR DANCES, in their authentic form, will be familiar to any rugby fans.

On 9 November, you will successfully observe the TRANSIT OF MERCURY, before circumnavigating the South Island. You will find a good berth for fishing and supplies of fresh water at MURDERERS BAY near Queen Charlotte Sound, and leave New Zealand on 1 April.

AUSTRALIA (NEW HOLLAND)
19 APRIL–22 AUGUST 1770

On 19 April comes a historic moment as the lookout spots the coastline of what Cook calls *Terra Australia Incognita*. Searching for a place to drop anchor, Cook passes and names a series of features – Cape Upright, Pigeon House, Cape St George, Long Nose and Red Point – before landing at a spot that is soon dubbed BOTANY BAY.

As you enter the bay, on 29 April, you will get your first glimpse of ABORIGINES. There will be a group of huts on shore, and two of the inhabitants, one old, one young, will approach the *Endeavour*. Due to mutual incomprehension and suspicion, spears will be thrown and muskets fired, leaving one Aborigine slightly wounded and their huts abandoned. Despite this inauspicious beginning, subsequent contacts with the Aborigines will be peaceable, if tentative. You will notice that the males have beards, bone piercings through their noses, and faces and bodies painted with white pigments. They usually appear armed, carrying three-foot wooden sticks that propel four-pointed bone darts, shields and boomerangs (be aware that none of Cook's company will know how these work). The women, wearing not much apart from shell necklaces and bracelets, will keep their distance from you.

Botany Bay is a natural choice for the landing site, as the botanists will have a field day. The wildlife is bewitching and (to your companions) entirely unfamiliar: kangaroos and dingoes, fruit bats, lizards, snakes, huge caterpillars and butterflies, green ants, scorpions, tropical parrots ...

Moving on, you pass PORT JACKSON (Sydney Harbour), POINT DANGER, CAPE MORETON and CAPE CAPRICORN, before reaching the beautiful but hazardous GREAT BARRIER REEF. On 11 June, it bares its fangs and a stretch of razor-sharp coral will rip a hole in the ship. Cook knows the only hope is to get to shallower water or run aground, so once the sails have been lowered you will immediately set about lightening the load; iron and stone ballast, rotten stores and all but four of the guns will be thrown overboard.

By the next day, *Endeavour* will be taking on a lot of water and you and every available hand will be manning the pumps. This continuous effort will pay dividends, especially after Cook manages to wrest the ship free and even more water pours in. This will be the crew's finest hour, working together as a well-oiled machine that will prompt the normally sanguine Cook to declare that 'no man ever behaved better than they have done on this occasion'.

However, you are still twenty-four miles from shore and still slowly sinking, until one of the crew, Jonathan Monkhouse, comes to the rescue and 'fothers' the hole. This entails sewing bits of oakum and wool together into an old sail, then drawing it under the ship to allow the water pressure to force it into the yawning gap in the hull, thereby blocking it and stopping the sea coming in. Job done, you will drift towards shore and come to a halt there on the morning of the 17th.

It will take two weeks to complete the repairs to the *Endeavour*; fixing the hole, scraping barnacles from the hull and mending the torn sails. You will be engaged in helping to speed this work along but there will be time for a little r & r as you camp out on the beach.

By 5 August, you are back at sea, inching your way across the Great Barrier Reef. Its spectacular colours are seductive but the crew never lose sight of the threat lurking beneath the surface: one false move and the reef will tear you up again. There are a hair-raising few hours when the sea falls calm and light winds start easing the *Endeavour* towards certain destruction. Feel free to join the prayers at this point. You will be delivered at the last moment when the wind shifts course and pulls you away from danger.

Having sailed along the whole east coast, you will come to CAPE YORK on 22 August. Here Cook will name the territory NEW SOUTH WALES and you will stand on deck as he and a few

THE ENDEAVOUR UNDERGOING REPAIRS OFF THE EAST COAST OF
AUSTRALIA.

men land on the tiny Possession Island, where you will see them
raise the British flag, a ceremony marked by three musket shots,
answered by three volleys from the *Endeavour's* guns and three
cheers from the rest of you.

HOMEWARD BOUND
23 AUGUST 1770–12 JULY 1771

The ailing *Endeavour* – its timber riddled with shipworms, its
pumps worn and its bottom still leaking – will now limp towards
the known world, the DUTCH EAST INDIES, and sail past TIMOR,
JAVA and SUVA before dropping anchor alongside Dutch ships and
a lone English merchantman in the harbour at BATAVIA.

The Dutch-governed settlement of Batavia has a mixed population – European, Polynesian and Chinese – of around 20,000 in the city and another 100,000 in the suburbs, and boasts a town hall, churches and a network of canals, designed to mirror Amsterdam. Unfortunately, after an earthquake blocked the flow of fresh water, the canals have become stagnant pools teeming with millions of mosquitos and caked in foul-smelling mud littered with human waste and dead animals. It is an ideal breeding ground for malaria and dysentery, and within days the majority of the *Endeavour*'s crew are on the sick list. (To avoid this calamity, you will be met soon after landing by a company representative disguised as a Dutch merchant sailor. While engaging you in idle chatter, he will slip you antimalarial medication and pills to ward off dysentery; it is enough to protect you, and you alone, from infection.) By the end of your stay in Batavia, prolonged by the repair work needed to reinvigorate the *Endeavour*, seven crew will be dead from malaria, and forty too sick to perform their duties; Tupia, your Tahitian guide, is the first to succumb.

Back at sea, after a swift stop off at Prince's Island to take on water, dysentery will raise its ugly head. Over the next few months another thirty-two of the party will pass away. This will be your darkest hour. Half your shipmates will have perished, along with the two Scandinavian botanists, the remaining artist and the astronomer.

Everyone's spirits will be lifted a little, though, when the CAPE OF GOOD HOPE is sighted. Two days later, on 15 March 1771, you will arrive in CAPE TOWN. In the idyllic setting of this sleepy outpost, with its whitewashed colonial-style buildings, its vineyards, orchards and kitchen gardens, and Table Mountain hovering in the background, you can shed some of the stress of the last few months. You will be able to take leisurely strolls through its picturesque streets and visit the local MENAGERIE with its ostriches, antelopes and zebras. You will also eat well courtesy of the Captain: Cook will purchase a whole ox for you to enjoy.

Somewhat refreshed, the surviving party will gird its loins for the final stretch of the journey. As you CROSS THE ATLANTIC, you will have merchant ships for company, and on 15 May you will witness an ECLIPSE OF THE SUN. When you clear the BAY OF BISCAY on 7 July, you will know the end is in sight. Your first glimpse of England will be on the 10th. By the 12th you will have reached Beachy Head: that afternoon you will drop anchor at the port of DEAL in Kent.

DEPARTURE

It is important not to get caught up in the riotous celebrations that will greet the *Endeavour's* return. Deal is a small but bustling port with a reputation for hard drinking, brawling and vice in all its forms. It is also a favoured hunting ground for the Impress Service; you could easily find yourself press ganged again and on a ship going god knows where. Instead, find the Dover Road and walk south for about two miles until you reach the village of UPPER WALMER. There you can safely stop at the ROYAL STANDARD INN for a quick drink to toast your survival before strolling a short distance to OLD ST MARY'S CHURCH, from where you will DEPART.

PART FIVE

EXTREME
EVENTS

The Eruption
of Vesuvius

23–25 AUGUST AD 79 ✵ POMPEII

THE ERUPTION OF MOUNT VESUVIUS WAS not the largest or deadliest in history. Yet it holds a special place in our imagination thanks to the ruins it left behind. Year after year, thousands troop round the excavations at Pompeii and Herculaneum hoping to recapture something of their Roman life, so movingly 'caught in time'. Now you can experience it in *real time*. This extreme travel trip gives you the chance to sample the day-to-day life of these energetic and cosmopolitan Roman towns – as well as to witness an awesome and spectacular act of nature. Having done so, you will be in a position to fully appreciate the scale of the tragedy as it unfolds before your eyes. At some point during your stay, you may become overwhelmed by the impulse to suggest to some of the locals that they might want to leave town for a few days. And take all their possessions with them. This is strictly forbidden. If you feel you are unable to control your charitable, humane instincts, then

Vesuvius is not the trip for you. Interaction with the citizens must not become too intimate or friendly.

You will spend a day and night in POMPEII and a day in the seaside town of HERCULANEUM, before boarding a specially chartered SHIP in the Bay of Naples, from where you will watch the cataclysm. The pitch black clouds of ash and debris produced by the eruption cloak the surrounding countryside for miles in all directions, making it impossible to find a decent vantage point on land. At sea, however, you will get an unobstructed, if long-distance, view of the ghastly proceedings.

BRIEFING: VESUVIUS

POMPEII's extremely pleasant climate, proximity to the sea and fertile soil has meant there has been a settlement here since the sixth century BC. The city came under the control of Rome somewhat reluctantly in the fourth century BC and joined a failed rebellion against its masters in 89 BC. After that, however, it was integrated peacefully into the Empire and has thrived; its population is currently around 12,000, with another 24,000 in its rural area. They are sustained by some of the best agricultural soil in Italy – the mineral-rich volcanic earth produces an abundance of cereals, grapes, olives, apricots, figs, peaches, almonds and walnuts, as well as being ideal for grazing sheep. This plethora of goods is traded in the city and exported across the Empire, while imports of more exotic fare – spices, perfumes, cloths, jewellery – flow in, making Pompeii an important centre for merchants.

HERCULANEUM shares a similar history to Pompeii, though it is a little smaller, and wealthier. It has some of the Empire's finest villas in the town and vicinity.

VESUVIUS, the author of both cities' destruction, is a so-called 'humpbacked' mountain, formed by a collision of two tectonic plates, the African and Eurasian, roughly 25,000 years ago. Before AD 79, there have been at least three other major eruptions, but none matched the ferocity of what you are about to witness, in which Vesuvius spewed out molten rock and pulverised pumice at a rate of 1.5 million tons per second, forming hydrothermal pyroclastic flows – molten lava with an accumulated thermal energy 100,000 times greater than the atomic bomb that levelled Hiroshima.

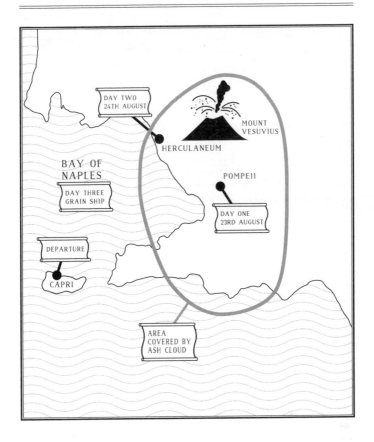

THE TRIP

You will arrive just outside the city of POMPEII, near family burial grounds marked by memorials of all kinds, ranging from large, ornate, multistorey structures honouring the rich and powerful, to the simplest of gravestones. You will be wearing a brightly coloured toga to help you blend into your environment; Pompeii is a city that likes its colours, and the houses are painted in bright reds, yellows and blues. After a short walk, you will enter the city via the NORTH-EASTERN GATE.

ROOMS, FOOD AND NIGHTLIFE

You will be staying in exclusive RENTED APARTMENTS on the upper floors of multipurpose buildings near the centre of Pompeii. These light, airy and spacious condos, with large windows and terraces, luxury fixtures and fittings, and their own TOILET (a wooden seat over a chute carved in the wall, emptying into a cesspit down below), will give you the chance to relax and unwind after the day's exertions. A small potable oven (*farnus*), with its own grill, provides a self-catering option.

There are, however, plenty of eating options around the city, and the fresh FISH DISHES are highly recommended. Do take the opportunity to sample garum, the fish sauce that is something of a speciality. Made from a mixture of sea salt and seafood, fermented in a vat for a few months in the sun then decanted into jugs, the very best comes from pure mackerel (liquaminis flos). But be wary: the low-grade stuff is no better than eating rotten seafood.

For carnivores, the most often served meat is PORK, which usually comes in the form of sausages or black pudding. For the unsqueamish, there is the Roman delicacy of DORMICE. Fed on nuts, the dormice are fattened up in specially designed jars, before being stuffed with pork, peppers and nuts, all glued together by garum, and cooked until tender. Some of the best-quality produce can be found in taverns around the MACELLUM (meat market) situated in the FORUM.

Another option is STREET FOOD or buying directly from retailers. There are BAKERS everywhere supplying fresh bread from their premises, using big ovens, not unlike present-day pizza ones. The dough is prepared in an adjacent room, while out back is the flour mill powered by a beast of burden. A loaf of bread with some local cheese and olive oil may be all you need for lunch. Don't hesitate to sample the LOCAL WINES. They have a decent reputation, particularly the Falernian brand.

You may want to take your evening meal early, as if you venture out after dark you'll need to keep your wits about you. With no light except the stars above, and all the houses, shops and workshops shuttered up, the streets are monopolised by drunken revellers and muggers.

If you do want to take in some local nightlife, though, you can take your pick from plenty of TAVERNAS. Asides from drinking, these play host to dice-based board games. GAMBLING is the norm, and if you want to avoid trouble it's best to watch rather than participate. Note also that these tavernas are exceptionally male environments. Female travellers may find the ambience intimidating and will almost certainly attract unwanted attention, as the assumption will be that you are a woman of easy virtue.

23 AUGUST: POMPEII STREET LIFE:

POMPEII is not a large city and the best way to explore it is on foot. Wheeled transport is a nightmare, the narrow, single lane roads choked with traffic as traders move their wares in carts drawn by donkeys or mules, leaving no room for manoeuvre. Congestion is such a problem that you will see traffic-calming measures all over the place, including bollards and one-way streets.

Even crossing the road can be a hazardous affair, due to the garbage and waste, both human and animal, scattered in your path. Thankfully there are high, sturdy pavements and, to avoid treading in anything untoward, there are stepping stones from one side of the street to another, with gaps between for cart wheels to pass through. It's going to get hot in the August sunshine, so remember to keep hydrated. Luckily the locals have that covered: at regular intervals, often at major junctions or crossroads, are WATER FOUNTAINS with large spouts and continuously running water supplied by a tank underneath. The city's water is entirely safe to drink. It comes from an aqueduct that sends it down the mountain to a tall water castle just outside the walls. It then distributes the water to a dozen or so towers made of stone and brick, up to twenty feet tall, with a lead tank at the top, which control and contain the flow of water through pipes below the pavements.

Pompeii is full of vivid, vibrant imagery everywhere you turn. There are large formal SCULPTURES of prominent citizens and figures from history, and shrines dedicated to the ever-present gods. Look more closely and you will also see dozens of smaller figures carved into the street or next to shops and businesses. Particularly common are dwarf-like figures with huge PHALLUSES; aside from being a symbol of fertility and male power, the phallus also represents good luck.

Most striking is the GRAFFITI. The life of the city is recorded in these scrawls, etched into every available surface. The walls will speak to you of politics and public affairs. They advertise forthcoming events and honour local celebrities. They boast of sexual

VESUVIUS DEPICTED IN A FRESCO OF BACCHUS AT POMPEII.
THE MOUNTAIN WILL NEVER LOOK LIKE THIS AGAIN, AS ITS
ENTIRE CONE WILL BE BLOWN OFF BY THE ERUPTION.

conquest and desire, of love gained and lost, and feature quotes
from the great poets and writers of antiquity.

This tradition of popular artistic expression extends to the
SIGNS outside shops. The best feature intricate, detailed images,
such as a builder's with symbols of his trade – tools, chisels, mallet
and the ubiquitous phallus. The sheer volume and diversity of retailers and craftsmen – textile merchants, fashion houses, barbers,
perfumers, jewellers, cobblers, spice stalls and so on – makes for

excellent window shopping. You will probably notice a number of brothels (*lupanari*), too. Pompeii has quite a reputation in this respect and Roman men will pop in during the day for a service.

As you wander round, you will notice that large parts of Pompeii are undergoing RECONSTRUCTION AND RENOVATION, with many of its most prominent public buildings out of commission. In some cases the rebuilding work is well advanced, in others there is little to see except rubble. For example, the AMPHITHEATRE, site of gruelling gladiatorial contests and blood-soaked spectacles involving wild animals, is closed due to construction work. This disruption is the result of a major earthquake that struck the city on 5 February 62 AD, measuring 5 to 6 on the Richter scale. On the day of the quake, the Forum had been packed with people attending two sacrifices to mark the anniversary of Emperor Augustus taking power and a feast to honour city gods, adding to the chaos and the death toll.

Entering the FORUM, a great open space in the heart of the city, the impact of the earthquake will be evident. Flanked by colonnades of columns on all sides, it is the home of two major temples; the TEMPLE OF APOLLO, the current version dating back to the second century BC, and the TEMPLE OF JUPITER, JUNO AND MINERVA, which was severely hit by the quake. There is also a house dedicated to the priestess EUMACHIA, daughter of a well-to-do wine merchant, plus the BASILICA, the largest public building in Pompeii, the surface of which is covered in graffiti. Resist the temptation to add your own 'I was here' to the hundreds of messages already carved into its façade.

The TEMPLE OF APOLLO, with its exterior columns and triangular gables, is well worth a look. Climb the steps up to a podium and then go in through its high doors and you will be greeted by statues of the relevant gods and goddesses, alongside dedications and tributes left by worshippers. Otherwise, the interior is relatively austere, a plain, simple space, not designed for major religious ceremonies or rituals (which took place in the Forum proper).

UP POMPEII! ROMANS HAVE A RELAXED ATTITUDE TO SEX AND
YOU'LL SEE A RICH VARIETY OF ACTS DEPICTED IN BOTH
PUBLIC AND PRIVATE BUILDINGS.

No day in Pompeii would be complete without a visit to the
BATHS. You will need to be comfortable with nudity, as everybody
will be naked, though currently the facilities are segregated by
sex. Travellers hoping to indulge in mixed bathing will be disappointed that the Central Baths, the only venue in the city where
men and women mingle together, is still undergoing repair work
from the earthquake.

Once inside the baths – the front entrance is for men, a side
entrance for women – you ditch your toga in the changing rooms

(*apodyterium*). This is worth a close look, as, to help you find where you have left your clothing, there are a series of erotic murals featuring depictions of unashamed cunnilingus and even a three-some involving two men and one woman. These are part of the Roman acceptance of the erotic and not given more than a passing look by your fellow bathers.

Toga off, you are free to exercise, swim, sunbathe, have your skin scraped or get a rubdown. The main attractions are the various rooms offering a full range of temperatures to immerse yourself in: a cold room (*frigidarium*), a warm room (*tepidarium*), a hot room (*caldarium*) and, for the hardcore enthusiast, the hot sweat room (*laconium*). The one thing we'd not advise is a dip in the pool, which is a breeding ground for bacteria of all kinds.

At some point in the day you may well need to relieve yourself. There are a number of PUBLIC TOILET facilities available, but don't expect the privacy of your own cubicle; emptying your bowels is a communal activity in Pompeii. You will squat in a row next to your neighbour on a keyhole-shaped seat cut out of a length of marble slab, with a trench directly underneath to collect and flush away the waste, and a small trough in the floor in front of you filled with fresh water. Once you're done, take a SPONGIA (a sea sponge attached to a stick), dip it in the trough, slip it discreetly under your toga and clean up as necessary.

24 AUGUST: HERCULANEUM

You will rendezvous early next morning at the arrival point, then head to the nearby town of HERCULANEUM. Small, with a high percentage of wealthy citizens occupying large, opulent homes, Herculaneum's position by the sea makes it an ideal spot for holiday homes for the Roman elite. It is also the perfect spot to view the FIRST ERUPTION.

At 1pm on 24 August, VESUVIUS bursts into life, propelling a thick cloud of ash and stones thousands of yards skywards. While this thick cloud cloaks Pompeii, Herculaneum, which is to the west of Vesuvius, only gets a very fine dusting, leaving a sooty layer a few inches deep. Though you might be troubled by irritated eyes, a dry throat, tight chest and nasal congestion, you will get a clear view of the action over Pompeii as the blanket of foul ash descends on it.

Though some of Herculaneum's residents stay put, hoping the worst is over, most abandon their homes and hit the road. With many fine dwellings abandoned, this is an excellent opportunity to explore.

Once you have selected a suitably DESERTED HOUSE, you will find yourself entering an open courtyard, the ATRIUM, from which you will be able to access the maze of rooms. There will be much to admire: shrines to the household gods (*lares*), ornate mirrors, oil lamps and bronze sculptures, and FRESCOES covering walls, ceilings and even floors, depicting scenes from mythology, erotic exploits, and hunting expeditions. Domestic GARDENS are a source of pride for their owners. Some will be wild, overrun with trees and vines; others more formal, with neatly arranged flowerbeds, or ornamental in style, featuring fishponds, shimmering pools and exquisite shrines. As you investigate, you will be struck by the eerie silence and ghostly hush that has descended on these homes, where only inanimate relics – the unoccupied dining room couches, the half-eaten food, the clothes dumped carelessly – bear witness to lives suddenly interrupted. They will remain in this state of suspended animation for a few more hours until the deluge consumes them.

By NIGHTFALL, you should be heading for the shoreline where small rowing boats will be waiting to take you out into the Bay of Naples, where you will transfer onto a larger vessel. The last shuttle will wait until 11.30pm, not a moment later. Anybody who fails to make the rendezvous in time will be stranded with no way back to the present. It is not a good prospect. Herculaneum will be flattened by hot gases sweeping through it at 100 miles per hour, reaching a temperature of 932° F (500° C), then buried under sixty foot of ash.

24 AUGUST: BAY OF NAPLES

Your rowing boat will help you transfer to our charter, a GRAIN SHIP with two sails, capable of an average speed of 4-5 knots in a favourable wind. It is controlled by side rudders and steering oars located at the stern of ship; these are manipulated by a system of cables rotated on an axis which are operated by the steersman who works the tiller (*clavus*), a bar set perpendicular to the oar. The steersman and the rest of the crew are all highly trained company employees. Light refreshments – soft-boiled eggs in pine-nut sauce, lentils with coriander, fresh oysters, sliced roast boar – will be served.

Gathered on deck, you will be ready for the main event later that night. When the initial ash cloud produced by VESUVIUS collapses, the gases it releases expand to create a PYROCLASTIC SURGE. This process will keep repeating itself in a series of devastating pulses, generating temperatures of up to 572° F (300° C). The third and fourth waves will level POMPEII, either incinerating or suffocating every living thing in its path.

From the boat you will see the top of Vesuvius smouldering away, burning brightly in darkness so thick it blots out the heavens as night merges seamlessly into day. Dotted across the landscape, the intense heat produces spots of glowing light like hundreds of bonfires.

You should also be able to make out the frantic activity on the shoreline as desperate throngs of people try to escape, trapped between increasingly choppy waters and the encroaching eruption. Many perish under hails of flaming debris – great masses of rocks and stones that have been transformed into lethal white-hot coals. As the catastrophe unfolds on land, you will notice the sea getting decidedly rougher, with huge, rolling waves slamming into the boat, tossing it hither and thither. This is because of seismic activity; the eruptions create tremors that ripple through the seabed.

Even on your boat, this is not a trip for the cautious. Sea-sickness may be an issue and you can expect slippery decks, an occasional soaking and moments when it will seem like the boat is about to sink without trace. Try to stay calm. It is a sturdy vessel and should be able to cope with the extreme conditions. We haven't lost one yet.

Shortly after the sixth and final pyroclastic surge, the ship will sail to the island of CAPRI and deposit you on a beach, ready for departure.

The Peasants' Revolt

12–15 JUNE 1381

MERRY OLD ENGLAND HAS REACHED boiling point. King Richard II, just fourteen, is perceived to be in thrall to a coterie of traitors and evil advisors: John of Gaunt, Duke of Lancaster and effectively regent during his nephew's minority, Archbishop of Canterbury Simon of Sudbury, and the Royal Treasurer Robert Hales. After three decades of social upheaval and swingeing taxation, join the peasants, yeomen and free townspeople of Kent, Essex and London as they rise up against their oppressors. You will join the rebel bands at Blackheath, consort with its leaders WAT TYLER, JACK STRAW and the radical preacher JOHN BALL; meet the KING'S BARGE AT ROTHERHITHE and then, with the angry London mob, STORM LONDON BRIDGE and take the city on the feast of Corpus Christi. This is an unparalleled opportunity to experience medieval London, its architectural eccentricities, rich social mix and odours, but don't linger for too long; all across the city you can see and join the febrile arc of rebellion, mob anarchy and counterrevolution.

BRIEFING: ENGLAND IN REVOLT

The PEASANTS' REVOLT emerged from three decades of tumult in medieval England. The Black Death that had swept Eurasia in the 1340s and 1350s killed over one third of the population of England. With land plentiful and labour in short supply the fundamental balance of power between the nobility and the peasantry shifted in favour of the latter. Bondsmen evaded their obligations, and moved to other manors or towns and the cost of labour soared despite repeated attempts to legally control wages. Serfdom was collapsing despite the draconian ORDINANCE OF LABOURERS and STATUTE OF LABOURERS that tried to keep them in place.

A widespread breakdown in feudal authority was made worse by the death of Edward III in 1377, when his son, now Richard II, was only ten; rule by his regent, his uncle John of Gaunt, the Duke of Lancaster, was widely reviled. The disastrous foreign policy conducted by Gaunt (who will be in the north of England during the rebellion signing another peace deal with the Scots) – above all the long-running and unwinnable Hundred Years' War with the French – required the levying of three monumentally costly POLL TAXES on the whole English population in 1377, 1379 and 1381. The first two had been met by some resistance and much evasion, but it was the third poll tax, due to be collected in June 1381, that finally ignited widespread protests in Essex and Kent. These led to systematic attacks on tax collectors and landowners and the organised BURNING OF LEGAL RECORDS of estates, churches and religious orders that specified feudal obligations and rents.

The rebel movement positioned itself politically by claiming to be for 'KING RICHARD AND THE COMMONS', and only against the traitors and incompetents who had led him astray. So when the message came to the Kentish rebels that the King would receive them near Blackheath, then outside London, they marched on the capital in their tens of thousands.

THE TRIP

Visitors will be arriving around lunchtime on Tuesday 12 June 1381 on the scrubby open lands of BLACKHEATH. These lie on the south side of the Thames about a mile upriver from the Tower of London and the City itself. You will find yourself among a

THE PRIEST JOHN BALL (ON HORSEBACK) ENCOURAGING WAT TYLER'S
REBELS – DEPICTED, ODDLY, IN FULL ARMOUR IN THIS 1470 MANUSCRIPT
OF JEAN FROISSART'S CHRONICLES.

gathering band of provincial rebels and lower-class Londoners,
awaiting a meeting with King Richard II.

For our more intrepid medievalists, we are now making available two longer excursions. These will allow you to experience the
initial risings in Essex and Kent before arriving at Blackheath;
though note that a basic level of equestrian skills and physical
fitness will be required.

ESSEX ARISE

A full twelve days longer than the London-only excursion, this
trip puts you down on 30 MAY at the edge of the market town
of BRENTWOOD, ESSEX, where a meeting of the local Justices

of the Peace with villagers will erupt into organised protest, the crowd refusing to pay their taxes before they run the King's representatives out of town. A short ride on WHITSUN SUNDAY to the village of BOCKING will allow you to join a great gathering of Essex men and witness the explosion of discontent and its organised export across the county.

Over the next week, the southern half of Essex, all of it within a day's ride, offers wildfire action of all kinds. Visitors will be expected to join the gathering of Essex rebels on 10 JUNE at CRESSING TEMPLE near the village of Coggeshall, where the Sheriff of Essex will be killed that evening by rebel bands. The MARCH ON LONDON begins on 11 JUNE via the town of CHELMSFORD, where there will be a spectacular display of RECORD BURNING. Please note that this march will terminate at Aldgate or Ludgate, on the north bank of the Thames. You will need to make your own way south across London Bridge to Blackheath, though you may find that the gates to the city are firmly shut. You should, however, be able to catch a ferryman on the wharves east of the Tower of London.

KENT IN FLAMES

Visitors will arrive in DARTFORD, the epicentre of the revolt in Kent, on 5 JUNE. Rebels have been riding out to the surrounding villages to gather support and you should find a couple of thousand armed men mustering there. On the following day, 6 JUNE, you will join them on their short march to ROCHESTER, where they will take the thinly defended CASTLE and take hostage the Constable of the Castle, Sir Roger Newenton. The 7th takes you to MAIDSTONE, where the mob will be STORMING THE JAIL and releasing the charismatic and heretical preacher of liberty JOHN BALL, whose Rotherhithe sermon later in the week is not to be missed

The most energetic visitors will then be able to join the emerging rebel leader WAT TYLER, whose bands will be marching on CANTERBURY some thirty miles to the south. On 10 JUNE you will be able to join Tyler on his entrance to CANTERBURY CATHEDRAL where he will call for the election of a new Archbishop, given the corruption of the old one. He will also call for the townspeople to name any 'traitors' in their midst. Three beheadings and a town-wide riot will follow while the rebels take the castle and break open the jail. On the following morning Tyler will recieve a royal messenger with the proposal that the rebels meet KING RICHARD in person near BLACKHEATH. For those who would like to take a mid-revolt breather, we recommend waiting things out in MAID-STONE or DARTFORD (Rochester is particularly prone to fire and riot), from where you will be able to rejoin Tyler's returning band as it heads towards Blackheath in the late afternoon of 11 June.

Whichever package you have chosen, and whatever route has brought you to BLACKHEATH, take a moment now to orient yourself; you will need to return here for your departure on the morning of June 16th. The small hamlet of GREENWICH is immediately to your north and it is here, on the low hill, that most of the leadership of the rebellion will be gathering. Follow the track across the heath away from the river and you will see two right hand turns. The first will take you down to ROTHERHITHE, where the rebels will be meeting King Richard; the second takes you to SOUTHWARK, the notorious suburb that sits on the south side of the river opposite London Bridge.

CITY LIFE

There are 354 TAVERNS within the walls of the City of London, so getting a drink shouldn't be a problem. Note, taverns are the upper end of the market serving only wine and food. The presence of linen tablecloths is a good guide to the best of them. The standard tipple is a BORDEAUX RED at a penny a cup; don't ask for claret, as the term won't come into use for another couple of centuries. Alternatively LEPE and OSEY are decent and strong Iberian whites. Better, but more expensive, RHENISH WINES at 2d a cup should also be available. Food in these establishments will revolve around ROAST MEATS and PIES.

London also boasts innumerable ALE HOUSES, with an altogether rougher clientele and more raucous atmosphere. Do keep an eye on your purse and your back in these establishments. As well as ALE, CIDER and MEAD should be on sale and basic nibbles like DARK BREAD and CHEESE. Street-food sellers are normally a big feature of fourteenth-century London, but the state of chaos that will prevail for most of your visit means that they will be around less than normal. Nonetheless, do look out for enterprising PIEMEN, BAKERS and FRUIT SELLERS. A word of warning on MEAT PIES: unscrupulous bakers have been known to mince up rotting carcasses to fill their wares.

London food markets and merchants would normally be a healthier alternative: in the month of June they should be full of soft fruits and spring vegetables. But, again, conditions of urban riot and mob rule will make trading difficult over the Corpus Christi weekend.

WHAT TO WEAR

The changing class structure of fourteenth-century England, and the threat to the established order of social mobility from below, has seen the introduction of increasingly punitive sumptuary laws. These have specified the kinds of fur, emblems, cloth and types of clothing that each layer of the social hierarchy can wear. But, like the rest of the feudal law, it has been breaking down. Over the main weekend of the Peasants' Revolt, for security reasons it will be best to dress modestly. It would be unfortunate to be mistaken for a lawyer, tax collector or juror during the worst of the mob violence in London. For both men and women travellers, we suggest clothes befitting someone above the rank of yeoman, perhaps a lowly townsperson or a junior scribe. We recommend: for gentlemen, HOSE (but not brightly coloured), a THIGH-LENGTH COAT and DOUBLET (go easy on the fur on the cuffs and the collars); for ladies, a LINEN SMOCK, a plain GROUND-LENGTH TUNIC, or KIRTLE, with narrow sleeves and surcoat.

ACCOMMODATION

Advance reservations have been made for you in two locations: outside of the city walls at the TABARD INN in Southwark and within the city walls at the LAMB TAVERN in Leadenhall Market. The former will be a safer and more secure evening venue, but the Lamb Tavern does keep you very close to the action. Feel free to use both. Payment will be required in advance and on arrival. Normal prices would be in the region of 1d for a bed for the night, 2d for a meal (more for meat and wine). We suggest budgeting for 4d per person at least. Your HORSES will need stabling and fodder, and that's another 2d each. Given the breakdown in social order, be prepared for a certain degree of price inflation. Beds are basic wooden frames strung with rope, but you can expect at least two straw and hemp mattresses per person.

HEALTH CARE

The last major outbreak of bubonic plague in southern England was in 1369; nonetheless all travellers will need to be fully up to date with PLAGUE VACCINE. In addition visitors must be inoculated against TYPHOID, TUBERCULOSIS and HEPATITIS. However, the most likely medical problem you will encounter will be in your guts and bowel. Emergency supplies of imodium will be supplied to travellers.

On such a short trip the danger of contracting LEPROSY is very slight; so do not be alarmed by the presence of lepers in London and on the roads in Essex and Kent.

TUESDAY 12 JUNE:
MEETING THE REBELS

The crowd on BLACKHEATH will be tired, hungry and expectant. Much of the day will be consumed by gathering firewood for the night ahead, pitching what little cover people have brought with them and waiting for a message from the King. Listen out for the FANTASTICAL RUMOURS that are sweeping through this volatile temporary encampment; Queen Joan apparently has blessed the rebellion, and the Earl of Buckinghamshire is about to declare for the people. The rebel leadership, on the hill near the river, will send their hostage, SIR JOHN NEWENTON, to the Tower of

London just a mile or so away. In the late afternoon, you may see two mounted royal heralds approach the hill. They will be delivering a summons from the King to meet at Rotherhithe the next morning.

An interesting afternoon and comfortable evening is available in SOUTHWARK (where you have a room booked at the Tabard Inn). We suggest that you arrive there by 4pm at the latest, as by 6pm much of the neighbourhood will be in flames. The first target of the rebels, who you will see joined by many Southwark towns-men, will be the MARSHALSEA PRISON next door to the inn. Over

RICHARD II ALMOST MEETS THE REBELS AT BLACKHEATH. THE TOWER OF
LONDON IS DEPICTED BEHIND THE ROYAL BARGE.

the course of the evening a number of houses belonging to Richard Imworth, keeper of the King's Bench Prison at Southwark and a local hate figure, will be burned, as will the houses and records of identified jurors and tax collectors. In the late evening many rebels will head west out of Southwark and march on LAMBETH PALACE, the home of the Archbishop of Canterbury. You should find this mob relatively restrained. The main purposes of the occupation will be finding and burning archiepiscopal records and the opening of the Bishop's casks of wine. The party going on at the palace kitchen is particularly lively; listen out for the popular song of the day, 'A Revel and a Revel'.

WEDNESDAY 13 JUNE: TYLER, THE KING AND AN EVENING OF BONFIRES

Whether you spend the night at Blackheath or bed down in Southwark you will need to be up early this morning to JOIN WAT TYLER and around a tenth of the rebel army on the south bank of the Thames at the royal manor of Rotherhithe. Tyler should be near the two large St George flags flying above the crowd. While you are waiting for King Richard and his entourage to put in a showing, the highlight of the morning will be the sermon given by JOHN BALL, the radical preacher freed by the Kentish mob in Rochester on 6 June. Listen out for his use of the well-known proverb 'When Adam Delved and Eve Span, who then was the Gentleman?' It's the kind of simple egalitarianism that sends shivers down the spine of any feudal ruling class.

Keep your eyes to the left. KING RICHARD'S BARGE and four accompanying vessels will appear around the long curve of the Thames. The King will be accompanied by ARCHBISHOP SUDBURY, Treasurer SIR ROBERT HALES and the EARLS OF WARWICK AND SALISBURY. Expect a lot of baying and ballyhoo onshore until the royal fleet pulls up about thirty yards away and refuses to land. There will be some discussion across the water and then a flurry of activity as the rebel leaders respond to the King's request for a

WRITTEN PETITION. One man will walk out into the water with the document and hand it over. It is a long list of required reforms and specific calls for the execution of leading members of Richard's court like John of Gaunt and Bishop Courtney of London, as well as Archbishop Sudbury and Treasurer Hales, who are on the boat. After some discussion, the royal retinue will turn around and row off upriver, leaving the Kentish rebels on the shore in a state of uproar.

From late morning onwards, the now angry rebels will be marching from Rotherhithe and Blackheath towards Southwark and London Bridge. Look out for the BROTHEL by SOUTHWARK FISHPONDS, owned by William Walworth, Mayor of London, which will go up in flames as the rebel army passes by. Many rebels will then gather on the southern third of LONDON BRIDGE, their path blocked by its raised drawbridge. On the other side, past the shops and the chapel that line the stone bridge, a large crowd can be seen, many of whom will appear to be welcoming the arrival of the rebels. At this point it is is widely believed that they are not a mob, and that they have come only to serve notice on traitors and have promised to pay market prices for victuals in the city. It won't quite work out that way. The drawbridge will eventually be lowered and, to cacophonic hooting and wailing, the crowd will pour across it and into the city.

Once you are across and heading north on BRIDGE STREET, take a moment to pause at the first junction; BILLINGSGATE is on your right and THE ROPERY is on your left. Some of the crowd streaming around you will turn right down Billingsgate and head for the TOWER OF LONDON, where a large crowd will be gathering on Tower Hill taunting the royal retinue trapped inside. Some will head straight on towards Fenchurch Street and then to ALDGATE, where the massed ranks of many of the Essex rebels are waiting to enter the city. While in this part of town do look out for GEOFFREY CHAUCER, who is currently renting an apartment above Aldgate. Most of the crowd will be turning left and heading west towards Ludgate and Newgate, where once again many other rebels are encamped. The NEWGATE MOB will be making for two locations on the other side of the city walls: NEWGATE PRISON and, three-quarters of a mile north up Golden Lane, the PRIORY OF ST MARY in Clerkenwell, the headquarters of the Knights Hospitaller.

By far the largest mob will be heading west towards Ludgate; follow them and keep the spire of St Paul's Cathedral to your right. LUDGATE itself is worth a look. It has recently been rebuilt using stones taken from the houses of rich Jewish merchants (killed or expelled in the thirteenth century) and is adorned with statues of ancient Britannic monarchs – including the legendary King Lud. Beyond the gate the city will give way to the pastures, estates, orchards and grand manors of the Bishop of Salisbury and the CARMELITES, or the White Friars as they are known. Very few rebels will enter these properties, though a small detachment will turn north to break down the doors of FLEET PRISON. Nearly everyone else will be heading along Fleet Street to either THE TEMPLE or, another mile down the Strand, to the largest house of all – John of Gaunt's SAVOY PALACE.

The Temple had originally served as the headquarters of the Knights Templar in the twelfth century but after their dissolution has fallen into the hands of Knights Hospitaller. They in turn had then leased the whole place out to the London legal profession, providing lodgings for trainee lawyers and repositories for legal documents. Around 4pm the grounds will be stormed by the rebels, some of whom will actually dismantle the outbuildings, while a gigantic BONFIRE of rolls, remittances, books and case notes will go up in flames in the gardens.

Attention will then turn to the Strand, the continuation of Fleet Street heading west. Here you will find the great houses of the Bishops of Exeter, Bath, Llandaff, Coventry and Worcester, but more opulent than any of these is the SAVOY PALACE standing on the south side of the Strand about halfway between the City and Westminster. There will most likely be a considerable crowd here by the time you arrive and the large gates in the palace's formidable stone walls will already be off their hinges. Still true to their original intent of punishing but not looting, the sack of the Savoy Palace is strangely ordered. Its napery, clothes and cloth will be burned to a cinder. Jewels will be ground to dust rather than being pocketed; gilt plate, both silver and gold, will be beaten out of shape rather than stolen. One attempt, mid-evening, by a rebel to pilfer some of the palace's plate will result in an impromptu court and punishment. Please don't be tempted inside the building by the sounds of the drunk laughing or the righteous calling; the small fires already lit inside the palace will be turning into a raging conflagration when three barrels of gunpowder inside are accidentally ignited.

EVENING

Towards evening, the action turns to CHEAPSIDE, which should be approached with some caution. This rare public space, right in the heart of the city, has long been a place of preaching, public punishments, and general milling about. It sits at the intersection of Milk Street, Bread Street and Wood Street and can be easily identified by its ELEANOR CROSS, a structure made of four hexagonal stone steps crowned by six statues of the late Queen Eleanor (it was built by Edward I, mourning the journey of his dead wife's body from Lincoln to Westminster Abbey). This evening, and for the next few days, it is going to be a site of EXECUTIONS by clumsy beheadings. The mob will be looking for a variety of known tax collectors and questermongers all over the city, and in particular the notorious ROGER LEGETT. Legett will be cornered by the mob at the church of St Martins le Grand on Newgate Street, a traditional place of sanctuary. The mob, however, will be having none of it. Legett will be dragged out of the church, and down West Cheap to Cheapside and his doom.

Alternatively you can join the crowds heading north along the Holborn river towards the open fields of CLERKENWELL. En route, the mob will be burning a series of properties owned by Legett, but the main prize is the PRIORY OF ST JOHN OF JERUSALEM – the home of the Knights Hospitaller, a fabulously wealthy military order. The entire complex will be torched and the remains will burn for over a week.

If you need to get away from the claustrophobia of the city streets or the mania of large-scale arson, head west toward the TOWER OF LONDON. In addition to the gathering on Tower Hill, you will now find a REBEL VILLAGE forming on the fields of the HOSPITAL OF ST KATHARINE on the far eastern side of the Tower. Late in the evening two ROYAL KNIGHTS will arrive at St Katherine's with a parchment bearing the King's own seal. One man among the crowd will stand on a hastily provided chair and read out their message, which is to the effect that 'everyone will be pardoned if they'd just go home now and then could they all to put their complaints in writing'. This will elicit a very strong reaction from the overwhelmingly illiterate crowd, who have been burning written records for the last week. Some of them will set off back to the City this evening to burn the houses and papers of lawyers and recorders.

Travellers who can't face the walk back to their rooms in Southwark or Leadenhall might like to bed down here for the night. Tower Hill and St Katharine's will be peaceful and well provisioned with wine and food, much of it intercepted on the way to the Tower and the rest given to them by Londoners. The party will go on all night long.

THURSDAY 14 JUNE: THE KING AT MILE END AND STORMING THE TOWER

Today you will need to choose one of three locations to focus on in the morning: HIGHBURY, MILE END or the TOWER OF LONDON.

The village of HIGHBURY lies to the the north of the city and is home to a number of estates owned by Treasurer Hales. From early morning a very large band of rebels, led by JACK STRAW, will have been systematically torching their great houses and stone barns. This group will be joined by a large body of townspeople from St Albans, alerted to the rebellion in London, and heading south to join it. Straw will later gather them together and ask them to collectively swear the rebel oath of allegiance 'To King Richard and the Commons'. Note that it is a three-mile hike to Highbury from the City: leave through Aldersgate and head north along Aldersgate Road and then Goswell Road.

The main political action of the day will be taking place just east of the city on the open fields of MILE END. After a night-long war council, KING RICHARD has decided to continue with his strategy of appeasement, and will be sending out messages to every quarter of the city to meet him at Mile End this morning. He will be riding out with a small retinue, including the Earls of Warwick and Oxford, his half-brothers, Thomas and John Holland, Sir Aubrey de Vere who will be carrying the King's sword, his leading soldiers Sir Robert Knolles and Sir Thomas Percy, and Mayor Walworth. QUEEN JOAN will be bringing up the rear in a whirligig. Look out for the London captain THOMAS FARRINGDON, who accosts the King on a number of occasions, grabs the reins of his horse, and calls for the execution of Treasurer Hales – 'That false traitor the prior.' If you want to beat the crowds, head out before dawn through Aldgate and get yourself to Mile End, where most of the rebel army and much of the London mob will be gathering. Look out for two enormous books looted in Essex from the library of Admiral Edmund de la Mare; they will be carried around the field on the prongs of pitchforks, serving as strange rebel totems.

The choreography of the morning will be as follows. A small number of REBEL LEADERS WILL APPROACH KING RICHARD, initially addressing him on bended knee. They will make a long list of requests and complaints, generally concerning conditions of serfdom and work, and calls for an end to feudal fines and manorial controls. After a certain amount of this Richard will say 'Yes' to all that, and call for the mob to line up in two long ranks so that he can confer a new charter of liberties on them. The King, at this point, for no obvious good reason, will loudly proclaim that, in addition to the freedom charters, the rebels are now free to go and catch traitors all across the realm of England, who they should then bring to him for trial according to the due process of the law. Quite how much of that everyone hears is a moot point. You will find that within minutes most rebels have decided either to go home or, ignited by the Royal Command, are baying to go and catch traitors in London. The due process of law will have to wait.

The news that King Richard has asked the rebels to seek out traitors will reach the TOWER OF LONDON by around 9.30am, and a large number of rebels will arrive there soon after from Mile End. The Tower, although appearing impregnable, will be captured by the rebels over the next hour; we have reports of the drawbridge being voluntarily lowered, the guards abandoning their positions on sighting a Royal Standard of England amongst the mob, and sympathisers within the Tower opening secret doors to the rebels.

Visitors may join the STORMING OF THE TOWER, but bearing in mind how easy it is to get lost in its maze of corridors and rooms, and how unsavoury it is going to be, it might be better to sit this one out. If you do go in, you are not, on any account, to reveal the hiding place of HENRY BOLINGBROKE, son of John of Gaunt, who in eighteen years is going to be crowned Henry IV of England. Over the next couple of hours rebel forces will reappear with four important prisoners: Archbishop of Canterbury SIMON OF SUDBURY, Royal Treasurer SIR ROBERT HALES, the King's Sergeant-at-Arms JOHN LEGGE and the Franciscan friar WILLIAM APPLETON, physician to John of Gaunt. All will be beheaded on Tower Hill. Sudbury's execution will be particularly cack-handed, requiring eight blows from an axe to sever his head from his body.

Look out later on in the morning for QUEEN JOAN escaping on on a barge to join the rest of the royals at their bolthole, CASTLE BAYNARD, in the west of the city.

AFTERNOON AND EVENING

The day is going to turn ever more gruesome. The anti-foreigner feeling among the London mob, in particular, will be given free rein. The ITALIAN BANKERS gathered around Lombard Street will be battening down the hatches, but by far the worst fate awaits the FLEMINGS or Flemish who are concentrated in the Vintry Ward, in the lanes south of Trinity Street running down to the Thames. At the junction of Queen Street and Upper Thames Street, you will find the mob gathering. They will eventually break down the church doors of the St Martin in the Vintry, where over forty Flemings will be hiding, and then they will behead them all. Another victim of the mob in the Vintry this afternoon will be the fabulously wealthy London merchant RICHARD LYONS, who will be snatched from his house and dragged through the streets of the Cordwainer Ward to the north before being beheaded on Cheapside. Look out for what one contemporary describes as, a man 'Very fair and large, with his hair rounded by his ears and curled, a little beard forked, a gown, girt to him down to his feet, of branched damasks, wrought with the lines of flowers, a large purse on his right side, hanging in a belt from his left shoulder: a plain hood about his neck, covering his shoulders and hanging back behind him.'

The heads of a number of those decapitated at Tower Hill in the morning will make their way across town to the ELEANOR CROSS in the hamlet of CHARRING, where rebel leaders will be orchestrating their display. Archbishop Sudbury, his red mitre nailed to his head, will be on show, joined by Sir Robert Hales, Roger Legget, William Appleton and the juror Robert Somenour, all of them atop high spears or lances. In the late afternoon you can follow a raucous TOUR OF THE FIVE HEADS to Westminster and then back to the city finishing at London Bridge, where they will be left on display.

FRIDAY 15 JUNE: WESTMINSTER ABBEY AND THE DEATH OF WAT TYLER

Early birds and royal watchers might like to base themselves in Westminster from dawn on Friday morning. RICHARD IMWORTH, the keeper of the King's Bench Prison in Southwark,

THIS REALLY IS SIMON OF SUDBURY – OR AT LEAST A RECONSTRUCTION
OF HIS HEAD, CREATED BY A FORENSIC ARTIST FROM THE ARCHBISHOP'S
SKULL, SIX HUNDRED YEARS AFTER IT PARTS COMPANY WITH HIS BODY.

is one of the main targets of the rebels still abroad. He has fled his
Southwark estates and taken refuge in WESTMINSTER ABBEY. At
approximately 9am a large detachment of rebels will approach and
enter the Abbey and will head for the High Altar, where Imworth
will be hiding – and is taken captive. You can then follow the
crowd back to Cheapside where Imworth will be beheaded in the
early afternoon.

As you approach Bread Street on your return, look out for the
unfortunate JOHN OF GREENFIELD, a valet who has apparently
spoken well of John of Gaunt's physician William Appleton (who
was beheaded yesterday). For this, he will be dragged by the mob
down to Queenhithe and the banks of the Thames before being
dragged back up to Cheapside, where he will be executed.

If you decide to stay in Westminster, await the ARRIVAL OF
KING RICHARD. He and his retinue of over 200 will be met by
a procession of the canons from St Stephen's Church, who will
then accompany the King to Westminster Abbey for private
prayers in the shrine of Edward the Confessor. Entry to the

Abbey will not be possible, and we recommend that you join the tail of the royal retinue when they depart an hour later for Smithfield.

EVENING

Visitors who choose to begin the day in the city centre should keep their ears open for the news that King Richard has called the rebels to a third meeting, which today is designated at SMITHFIELD – a large open space north of the city commonly used for fairs, festivals and public executions. After lunch you will find a steady flow of people walking up to Newgate and Aldersgate – follow them. By around 5pm most of the remaining rebel forces in London will have gathered on Smithfield, and you will notice that WAT TYLER is once again on horseback and in command.

The royal retinue will arrive and assemble at some distance from the rebel army, in front of the hospital and the large stone Priory of St Bartholomew. You are unlikely to be able to get very close to the action to come, certainly not near enough to hear it, so a certain amount of interpreting body language will be required to make sense of events. You should be able to see Wat Tyler ride out towards Richard and his retinue. At distance it is hard to see, but Tyler does appear to treat the King with a degree of contempt. There will be no bended knee this time; an over-firm handshake with the royal glove follows, and then you should see a long barracking during which Tyler purportedly outlines a UTOPIAN VISION OF ENGLAND in which much of the legal and spiritual apparatus of Plantagenet feudalism is dismantled. At some point here there will be an altercation between Mayor Walworth and Tyler, daggers will be drawn and used, and then, after further commotion, one of the royal retinue, RALPH STANDISH, will run Tyler through with a sword.

Confusion will reign all around, but keep your eyes on the King, who will call to the rebel army to follow him, and with

MEDIEVAL COMIC BOOK CAPERS. RICHARD II WATCHES LONDON
MAYOR RALPH STANDISH KILL WAT TYLER, AND TALKS TO THE
PEASANTS AT THE SAME TIME.

his bodyguard will ride off in the direction of Clerkenwell Field;
after some indecision, much of the rebel force will follow him.
Later on in the afternoon, MAYOR WALWORTH will return to
Clerkenwell at the head of a small army of mercenary officers
who will quickly surround the now demoralised and confused
rebel forces. On Richard's order, and in the face of the newly
arrived troops, you will see the rebel army slowly melt away, with
much of the Essex contingent heading for home. If you can get
close enough to the royal retinue at this point, you should be
able to see Richard confer knighthoods on Mayor Walworth and
three other aldermen: Nicholas Brembre, Robert Launde and
Ralph Standish.

DEPARTURE

We recommend that you make this your last port of call on this visit. Try and resist the urge to follow the Essex rebels home, or to explore the waves of rebellion and then counterterror that will ripple out across the country over the coming weeks from Bridgeport in Somerset to Cambridge and York.

First Battle of Bull Run

21 JULY 1861 ❋ WASHINGTON D.C. & VIRGINIA, US

 JOIN THE ELITES OF THE UNION AT THE first major battle of the American Civil War. Dine at WILLARD'S HOTEL, the centre of Washington D.C.'s social life and smell the hubris; take a carriage to CENTREVILLE, Virginia where the Union army of the Potomac is massing; sample the atmosphere on the CENTREVILLE KNOLL, where journalists, politicians and the curious gather. For the intrepid, see and hear the battle from forward positions. But be warned: the devastating retreat and then rout of the Union army is to come ... and you'll be just ahead of the pack skittering up the Warrenton Turnpike and back to Washington.

BRIEFING: EXPECTING A SWIFT VICTORY

In the early days of the American Civil War, the Union's politicians and press were calling for a quick and decisive victory over the rebel confederacy in northern Virginia, paving the way for an assault on their capital in Richmond.

Under political pressure, and with some reluctance, given the untried nature of his forces, GENERAL IRVING MCDOWELL manoeuvred the UNION ARMY OF THE POTOMAC, 35,000 strong, southwest of Washington. There, the CONFEDERACY FORCES led by PIERRE GUSTAVE TOUTANT BEAUREGARD had massed at Manassas railway junction, on the far side of the BULL RUN RIVER.

The Washington political elite thought they were going to send the Confederacy packing at BULL RUN. Hundreds of civilians travelled the thirty miles from the capital to join General McDowell's army around the hamlet of CENTREVILLE, expecting a swift victory.

It won't quite work out that way. McDowell, due to a mixture

A UNION ARTILLERY UNIT ON THE BATTLEFIELD OF BULL RUN.

of poor scouting, inexperience and bad luck, will find himself unable to concentrate his larger forces at the decisive moments of the battle. In particular, the great flanking movement of two of his divisions on the west of the battlefield will be slowed to a snail's pace by treacherous conditions. By contrast, Beauregard will be able to turn the tide of the battle when reinforcements arrive by rail. When the Union's line breaks at around 5pm the discipline of this very inexperienced and now brutalised army will crack. Thousands of men will pour back to Centreville and when harried by Confederate artillery and cavalry it will become a rout.

Both armies are desperately naive and ill co-ordinated. All are shocked by the scale of the slaughter and by the harsh psychological and emotional conditions of battle. After Bull Run, it will become clear to all that the war will be long, gruelling and costly.

THE TRIP

You will be arriving in WASHINGTON DC in late afternoon, Saturday 20 July 1861. The weather will be warm and the air humid as you step out onto the south-east corner of the junction of PENNSYLVANIA AVENUE AND 14TH STREET. Please return here by midnight on Monday 22 July for departure.

Washington, despite its apparent grandeur, is a new, small and desperately underdeveloped city. Garbage disposal and sanitation are particularly poorly provided for – a situation made worse by the marshy and mosquito-ridden landscape on which the new capital has been constructed. Sniff the air. The rotten aromas of the city's putrid drainage canal, a quarter of a mile away, will be unmistakable.

Directly opposite you, however, is the beautiful curving corner of WILLARD'S HOTEL, a five-storey Beaux Arts concoction that serves as the capital's most prestigious visiting address. Home to President Lincoln before his inauguration earlier this year, and the site of the last desperate and failed peace conference before the war, it is now the centre of Washington's political and social life. Its salons and dining rooms are filled with politicians, lobbyists, senior military officers, journalists and businessmen, not to mention, as the writer Nathaniel Hawthorne, who will be visiting Willard's in 1862, put it, 'office seekers, wire pullers, inventors, artists, attachés of foreign powers, long-winded talkers, contractors and railway directors'. Note the small patches of smoke and water damage on the building's walls. Just two months prior to your arrival, a fire in a small barber's shop next door threatened to engulf the hotel. A battalion of New York firemen, enlisted in the Union army as the 11th New York Zouaves (whom you will be meeting later), came to the rescue, forming human pyramids to carry water and hoses.

This is a good opportunity to take a look at the WHITE HOUSE just to your west and the WASHINGTON MONUMENT, five minutes' walk due south along 14th Street. CAPITOL HILL is a few minutes' ride by carriage or the regular omnibus service southwest along Pennsylvania Avenue.

You may be surprised by the architectural mayhem of the street. Broad and lined with alianthus trees, it is populated by a mixture of grand marble town houses, official buildings, rough wood-plank commercial premises and tumbledown plots. The Capitol building itself is undergoing major works, its roofline covered with half-finished marble towers, ironwork and cranes; the old dome on the building is being supplanted by a new and much bigger dome.

When you are ready to eat, head back to Willard's, walk into the lobby and look for the dining rooms – reservations are not necessary. We recommend that you eat heartily while you can, as dining at Bull Run will be a much more haphazard affair. The menu features baked pike in claret sauce, roasted leg of mutton with capers, and broiled quails. For those with a sweet tooth, try the Lady Cake, cream pies and jelly tart. As you will see from your fellow diners, PICNIC HAMPERS, SANDWICHES AND BEER can also be ordered here for your journey.

We recommend you call for your carriage no later than midnight and preferably much earlier. Those who wish to see the Union Army's pre-dawn mobilisation should be gone by 7pm.

CENTREVILLE

Your carriage will be taking you west through GEORGETOWN and
then south across the Potomac River before heading for CENTRE-
VILLE in Prince William County, Virginia; it is about 30 miles – a
seven-hour drive. Centreville is a tiny place, tired-looking at the
best of times. On the morning of 21 July you will find the town a
great ragged military encampment.

To its east are three UNION DIVISIONS commanded by
COLONELS HUNTER, HEINTZELMAN and MILES. To the west,
about half a mile from town, is the division led by BRIGADIER
GENERAL TYLER. The two encampments are connected by the
Warrenton Turnpike, which serves as the town's main street. There
are shutterboard houses, a small hotel and a chapel but little to
trouble the visitor. The Union's commander-in-chief, GENERAL
MCDOWELL, is camped close to the town on the west side. You
might, while wandering near the camp, hear the general vomiting;
he will be struck by a violent episode of food poisoning this evening.

Around 2.30am you will begin to hear the army stir: expect
bugles, drum rolls and beats, and hundreds of campfires bursting
into flame. Breakfast for most of the troops will be grim boiled
coffee, pressed beef, hard tack biscuits and tobacco. Wagons will
creek into action, horse harnesses will jangle, troops will be check-
ing their weapons and then there will be a rising crescendo of
barked orders and movement. It will already be a pleasant temperature and will be considerably warmer by early morning. At
the peak of the battle later in the day, it will be searing and many
soldiers on both sides will suffer from severe dehydration. Now is
the moment to make sure you have plenty of water supplies.

UNIFORMS

As the army mobilises, you will notice that there is no single, common uniform among the troops. Although the UNION has broadly opted for NAVY BLUE and the CONFEDERACY for GREY, there will be plenty of soldiers in both colours or the opponents' colours, for

THE ZOUAVE LOOK AS MODELLED BY A UNION SOLDIER.

neither side has established centralised quartermasters operations or imposed a common uniform. This sartorial irregularity is made worse by the fact that regiments are often kitted out by their city or state patrons, and officers have to buy their own uniforms. In any case, there will be so much dust, smoke and mud at Bull Run later in the day that it will often be impossible to know who is who.

Two distinctive uniforms to look out for, however, are:

11TH NEW YORK INFANTRY (aka Ellsworth or First Fire Zouaves). The zouaves are distinguished by red cuffs and trim on their navy jackets as well as a red fireman's undershirt. They will be wearing a mixture of blue and red fezes and blue and red kepis.

14TH NEW YORK MILITIA (aka 14th Brooklyn or Red Legged Devils). The devils team their blue chasseur jackets with red pantaloons, a red-and-blue-banded kepi and havelocks – white cloth-neck and head covers.

The ARMY'S MANOEUVRES, which will begin at about 4.30am, are simple in design but, as you will see, enormously complicated and fraught in practice. HUNTER AND HEINTZELMAN'S DIVISIONS – nearly 12,000 men, are camped equidistant form the turnpike but start marching simultaneously, leading to a terrible bottleneck of troops, horse and equipment on the main street of Centreville. Worse, by the time the leading columns reach the west side of town, they will butt up against the rear of TYLER'S DIVISION still making its way down the Warrenton Turnpike to the STONE BRIDGE, having been delayed by fierce skirmishing along the path. Around 5.30am the jam will be cleared when General McDowell and his staff put in an appearance at the rickety wooden CUB RUN BRIDGE and order Tyler's remaining troops to get off the road and let Hunter and Heintzelman's divisions through.

For those visitors who want to experience SUDLEY FIELD HOSPITAL (see below), join the rear of Heintzelman's division as it turns off the Warrenton Turnpike a few hundred yards beyond the Cub Run Bridge. The march to Sudley Ford North and then back south through Sudley to the western edge of MATTHEWS HILL should take about five hours. Another two hundred yards along the turnpike you will find a blacksmith's, which has been turned into GENERAL MCDOWELL'S FORWARD FIELD HQ.

THE CENTREVILLE KNOLL

The GRASSY KNOLL to the south of Centreville is the main point at which civilian visitors to the battle will gather during the day. As you arrive in the early morning, a small number of journalists, politicians and their retinues will already have staked out positions. Over the next five hours, numbers will swell as carriages, city hacks and wagons roll in, joined by more visitors on horse or on foot. Amongst the early arrivals to look out for are WILLIAM HOWARD RUSSELL, correspondent for the *Times* of London, and the photographer MATTHEW BRADY, identifiable by his straw hat, long linen duster and the large wooden box (his camera) strapped

to his back. From Capitol Hill, look out for SENATORS HENRY
WILSON (Massachusetts); ZACHARIAH CHANDLER (Michigan);
BEN WADE (Ohio); JAMES GRIMES (Iowa); JIM LANE (Kan-
sas); LAFAYETTE FOSTER (Connecticut); and from the House of
Representatives, ALFRED ELY (New York); SCHUYLER COLFAX
(Indiana); and ELIHU WASHBURN and ISAAC ARNOLD (Illinois).
Senator Wilson and his servants will be handing out freshly made
sandwiches to troops for much of the morning. Do try and stay
clear of his buggy and horses; they will be struck by a Confederate
shell late in the afternoon, forcing the Senator to escape back to
Washington on a mule.

Other characters passing through the knoll will include JUDGE
DANIEL MCCOOK of Ohio and the leading abolitionist W.P.
THOMASSON, who is notable for his extremely high black silk top
hat. Later in the day he will pick up a rifle and join the 71st New
York in battle, as will CONGRESSMAN OWEN LOVEJOY of Illinois.
Two young Bostonians with a cart will pull up looking for the
corpse of their brother – a Union soldier killed in a skirmish at
Blackburn Ford, just south of the knoll, three days earlier. There
are at least two dozen women on the knoll as well, including
mothers of soldiers, wives of senators, and PIE AND SELTZER
SELLERS. Look out for MISS AUGUSTA FOSTER, the adopted
daughter and regimental mascot of the 2nd Maine.

In actual fact you will see very little of the battle from here.
Though the sound of cannon fire and the smell of gun smoke will
be prevalent all day, the main action on MATTHEW'S HILL and
HENRY HOUSE HILL is almost five miles away. At various points
during the day, especially late morning and lunchtime, Union
officers will ride up with good news from the front line – 'We've
whipped them at all points'; please do try not to give the game
away. If you do decide to spend all day here, we suggest that you
and your carriage are on the road out of Centreville by 6.30pm
before the rout makes horse-drawn traffic impossible.

The more adventurous among the crowd, however, especially
the senior republican senators and journalists, will be making

COLONEL DIXON MILES – HARD LIQUOR NOT DEPICTED.

their way closer to the battle field from 9am, heading for the WARRENTON TURNPIKE or the BULL RUN RIDGE (see below). More cautious travellers who would, nonetheless, like to get away from the knoll should explore BLACKBURN'S FORD and follow COLONEL DIXON MILES.

On a ridge about a mile south and slightly west of Centreville on the road to Manassas, you will find CAPTAIN JOHN TIDBALL and his artillery battery. From here you will have a good view of Bull Run creek and the narrow Blackburn's Ford at the bottom of the ravine. There will still be corpses and abandoned equipment here, left over from a skirmish on the previous Thursday. By lunchtime there will be a considerable crowd, with buggies and carts parked in an overflow field behind the artillery battery, and a throng around Tidball, questioning him, fruitlessly, about the progress of the battle.

For those able to track him on horseback, the peregrinations of COLONEL DIXON MILES make for an interesting afternoon. Placed in command of the reserves, the colonel can be found in the morning on the stoop of the CENTREVILLE HOTEL, which is serving as his HQ and as a field hospital. He will be sporting the bizarre but effective sun protection of two straw hats mashed together on his head, and he will already be a little the worse for wear on a combination of liquor and opiate-based medicines. Colonel Dixon Miles will be making his first visits to the artillery positions of Colonel Davies and Richardson in the morning but the afternoon return encounters will be the most colourful. Richardson in particular will refuse to accept Miles's orders and will publicly accuse him of being drunk. Hang around long enough at Richardson's position, and General McDowell himself will eventually show up and relieve Colonel Miles of his position.

BULL RUN RIDGE

Unquestionably the best vantage point from which to see at least some of the battle is the BULL RUN RIDGE just to the south of the Warrenton Turnpike. You can walk here across country but we suggest that you get on the turnpike and walk west. By late lunchtime the main reporters and senior senators will have gathered here with a view of a least parts of HENRY HOUSE HILL and MATTHEW'S HILL, where the main fighting will be concentrated. For the very intrepid, the best view of all can be gained another half a mile down the Warrenton Turnpike at the STONE BRIDGE over Bull Run.

Over the afternoon, JUDGE DANIEL MCCOOK will be lunching with one of his sons, serving that day on the battlefield, and tragically leaving with his corpse in his buggy after he is shot by a Confederate officer. CONGRESSMEN WASHBURNE, irate throughout the day, will be heading out on his reconnaissance mission in the afternoon. As ever, do make sure you are clear of the area by 5.30pm, when it will be overrun by the Confederate cavalry. CONGRESSMEN ELY will be taken prisoner by an infantry brigade.

BATTLEFIELD MEDICINE

The battle, although a mere skirmish compared to the massive encounters yet to come in the American Civil War, will appear unbelievably bloody and horrific to participants and observers. By the end of the day there will be 460 Union deaths and 1,124 wounded, while the Confederacy will lose 387 men and suffer 1,587 injuries. Many of the dead and injured will end up at one of the field hospitals established on the day.

For the medically minded among our travellers, UNION FIELD HOSPITALS can be found at: the four-room farmhouse by Stone Bridge; the Lewis House to the north of this; and on the Warrenton Turnpike beyond Bull Run Ridge. However, by far the largest and busiest is at SUDLEY SPRINGS, the village through which Hunter and Heintzelman's divisions marched in the morning.

Later in the day Sudley Springs cannot be approached across the battlefield, so you will have to follow Hunter and Heintzelman's men on their pre-dawn march. Here you will find that the church will be rapidly converted into a field hospital. Its pews will be removed and placed in the oak grove next to the church, and hay will be spread on the floor as improvised operating tables are set up inside.

The first AMBULANCE WAGONS, with their distinctive white canvas covers, will begin arriving from 10.30am, blood dripping from the carts and gathering in a puddle outside the church door. Over the course of the afternoon the medics will commandeer two nearby houses and a wheelwright's shop, but the churchyard will still fill to overflowing with the dead, the dying and the wounded. Alongside dressing wounds, staunching cuts and setting broken bones, the surgeons will be busy with amputations in an effort to save injured soldiers. Anaesthetics available include brandy, morphine and chloroform, but we do warn travellers that the sounds of the hospitals are even more fearsome than the sights and smells.

THE BATTLE

From the vantage points of either the Stone Bridge or Bull Run Ridge, visitors will be able to glimpse only elements of the battle: the Union troops of TYLER'S DIVISION pouring across the Stone Bridge in mid-afternoon, skittish lines of troops crossing fields, plumes of smoke from the copses that dot the hillsides. Nonetheless, from these limited signals you should be able to put together the key choreography.

In the morning – from around 9.30am to 11.30am – Union and Confederate forces will clash on MATTHEWS HILL. You should be able to make out BRIGADIER GENERAL NATHAN EVANS' SEVENTH BRIGADE shift position from in front of the Stone Bridge to the west side of Matthews Hill, where the the main body of Union troops are beginning to arrive via Sudley Ford. Be alert to the advance of COLONEL SHERMAN'S SECOND BRIGADE, over Farm Ford a few hundred yards north of Stone Bridge. This pincer movement from the Union forces will, by around 11.30am, force the Confederate lines on Matthew's Hill to break. Visitors will be able to see them make their RETREAT south onto Henry House Hill.

Over the next hour or so, expect a steady ARTILLERY DUEL between the Union forces now massing on Matthew's Hill and the reassembling Confederate lines on Henry House Hill. Between

IF THE BATTLE LOOKS LIKE THIS TO YOU (AND YOU'RE LOOKING HERE AT A UNION ATTACK), THEN YOU'RE PROBABLY TOO CLOSE. PLEASE RETURN TO THE BULL RUN RIDGE.

1pm and 3pm, repeated UNION ATTACKS will be beaten off, including the now famous, but probably apocryphal, moment when Virginian COLONEL JACKSON's regiment stands firm at the centre of the Confederate lines 'like a stonewall'.

It will not be immediately apparent from your vantage points, but after 3.30pm the TIDE OF BATTLE WILL BEGIN TO TURN. The Union's troops, many of them completely exhausted by their long march and lack of food and water, are beginning to wilt. At the same time a large number of CONFEDERATE REINFORCEMENTS will arrive from the Shenandoah Valley by train. When they are thrown into the battle the UNION LINES WILL BREAK, first on the CHINN RIDGE on the eastern edge of the battlefield and then in the centre at the foot of Henry House Hill. By 5.00pm the Union army will be in HEADLONG RETREAT. Some will head north back to Sudley, but above all they will be flowing east over the Stone Bridge and back up the Warrenton Turnpike.

FEDERAL CAVALRY AT SUDLEY FORD AFTER THE BATTLE.

SENATORS ZACHARIAH CHANDLER AND BENJAMIN WADE.

THE RETREAT

The first signs of THE RETREAT will become apparent on Bull Run Ridge around 5pm. Fleeing soldiers will cry, 'Turn back, turn back, we're whipped!' At this, expect SENATOR ZACHARIAH CHANDLER to respond by attempting to singlehandedly block the road, demanding that soldiers stop retreating. SENATOR BEN WADE will train a rifle on his troops, but in vain. It is now imperative that you get beyond the CUB RUN BRIDGE, a mile up the road, by 6pm; after that, Confederate fire will reach the bridge and induce the greatest moment of panic. A wagon on the bridge will swerve and turn over, blocking the path and forcing the streaming mass of people into the creek. At this point the retreat will become a ROUT. Soldiers will abandon their weapons, haversacks and even uniforms, leaving a trail of ammunition boxes, hay bales and bags of oats. Shells will be bursting overhead. Troops will clamber aboard ambulances, wagons, captured mules and stray horses. Officers and men alike will be running pell-mell for Centreville, yelling with rage and fear; it is best not to get in their way.

Safety lies another mile up the turnpike, where COLONEL BLENKER'S GERMAN BRIGADE – three infantry regiments plus cannon – will be covering the Union retreat and enforcing a modicum of order on the road. Some troops will be heading home, some will be heading to Washington, most will go to their camps in Centreville and grab what they can before beginning the thirty-mile walk back to the capital. General McDowell will order a COMPLETE RETREAT at midnight. If you can't get a carriage or a mule and have to walk, you might want to try and hook up with the Rhode Islanders who will maintain the best morale and the best singing on the way back. It may be very gruesome; expect the walking wounded to include recent amputees, soldiers with severed tongues and holes in their thighs and scrotums. As with the rest of the day, fresh water remains much in demand and in desperately short supply.

Past, present & future reading

 Alongside their own on-the-spot investigations and observations, WAG TIME INSPECTORS have made use of work by scholars and participants unable to access Chronoswoosh™ technologies. We can attest to the fidelity of the following books despite fixity in their own time–space continuum. They are all recommended pre-holiday reads – but should, of course, on no account be carried in your hand luggage.

The Field of the Cloth of Gold

Glenn Richardson ✳ *The Field of Cloth of Gold* (2013).

The Great Exhibition

Michael Leapman ✳ *The World for a Shilling: How the Great Exhibition of 1851 Shaped a Nation* (2001).

VE Day

Russell Miller | *VE Day: The People's Story* (2007).

Woodstock Festival

James E. Perone ✳ *Woodstock: An Encyclopaedia of the Music and Art Fair* (2005).

Joel Makower ✳ *Woodstock: An Oral History* (1989).

The Execution of Charles I

Ben Coates ✳ *The Impact of the English Civil War on the Economy of London 1642–50* (2004).

Charles Spencer ✳ *Killers of the King: The Men Who Dared to Execute Charles I* (2014).

C.V. Wedgwood ✳ *A King Condemned: The Trial and Execution of Charles I* (1964).

The Women's March on Versailles

George Rudé ✳ *The Crowd in the French Revolution* (1959).

Simon Schama * *Citizens: A Chronicle of the French Revolution* (1989).

The Assassination of Archduke Ferdinand

Christopher Clark * *The Sleepwalkers: How Europe Went to War in 1914* (2012).

David James Smith * *One Morning in Sarajevo: 28 June 1914* (2008).

The Fall of the Berlin Wall

Mary Elise Sarotte * *The Collapse: The Accidental Opening of the Berlin Wall* (2014).

The 235th Olympiad

Nigel Spivey * *The Ancient Olympics: A History* (2005).

Shakespeare's Globe

Peter Ackroyd * *Shakespeare: The Biography* (2005).

James Shapiro * *1599: A Year in the Life of William Shakespeare* (2005).

The Birth of Bebop

Stanley Crouch * *Kansas City Lightning: The Rise and Times of Charlie Parker* (2013).

Ira Gitler * *Swing to Bop: An Oral History of the Transition in Jazz in the 1940s* (1985).

Robin D.G. Kelley * *Thelonious Monk: The Life and Times of an American Original* (2010).

The Beatles in Hamburg

Mark Lewisohn * *The Beatles: All These Years – Volume 1, Tune In* (2013).

The Rumble in the Jungle

Norman Mailer * *The Fight* (1975).

In Xanadu with Marco Polo

Marco Polo * *The Travels* (1299).

John Man * *Xanadu: Marco Polo and Europe's Discovery of the East* (2009).

Captain Cook's First Epic Voyage

Peter Aughton * *Endeavour: The Story of Captain Cook's First Great Epic Voyage* (2002).

James Cook * *The Journals of Captain Cook* (1768–71).

Frank McLynn * *Captain Cook: Master of the Seas* (2011).

The Eruption of Vesuvius

Mary Beard * *Pompeii: The Life of a Roman Town* (2008).

The Peasants' Revolt

Judith Barker * *1381: The Year of the Peasants' Revolt* (2014).

Dan Jones * *Summer of Blood: The Peasants' Revolt of 1381* (2010).

First Battle of Bull Run

David Detzer * *Donnybrook: The Battle of Bull Run, 1861* (2004).

THE WAG TIME TRAVEL AGENCY

James Wyllie is a history writer and award-winning screenwriter. His latest book is *The Codebreakers* – the story of the secret intelligence team that changed the course of the First World War.

Johnny 'Lord' Acton has written books on everything from food (*Preserved* with Hugh Fearnley-Whittingstall) to the history of balloons (*The Man Who Touched the Sky*), and co-authored, with David Goldblatt, *How to Watch the Olympics*.

David Goldblatt is the author of the definitive, doorstopping football histories, *The Ball is Round* and *The Game of Our Lives*. He writes and broadcasts on the politics of sport for the *Guardian* and BBC radio.